NATIVE AMERICAN JUSTICE

Native American Justice

Laurence Armand French
Western New Mexico University

Burnham Inc., Publishers

CHICAGO

President: Kathleen Kusta
Vice-President: Brett J. Hallongren
Project Editor: Dorothy Anderson
Design/Production: Tamra Campbell-Phelps
Cover: "Freedom" by Julia DelNagro-Oehmke
Printer: Cushing-Malloy, Inc.

Library of Congress Cataloging-in-Publication Data

French, Laurence Armand.
    Native American justice / Laurence Armand French.
       p. cm.
Includes bibliographical references and index.
    ISBN 0-8304-1575-0 (pbk.)
    1. Indians of North America—Legal status, laws, etc. 2. Indian
courts—United States. I. Title.
      KF8205.F74 2002
      342.73'0872—dc21

                                                                    2001006677

Manufactured in the United States of America

10 9 8 7 6 5 4 3 2 1

∞   The paper used in this book meets the minimum
    requirements of American National Standard for
    Information Sciences—Permanence of Paper for
    Printed Library Materials, ANSI Z39.48-1984.

CONTENTS

Part I

INDIAN POLICIES, TREATIES, AND RIGHTS

CHAPTER TWO

**Civil Rights, Self-Determination, and the
New Federalism**   **43**

Part II

INDIAN JUSTICE   77

CHAPTER THREE

Aboriginal Justice: Cherokee Blood Vengeance   **79**

CHAPTER FOUR

**American Indian Religious Freedom within the
Criminal Justice Context: History, Current Status, and
Prospects for the Future** _by Little Rock Reed_   **97**

Part III

INDIAN COURTS AND JURISDICTIONS   127

CHAPTER FIVE
Unequal Justice and Punishment under the Law   129

CHAPTER SIX
Tribal Courts: Self-Determination and Limited Justice   141

CHAPTER SEVEN
The Navajo Court System   149

PART I

INDIAN POLICIES, TREATIES, AND RIGHTS

CHAPTER ONE

THE GENESIS OF INDIAN-U.S. RELATIONS

From the Colonial Era to Federal Control

During the colonial era of America, the British Crown recognized Indian tribes as foreign sovereign nations and made treaties and other alliances with American Indians much as the French did in their colonies. Given this recognition as independent nations, the British often had to play the role of protector for the indigenous natives from the settlers who desired their land. Indeed, various tribes of North America played a significant role in the European colonial wars up to the Declaration of Independence in 1776. It is not surprising, then, that most tribes sided with the British during the Revolutionary War.[1] Apparently, the British Crown was able to protect American Indians from slavery. However, some Indians were enslaved in all thirteen colonies and the Caribbean Islands and were credited with building Charlestown, South Carolina. Moreover, Indian slavery included all the horrors associated with the worst image of this practice: beatings, killings, separation of families, and so on. The 1708 census of the Carolina settlement illustrates the magnitude of this practice, with a population profile of 5,300 whites, 2,900 black slaves, and 1,400 Indian slaves. Indian slaves were often

3

used to quell black slave uprisings and vice versa. Members of the Lumbee Indians, an unrecognized tribe of over 40,000 members in North Carolina, clearly reflect the mixture of Indian and black slaves, a process initiated during the colonial era.

Of the three most influential colonial powers in North America, French colonists were the least likely to enslave American Indians, while the Mexicans continued this Spanish practice until the late nineteenth century.[2] Indeed, the prevailing view among Spanish and British colonists was that indigenous Indian tribes were a nuisance that interfered with their ethnocentric sense of Manifest Destiny. This view of American Indians led to the need for federal protection, on the one hand, and to the beginning of ethnic cleansing as a response to increased pressure from settlers to open up more Indian territory, on the other. An element of Manifest Destiny and its justification for initiating realistic conflict was based on the notion of the unquestionable superiority of the Euro-American Christian perspective over that of native groups. This process of boundary maintenance served to exacerbate the extremes of antagonistic reciprocity and the polarization associated with its corollary: out-group hostility increases in-group cohesion. Here, intergroup hatred fostered by this hostile interaction often leads to the out-group being labeled in terms that connote negative stereotypes, which, in the case of American Indians, led to a dehumanized image—one that justified physical genocide.[3]

Examples of out-group dehumanization were scalping and torture, practices long held up as clear examples of the dehumanized, vicious-animal image the Euro-American dominant society portrayed of American Indians and, subsequently, used as a justification for their eradication. The first known instance of scalping by white settlers in the New World occurred in 1725 at Wakefield, New Hampshire. Settlers killed ten Indians for their scalp bounty. Georg Friederici, a German researcher, investigated the scalping phenomenon in North America as part of his Doctor of Philosophy dissertation at the University of Leipzig. His findings were published in the 1906 *Annual Report of the Smithsonian Institution.* Friederici noted that certain tribes engaged in scalping prior to European contact and that Jacques Cartier wrote of this practice among the Huron-Iroquois, Montreal Indians living in what is now Quebec in 1535. Hernando De Soto also reported on this practice among the Muskhogean linguistic tribes of the Southeast in 1540. Apparently, this practice was part of keeping count of victims during blood feuds between competing enemy tribes.

However, Friederici noted that the increase in scalping was initiated by the European white settlers:

Scalping in its commonly known form and greatest extent was, as will be shown later, largely the result of the influences of white people, who introduced firearms, which increased the fatalities in a conflict, brought the steel knife, facilitating the taking of the scalp, and finally offered scalp premiums, which so stimulated the hunt for these objects the removing of whole heads was abandoned. . . . The Hudson Indians . . . gathered for a time a peculiar kind of war trophy, namely, the hand. The development of this peculiarity can be traced to the introduction by the Dutch of Negro slaves and the reward offered by the owners, according to a widespread habit in Africa, for the right hand of every slave fugitive. The Indians engaged in the pursuit of such fugitives just as the whites did. . . . With, or even before, the end of the Dutch dominion the usage ceased and was eventually replaced by the practice of taking scalps, for which premiums were offered by the English. . . .

The first group to offer premiums for the heads of their native enemies were, in 1637, the Puritans of New England. They asked for the heads, scalping being as yet unknown in that part of the country. As a result, the colonists and allied Indians in large numbers brought in heads of the Pequots. In 1680 scalp prizes were offered by the colonists of South Carolina. . . .

About this time we hear for the first time of scalp premiums offered by the French. In 1688 the French Canadians paid for every scalp of their enemies, whether white or Indian, 10 beaver skins, which was also a high price, equivalent in Montreal to the price of a gun with 4 pounds of powder and 40 pounds of lead. . . .

In Mexico the first offers of head premiums of which the writer could find a record date from 1616 to 1618, preceding, therefore, by twenty years similar rewards given by the New Englanders during the Pequot war. . . . In 1835 the legislature of Sonora proclaimed a war of extermination against the Apaches and set the reward of $100 for every Apache scalp. Chihuahua followed in 1837 with an offer of $100 for every scalp of a male, $50 for that of a female and $25 for that of every Indian child. . . . Such a state of affairs lasted for several decades, continuing past the French invasion and well up to the eighties. The rewards offered reached, in 1863 to 1870, the large sums of $200 to $300 for each ordinary scalp and $500 for that of a chief of the Indians.[4]

The implication here is that the killing of American Indians was not only a sanctioned practice among New World white settlers, but the scalp trophy itself was a positive representation of one's status as a defender of the in-group. Outside Concord, New Hampshire, along the Merrimack River, is a monument honoring Hannah Dustin, a white female settler who killed and scalped two adult Indian males, two Indian females, and six Indian children while they slept. The colony paid her the scalp bounties, and Governor Nicholson rewarded her with an additional fee and promoted her to the status of "heroine" within the New England colonies. Later, Little Crow, chief of the Santee Sioux during the 1862 Great Sioux Uprising, was murdered, along with his sixteen-year-old son, while picking wild berries in Minnesota. The white hunters that stalked and killed them did so for the standing $25 Indian scalp bounty. But when government officials realized that this was the scalp and skull of Little Crow, the hunters were awarded an additional $500.[5] This introduction prepares us for the discussion of the often contravening nature of U.S.-Indian policy that follows.

European technologies, including the introduction of the horse, firearms, and steel weapons and tools, forever changed the American Indian aboriginal ways. European and African interactions also led to a sharing of customs and cultural attributes, as did the introduction of native foods and substances, notably corn, tomatoes, potatoes, and tobacco. Nonetheless, the European manner of alcohol production and consumption, perhaps more than any other interethnic exchange, made an impact on American Indians and is a major element of the subsequent federal intercourse acts regulating trade and exchange between members of the dominant U.S. society and the indigenous natives. In his book, *Addictions and Native Americans*, Laurence French noted:

> Many blame the Europeans for the introduction of alcohol, perhaps the most significant social ill associated with psychocultural marginality, but this is not the case: alcohol and other psychoactive agents have played a role among American Indians since aboriginal times, prior to Euro-American contact and influence. The major difference between aboriginal use and what transpired following the Euro-American influence was that, under the dictates of the harmony ethos, substance use was highly regulated and closely related to social customs and rituals. Another significant distinction was the potency of the psychoactive agent in these rituals.[6]

The United States made 394 Indian treaties between 1778 and 1868, not including those made by tribes with the Confederacy during the Civil War. Three years later, the Indian Appropriations Act of 1871 ended treaty making with Native Americans. William Canby suggested that initial federal intervention between settlers in states and territories and American Indians was to avoid more violence and yet another costly war.[7] U.S.-Indian policy was unclear under the Articles of Confederation but became better articulated under the Constitution when Congress was granted the power to regulate commerce with Indian tribes. The Constitution also authorized the U.S. president to make treaties, including Indian treaties, with ratification by the U.S. Senate. According to Costo and Henry, not all Indian treaties were ratified by Congress.[8] More significantly, there had always been strong opposition to Indian treaties, especially those that provide special lands and status to Native Americans. In reviewing U.S.-Indian policy, we see that clear mandates are absent. Instead, policy has waxed and waned depending on the prevailing interest of the parties in control of either the Executive Branch or the U.S. Congress. Regionalism has played a critical role in these challenges to self-determination within Indian country. One of the strongest anti-Indian groups has been the Western Conference of the Council of State Governments, which includes the western states where large Indian tribes reside and where the non-Indians have aired strong antigovernment sentiments, especially over the control of federal lands, including Indian reservations. This process of attempting to abrogate U.S.-Indian treaties and rights constitutes what I term "cultural genocide."

Removal as Ethnic Cleansing: U.S.-Indian Treaties and Policies from 1778 to 1870

A number of treaties were made during the early years of the new republic. Nineteen treaties were made during the late 1800s, often involving the same tribes, as the demands of the Revolutionary War and white settlers increased:

1778　Treaty with the Delaware.
1784　Treaty with the Six Nations.
1785　Treaty with the Wyandot, Delaware, Chippewa, and Ottawa
　　　(Treaty of Fort McIntosh); Treaty with the Cherokee
　　　(Hopewell Treaty).
1786　Treaty with the Choctaw;
　　　Treaty with the Chickasaw;
　　　Treaty with the Shawnee.
1789　Treaty with the Wyandot, Delaware, Ottawa, Chippewa, Potawatomi, and
　　　Sac Nations;
　　　Treaty with the Six Nations.
1790　Treaty with the Creeks.
1791　Treaty with the Cherokee.
1794　Treaty with the Cherokee;

Treaty with the Six Nations;

Treaty with the Oneida, Tuscarora, and Stockbridge.

1795 Treaty with the Wyandot, Delaware, Shawanoes, Ottawa, Chippewa, Potawatomi, Miami, Eel-River, Weea, Kickapoo, Piankashaw, and Kaskaskia.

1796 Treaty with the Seven Nations of Canada;

Treaty with the Creeks.

1797 Treaty with the Mohawk.

1798 Treaty with the Cherokee.[8]

Federal legal control over Indians in the newly created U.S. republic was vested in trade and intercourse acts. Early efforts by the Continental Congress were futile and ambiguous in that the federal government had little influence over curtailing the steady encroachment of white settlers in Indian country while at the same time searching for treaty loopholes that would open up new territories in Indian country. Especially problematic was the emerging battle over states rights, where states were more aggressive in their anti-Indian sentiments and sense of Manifest Destiny.[9]

The establishment of the War Department under the new U.S. Constitution in 1789 created the federal authority needed to regulate Indian policy. Indian affairs remained under the War Department until the establishment of the Interior Department in 1849.[10] Trade and intercourse acts, passed by the new U.S. Congress, established federal policy relevant to the nature of legal interactions between Indians and non-Indians, especially directing those relationships and exchanges between white communities and Indian tribes. Toward this end, these acts articulated the boundaries of Indian country and had proscriptions designed to protect the Indians in Indian country from exploitation outside of constitutionally based treaties. These acts, first established under President Washington, provided the initial foundation of federal Indian policy.

The initial *Trade and Intercourse Act* was enacted July 22, 1790, and was authorized only for the two-year congressional session. Section 4 stipulated that no sale of lands made by any Indians or by any nation or tribe of Indians within the United States can be made outside of federally approved treaties, while Section 5 set forth the first laws governing crime in Indian country.

And be it further enacted, That if any citizen or inhabitant of the United States, or of either of the territorial districts of the United States, shall go into any town, settlement or territory belonging to any nation or tribe of Indians, and shall they commit any crime upon, or trespass against, the person or property of any peaceable and friendly Indian or Indians, which, if committed within the jurisdiction of any state, or within the jurisdiction of either of the said districts, against a citizen or white inhabitant thereof, would be punishable by the laws of such state or district, such offender or offenders shall be proceeded against in the same manner as if the offence had been committed within the jurisdiction of the state or district to which he or they may belong, against a citizen or white inhabitant thereof.[11]

These temporary trade and intercourse acts started during the Washington administration were continued in 1796 and 1799 along with the establishment of Government Trading Houses authorized by the federal government for trade with certain Indian nations, a move that President Thomas Jefferson felt would help transform the Indians' economies from hunting and gathering to agriculture. In 1806, the position of superintendent of Indian trade was authorized to facilitate these trading houses. A more permanent Trade and Intercourse Act was established in 1802, while the trading houses and superintendent position were abolished in 1822. Again, the laws against crimes in Indian country continued to be stressed as well as the need for a federal license to trade with any Indian individual or tribe. An additional element was Section 21, which authorized the U.S. president to establish measures to prevent the vending or distribution of spirituous liquors among all or any of the Indian tribes.[12] Control over Indian trade was a difficult endeavor, with little help provided by states that bordered Indian reservations. Another problem was foreign trade with Indian tribes, especially that with the English. These factors led to the end of the federal Trade Houses and the English trade with the Indians. In 1824, the secretary of war established the first Bureau of Indian Affairs (BIA). Eight years later, the U.S. Congress approved the BIA and designated the position of commissioner of Indian affairs to head the BIA.

During this time, states were eager to remove Indians from their territory, leading to more treaties and the establishment of the controversial U.S. policy of ethnic cleansing. This conflict led to the Indian Removal Act of 1830 when the U.S. Congress authorized the president to exchange lands in the West for those held by Indian tribes in any state or territory. A strong proponent of "removal" as a mechanism of Manifest Destiny, President Andrew Jackson started the forceful removal of tribes, even the so-called Five Civilized Tribes (Cherokee, Choctaw, Creek, Chickasaw, Seminole) whose economic lifestyle could not be differentiated from that of their white counterparts. Although he did not live to see this action, President Jefferson set the stage for removal and listed this as a major reason for his consummation of the Louisiana Purchase in 1803. A portion of this land beyond the Mississippi River would now become designated Indian Territory.[13]

The final version of the Trade and Intercourse Act was passed in 1834, again keeping much of the content of previous versions. The difference was that this act was now applicable to the increased contact with Indian tribes as the United States itself expanded west. A major departure from previous guidelines for Indian interaction were those sections (20 and 21) addressing the liquor trade. The new act now prohibited the sale of alcohol to Indians anywhere in the United States. Thus began the longest era of prohibition in U.S. history, extending until repeal in 1953. Clearly, prohibition was intended as a mechanism of control over American Indians and was not devised as a humanitarian or benevolent act. During this time alcohol was transformed from its aboriginal positive and restricted use to that of illegal contraband whose unsanctioned use contributed to numerous social, economic, and legal problems—problems that still plague American Indians today.[14]

Removal, the United States' first formal policy on ethnic cleansing, set the stage for the dominant society to depersonalize American Indians, thus making them objects of abuse and violence. Hence, this policy provided the foundation for physical genocide. Removal also represented one of the major internal battles at the federal level of government, with the Executive Branch, Congress, and the Supreme Court often opposing each other in what became known as "the Indian problem." Between 1828 and 1830, the state of Georgia enacted laws dividing the Cherokee Nation. This was due in part to Georgia's frustration over the federal government's promise to extinguish Indian title to these lands if Georgia gave up its claims to western lands. In the 1831 case *Cherokee Nation v. Georgia*, the Cherokees filed a suit against the state of Georgia, which was attempting to extend state laws to the tribe. The Supreme Court, in its 1831 decision, refused to recognize Indian tribes as foreign nations but rather assigned them the status of "domestic dependent nations." In this ruling, the Court labeled American Indians as "wards" of the government, allowing anti-Indian groups to interpret this to mean that Indian tribes were incapable of self-government. This argument continues today with tribes, states, and the federal government arguing over who has control over Indian country.[15]

In 1832, the U.S. Supreme Court heard the case of white missionaries who were arrested and incarcerated by the state of Georgia (*Worcester v. Georgia*). Samuel A. Worcester was one of several white missionaries who resided among the Cherokee and refused to either obtain a permit from or swear an oath of allegiance to the state of Georgia as was required by state

law. The Reverend Samuel A. Worcester was well known among the Cherokee, having assisted the tribe by changing Sequoya's syllabary, the only written American Indian language using its own symbols, into a typeface and
using it to print the New Testament, hymns, and school texts. The Supreme
Court's decision maintained that the Cherokee, the largest of the so-called
Civilized Tribes, was indeed a nation independent of state jurisdiction. In his
decision, Chief Justice Marshall noted that both federal treaties and the rules
of the trade and intercourse acts recognized several Indian tribes, including
the Cherokee, as being distinct political entities with exclusive authority
within their own territorial boundaries.[16] President Jackson proceeded with
removal despite the Court's decision. He left office a year before the 1838
Trail of Tears when the bulk of the Cherokee Nation was rounded up by
General Winfield Scott. Despite numerous petitions by the Cherokee and
their supporters, neither President Van Buren nor Congress acted to overturn
the Cherokee removal. (General Scott also aided President Jackson in an earlier unconstitutional act—the attack on Spanish Florida, without a declaration of war, for the specific purpose of ridding the territory of the Seminole
Indians.) Removed to stockades at gunpoint, thousands of Cherokee were
herded on a thousand mile trek, in the dead of winter, to Indian Territory
(Oklahoma). Over a quarter of the Indians perished along the way.[17]

In addition to the Five Civilized Tribes (Cherokee, Choctaw, Chickasaw,
Creek, Seminole), the Trail of Tears was played out dozens of times during
the nineteenth century with other tribes that were eventually removed to
Indian Territory (Oklahoma): Apache; Caddo; Cheyenne-Arapaho;
Comanche; Delaware; Iowa; Kaw; Kialegee; Kickapoo; Kiowa; Miami;
Modoc; Osage; Oto-Missouri; Ottawa; Pawnee; Peoria; Ponca; Potawatomi;
Quapaw; Sac and Fox; Seneca-Cayuga; Shawnee; Thlopthlocco; Tonkawa;
Wichita; Wyandotte; and Yuchi.[18] Those not removed suffered from federal
and state policies of physical and cultural genocide. Indeed, physical genocide among the Plains Indians and the Apache of the Southwest extended
until the late 1800s. And some feel that this practice among the Sioux continued until the 1970s with Wounded Knee II.

Two examples of forced removal to areas other than Indian Territory
(Oklahoma) occurred during President Lincoln's administration. In 1837,
the Santee (Dakota) Sioux were forced from their tribal lands east of the Mississippi River, giving up 35 million acres of rich agricultural land to
encroaching white settlers. The U.S. government then reneged on the mon-
etary sum agreed upon in their removal, using it instead to pay white traders
and other white administrators. Denied their traditional woodland existence
and with little of the goods and services promised by the federal government,

starvation, disease, and disillusionment became the tools of physical and cultural genocide.

In 1851, the Santee Sioux were again forced to cede most of their lands to white settlers. And again the United States failed to provide the goods and services promised. This inaction led to the first major Sioux hostilities in what became known as the Great Sioux Uprising. In the fall of 1862, the Santee Sioux, on the verge of starvation, were led by Little Crow in attacks on white settlers. The Santee Sioux were then removed across the Missouri River from Minnesota to Nebraska, thus displacing the Spotted Tail band of Sioux, who moved north and west into what is now the Rosebud Sioux Reservation. The Spotted Tail (Brulé) Sioux replaced the Ponca in 1865 when the Ponca tribe was removed to Indian Territory (Oklahoma).

Steven L. Johnson, in his *Guide to American Indian Documents in the Congressional Serial Set: 1817–1899*, described the Ponca removals as a: "shameful treatment of the tribe by the government; reservation in Dakota granted under the treaties of March 12, 1858, and March 10, 1865, is ceded to the Sioux without consultation with them; removed to Indian territory."[19] The Ponca chief, Standing Bear, would later leave Oklahoma illegally. His arrest and trial led to a significant federal court decision in 1879. In *Standing Bear v. Crook*, General George Crook stated that Standing Bear had no recourse to a writ before the court because, under the law, he and other American Indians were not "persons." Judge Elmer S. Dundy, in his historical decision, proclaimed that "an Indian is a person within the meaning of the law of the United States."[20] Other tribes that moved about in this region at this time included the Winnebagoes, who were also removed from Minnesota by an act of Congress and relocated to a reservation in eastern Nebraska adjacent to the Omaha tribe.[21]

The federal government gave in to white and Mexican-American settlers and certain Pueblo tribes when it ordered Colonel Kit Carson to engage in a punitive expedition beginning in June 1863. This became known as the "Long Walk," the Navajos' Trail of Tears. Crops, herds, and villages were destroyed, and those who refused to be removed were hunted down and killed. Like the ordeal of the Cherokee and other forcefully removed tribes, the conditions of the trek were severe. Only children and the handicapped were allowed to ride in wagons. The rest walked the three hundred miles to Fort Sumner in New Mexico. Those who could not keep up were killed. Eight thousand Navajo were eventually removed to Fort Sumner, where many more died due to the poor living conditions in this concentration camp environment. In 1868 the Navajo were allowed back into their now greatly reduced tribal lands.[22]

Standing Bear's efforts led to the beginning of the end of the era of physical genocide and forced the federal government to now focus on the destruction of Indian cultures instead of the Indians per se. With the federal court decision recognizing American Indians as "persons," the de facto policy of Manifest Destiny and its new practice of cultural genocide was now shrouded in the theme of peace. The transition in U.S. policies justifying ethnic cleansing with forced removal *without* regard for American Indians as human beings to forced removal *with* regard for them as "persons" had its origin in President Ulysses S. Grant's "peace policy" plan for Indian accommodation.

Grant's main architect for the peace plan was his choice to head the Bureau of Indian Affairs, Commissioner of Indian Affairs Ely Parker. Parker was of mixed Indian (Seneca) and white blood and served as a brigadier general in the Union Army. A trusted protege of President Grant and strong supporter of this new dimension of ethnic cleansing, he supported these efforts to not only uproot tribes but also force them to abandon their traditional ways in lieu of the Western Christian perspective. Removal continued to be the primary vehicle for ridding lands desired by white settlers and the railroads of unwanted Indians. Congress aided the Executive Branch in this process by refusing to ratify any more Indian treaties. In 1854, the U.S. Senate, in executive session, read each unratified U.S.-Indian treaty three times, as required by law, and then denied ratification for all. The tribes involved were not notified of this clandestine move and had little recourse after the fact.

With the 1869 *Standing Bear* ruling elevating American Indians from the status of feral animals with bounties on their heads to "persons," albeit not persons equal to the white man, the federal government was forced to find a new justification for its continued policy of ethnic cleansing and the forced removal of Indians from traditional lands to small "concentration camps." In providing a review of his "peace policy," President Grant authorized a Board of Indian Commissioners. Their 1869 report noted that most of the so-called Indian problem lay with unscrupulous whites, including officials, who blatantly exploited the Indians for their own ends.

Parasocial as it may seem, the white man has been the chief obstacle in the way of Indian civilization. The benevolent measures attempted by the government for advancement have been almost uniformly thwarted by the agencies employed to carry them out. The soldiers, sent for their protection, too often carried demoralization and disease into their midst. The agent, appointed to be their friend and counsellor, business manager, and the almoner of the government bounties, frequently went among them only to enrich himself in the shortest possible time, at the cost of the Indians, and spent the largest available sum of the government money with the least ostensible beneficial result.

Whatever may have been the original character of the aborigines, many of them are now precisely what the course of treatment received from the whites must necessarily have made them—suspicious, revengeful, and cruel in their retaliation. In war they know no distinction between the innocent and the guilty. In his most savage vices the worst Indian is but the imitator of bad white men on the border. To assume that all of them, or even a majority of them, may be so characterized with any degree of truthfulness, would be no more just than to assume the same of all the white people upon the frontier.[23]

In spite of this indictment of abuses by members of the dominant white society, the commission went on to recommend that the planned policies of cultural genocide, civilization, and Christianization be implemented with a total disregard for the viability of traditional Indian communal lifestyle.

The policy of collecting the Indian tribes upon small reservations contiguous to each other, and within the limits of a large reservation, eventually to become a State of the Union, and of which the small reservations will probably be the counties, seems to be the best that can be devised. Many tribes may thus be collected in the present Indian territory. The larger the number that can be thus concentrated the better for the success of the plan; care being taken to separate hereditary enemies from each other. When upon the reservation they should be taught as soon as possible the advantage of individual ownership of property; and should be given land in severalty as soon as it is desired by any of them, and that tribal relations should be discouraged. . . .

The treaty system should be abandoned, and as soon as any just method can be devised to accomplish it, existing treaties should be abrogated.

The legal status of the uncivilized Indians should be that of wards of the government; the duty of the latter being to protect them, to educate them in industry, the arts of civilization, and the principles of Christianity; elevate them to the rights of citizenship, and to sustain and clothe them until they can support themselves. . . . The establishment of Christian missions should be encouraged, and their schools fostered. . . . The religion of our blessed Saviour is believed to be the most effective agent for the civilization of any people.[24]

President Grant, acting on the Board of Indian Commissioners' advice, spelled out his new "peace policy" in his Second Annual Message to Congress on December 6, 1870. Here he indicated his intent to make Indians wards of the United States and place them on reservations where they would learn the ways of the dominant society. Moreover, President Grant announced that religious societies would implement the civilization and Christianization resocialization component of indoctrination for dependent Indian wards on the reservations, replacing military personnel who had administrated the reservations in the past.[25] Already that year, the Kiowas, Comanches, Apaches, Arapahoes, Sacs, Foxes, and Cheyenne had been relocated (forcefully removed) to Indian territory (Oklahoma). And the following year, 1871, President Grant's fellow general, Commissioner of Indian Affairs Ely Parker, was forced to resign under a cloud of graft and corruption within the Bureau of Indian Affairs.[26] That same year Congress also followed the recommendations of the Board of Indian Commissioners and abolished treaty making with Indian tribes. Reservations created after 1871 were established by statute or by executive practice until Congress ended this executive practice as well in 1919. In Indian territory (Oklahoma) land was made available for these newly removed tribes by taking it away from the Five Civilized Tribes in violation of their removal treaties. This was justified as punishment for siding with the Confederacy during the Civil War. Five "agreements" are on record following the congressional termination of treaties with Indian tribes:

> 1872   Agreement with the Sisseton and Wahpeton bands of Sioux Indians. (Unratified)
> 1873   Amended agreement with certain Sioux tribes. (Ratified)
> 1880   Agreement with the Crow Indians. (Unratified)
> 1882–83   Agreement with certain Sioux tribes. (Unratified)
> 1883   Agreement with Columbia and Colville tribes. (Ratified)[27]

The idea of full assimilation for American Indians was never part of the peace policy or any U.S.-Indian policy for that fact. Even accommodation, with a shared but separate social structure, was never a viable plan, given the treatment of the Five Civilized Tribes during removal to Indian territory and later their punishment following the Civil War and the eventual dissolution of their tribes during the allotment era. Indian wars continued, despite the new peace policy, especially with the Apache of the Southwest and the Plains Indian tribes.

Treaties were made with the Siouan tribes and their neighbors, the Crow, Arapaho, and Cheyenne, in 1851, 1865, and lastly, in 1868. The 1851 Fort Laramie Treaty stipulated that the U.S. government had the right to establish roads and military and other posts in the Lakota Sioux, Crow, Cheyenne, and

Arapaho tribal lands (Article 2). However, it also promised to "protect the aforesaid Indian nations against the commission of all depredations by the people of the said United States, after ratification of this treaty" (Article 3).[28] The 1862 Great Sioux Uprising among the Santee (Dakota) Sioux marked the beginning of twenty-eight years of conflict, deceit, and massacre, culminating with the summary execution of the Hunkpapa Sioux medicine man, Sitting Bull, at the Fort Yates Reservation and the massacre of Big Foot and 146 members of his party at Wounded Knee on the Pine Ridge Reservation in December 1890.

The terms of the 1868 Fort Laramie Treaty were supposed to provide the Lakota Sioux with a large territory consisting of South Dakota, part of North Dakota, and the northwestern portion of Nebraska. The Great Sioux Reservation was to extend from the Missouri River to the Black Hills, and this thirty-five thousand square mile area, comprised of sacred hills and the buffalo plains, was to become home to some twenty thousand Sioux in perpetuity, without either white settlers or military intervention. This promise was similar to the one given to the eastern tribes when they were forcefully removed to Indian Territory (Oklahoma). The Sioux promise lasted only six years. Gold was found in the Black Hills, and the U.S. military began to protect the white intruders despite the conditions of the 1868 treaty. The Plains Indians knew that only a concerted effort on their part could stop the onslaught of settlers and attacks by the U.S. Army. Red Cloud, chief of the Oglala Sioux, was successful in mustering a force consisting of the Lakota bands as well as the Cheyenne. His plan was to fight a hit-and-run guerrilla campaign, a plan that led to their short-lived success at Little Big Horn in 1876. In what is clearly retaliation for Custer's death, Crazy Horse was killed in the stockade at Fort Robinson, Nebraska, in 1877. Another injustice forced upon the Plains Indians for Custer's defeat was carried out by General Philip H. Sheridan, commander of the Military Division of Missouri. His policy of dismounting the Sioux through pony seizures was designed to force the Indians to rely only on their feet for mobility, greatly exacerbating the hardships these Indians already suffered on the reservation. Sievers tied this process to the peace commission's plan for obtaining more tribal lands under the guise of the civilizing and Christianization of the Indians.

> As deep winter snows again blanketed the Upper Missouri countryside in the winter of 1868, Indian policy had been more clearly defined than ever before. More than twenty years would pass before the last shots of the Plains Indian conflict would be heard, but the Northwest Treaty Commission and the Peace Commission had prescribed the first steps in the government's

"civilizing" policy. Reevaluation of policy and attitudes had been pushed aside as concerned citizens and officials plotted the "civilizing" of the Indian and the restoration of peace. The Indians were to be removed, reservationized, agriculturalized, and assimilated at the altar of progress.[29]

The war with the Chiricahua Apache began with the 1848 Treaty of Guadalupe Hidalgo, which ended the Mexican War, and concluded in 1886 with the surrender of Geronimo and the incarceration and removal of the Chiricahua band. A treaty was made with the Apache in 1852 in Santa Fe, New Mexico, between Colonel Sumner, military commander for the Territory of New Mexico, John Creiner, Indian agent for the territory, and Cuentas, Azules, Blancito, Negrito, Capitan Simon, Capitan Vuelta, and Mangus Colorado, chiefs acting on the part of the Apache Nation of Indians. Article 9 of the 1852 treaty made provisions for separate territories for the various Apache bands:

> Relying confidently upon the justice and the liberality of the aforesaid government, and anxious to remove every possible cause that might disturb their peace and quiet, it is agreed by the aforesaid Apaches that the government of the United States shall at its earliest convenience designate, settle, and adjust their territorial boundaries, and pass and execute in their territory such laws as may be deemed conducive to the prosperity and happiness of said Indians.[30]

This, like all subsequent treaties made with the Apache Nation, was never approved by the U.S. Senate. The next year, the United States gained an additional million square miles of new territory in what are now the states of Texas, New Mexico, Arizona, Utah, Colorado, California, and parts of Nevada, Idaho, and Wyoming with the 1853 Gadsden Purchase from Mexico. In New Mexico Territory, the territorial governor made unauthorized treaties with the Jicarilla, who were sent from reservation to reservation, including the infamous Bosque Redondo at Fort Sumner, until they were finally granted their own place in 1880.

Conflict with the southern Apache bands, notably the Chiricahua, escalated in 1860 when Lieutenant George Bascom wrongly accused the Apache chief, Cochise, of kidnapping a twelve-year-old white boy, Felix Ward. Bascom attacked Cochise after he entered the army camp under a white-flag truce. The Camp Grant massacre of April 30, 1871, placed all Apache on notice that the white and Hispanic settlers' de facto policy of physical genocide was in effect within their traditional lands in Gran Apacheria. Under the supposed protection of the U.S. Army, hundreds of unarmed Apache were living at Camp Grant, located about sixty miles northeast of Tucson in Arizona Territory when they were attacked by a civilian posse from Tucson composed of Anglos, Mexicans, and Papago Indians. One hundred women and children were shot or clubbed to death. Twenty-nine Indian children survived and were taken captive; two escaped, five were turned over to the government, and the remaining twenty-two were sold as slaves in Mexico.

President Grant was instrumental in having 104 of the 148 posse members charged and adjudicated, but a local white jury acquitted all after only twenty minutes of deliberation. Both the *Denver News* and the *El Paso Morning Times* glorified these acts and endorsed these types of massacres as a means of ridding the area of the Apache. By 1876, four reservations, under the new concentration camp philosophy, were established for the various Apache bands. Many Apache groups left this impoverished environment to make raids into Mexico for horses and food, and it took a concerted effort by Mexico and the United States to finally get the last of the Chiricahua to surrender. This occurred on September 4, 1886, with Geronimo's surrender. In an unprecedented move the federal government classified all members of the Chiricahua Apache, including decorated U.S. Army scouts, as prisoners of war and forcefully exiled them to a military prison in Florida. Those who survived the squalid conditions were eventually moved to Alabama and then to Fort Sill, Oklahoma. Some Chiricahua now reside on the Mescalero Apache Reservation in eastern New Mexico.[31] These actions clearly equate the peace policy with cultural genocide and other attributes of intolerance associated with the white-man–oriented dictates of Manifest Destiny.

The Evolution of Laws and Courts in Indian Country

During the colonial era, most aboriginal tribal sanctions and folk justice were still enforced according to traditional methods. After the Revolution, the United States extended federal control and jurisdiction into Indian country. Foregoing the British and French policy of autonomous recognition of aboriginal groups, the United States extended its control and jurisdiction onto tribal lands, lands that were rapidly being reduced via numerous treaties. Federally recognized tribal boundaries thereby constituted both Indian country and the special conditions of federal Indian policy. As stated earlier, the first set of such policies to establish federal jurisdiction among tribes were the trade and intercourse acts, whose intent was to regulate and prosecute civil and criminal misconduct of non-Indians within Indian country.

Federal jurisdiction in Indian country was expanded with the Federal

Enclaves Act, also known as the General Crimes Act, of 1817. This act established exclusive federal jurisdiction in Indian country, superseding any state
or territorial jurisdictions. The earlier Federal Crimes Act of April 1790 dealt
with constitutional issues, such as treason, counterfeiting of securities, and
crimes upon the high seas, and did not specifically address Indian country.
The Federal Enclaves Act permitted punishment for all crimes committed by
non-Indians in Indian country as well as some crimes committed by Indians
against whites. Specifically omitted from federal jurisdiction under the Federal Enclaves Act were the following offenses: (a) crimes by Indians against
Indians, including consensual (victimless) acts between Indians that were trib-
ally sanctioned but deemed illegal within the larger dominant society (such as
adultery); (b) crimes by Indians that were already addressed by tribal recourse
(cultural double jeopardy clause); and (c) crimes where the tribe was granted
exclusive jurisdiction as a condition of a U.S.-tribal treaty:

> Except as otherwise expressly provided by law, the general laws of the
> United States as to the punishment of offenses committed in any place
> within the sole and exclusive jurisdiction of the United States, except the
> District of Columbia, shall extend to the Indian country. This section shall
> not extend to offenses committed by one Indian against the person or prop-
> erty of another Indian, nor to any Indian committing any offense in the
> Indian country who has been punished by the local law of the tribe, or to
> any case where, by treaty stipulations, the exclusive jurisdiction over such
> offenses is or may be secured to the Indian tribes respectively.[32]

In the 1820s, U.S. Representatives James Buchanan and Daniel Webster
saw a need for an expansion of the 1790 Federal Crimes Act to include federal jurisdiction over local statutes within U.S. territory where federal jurisdiction was deemed exclusive. Their effort resulted in passage of the Federal
Crimes Act of March 1825, also known as the Assimilative Crimes Act since
it assimilated local criminal statutes into the exclusive federal jurisdiction
(federal enclaves). Passage of this act automatically had an impact on the Federal Enclaves Act of 1817 relevant to Indian country, increasing the number
of offenses in tribal lands for which non-Indians could be charged.

> . . . [I]f any offence shall be committed in any of the places aforesaid, the
> punishment of which offence is not specially provided for by any law of the
> United States, such offence shall, upon a conviction in any court of the
> United States having cognisance thereof, be liable to, and receive the same
> punishment as the laws of the state in which such fort, dock-yard, navy-yard,
> arsenal, armory, or magazine, or other place, ceded as aforesaid, is situated,

provide for the like offence when committed within the body of any county of such state.[33]

The Federal Crimes Act of 1825 was amended in 1866 and incorporated into the Revised Statutes in 1874. In 1948, Congress revised the criminal code of the United States, thereby modifying the Assimilative Crimes Act to include all nonfederal laws in force in the local jurisdiction if committed in a federal enclave where federal jurisdiction was exclusive. This included the federal prosecution of minor offenses such as traffic violations as well as drunk driving, greatly increasing the rate of criminal prosecution in Indian country. The act is still in effect today and provides the model for state jurisdiction in Indian country as a component of Public Law 280, the 1953 congressional action that extended state jurisdiction over offenses committed by or against Indians in Indian country.

The Federal Enclaves Act and Assimilative Crimes Act were the norm in Indian country until the 1880s, when the turbulence with the Plains Indians and Apache of the Southwest forced a congressional reconsideration of Indian justice. Two major events occurred in 1883—the establishment of the Courts of Indian Offenses and the U.S. Supreme Court decision *Ex parte Crow Dog*. The Courts of Indian Offenses provided that pro-Christian Indian judges be appointed by Indian agents. Clearly, the intent was to have Indian judges who would support the prevailing theme of dominant society ethnocentrism, which perceived Indian culture as evil. These courts and their codes did not subscribe to indigenous tribal rituals and practices. Instead, the Courts of Indian Offenses imposed the federal dictates of Christian civilization. Here, religious dances, customary practices, including the purification sweat, vision quest, and sun dance, and plural marriages were outlawed. Secretary of the Interior Henry M. Teller initiated the Courts of Indian Offenses in order to eliminate what he termed the "heathenish practices" among Indians. The courts actually reinforced the enforcement of minor offenses in Indian country, defined by the already established Federal Enclaves and Assimilative Crimes Acts. Teller outlined his philosophy in his report to Congress on November 1, 1883:

> Many of the agencies are without law of any kind, and the necessity for some rule of government on the reservations grows more and more apparent each day. If it is the purpose of the Government to civilize the Indians, they must be compelled to desist from the savage and barbarous practices that are calculated to continue them in savagery, no matter what exterior influences are brought to bear on them. Very many of the progressive Indians have become

fully alive to the pernicious influences of these heathenish practices indulged in by their people, and have sought to abolish them; in such efforts they have been aided by their missionaries, teachers, and agents, but this has been found impossible even with the aid thus given. The Government furnishes the teachers, and the charitable people contribute to the support of missionaries, and much time, labor, and money is yearly expended for their elevation, and a few non-progressive, degraded Indians are allowed to exhibit before the young and susceptible children all the debauchery, diabolism, and savagery of the worst state of the Indian race. Every man familiar with Indian life will bear witness to the pernicious influence of these savage rites and heathenish customs.

. . . In accordance with the suggestions of this letter, the Commission of Indian Affairs established a tribunal at all agencies, except among the civilized Indians, consisting of three Indians, to be known as the Court of Indian Offenses. The members of this tribunal consist of the first three officers in rank of the police force, if such selection is approved by the agency; otherwise, the agent may select from among the members of the tribe three suitable persons to constitute such tribunal.

The Commissioner of Indian Affairs, with the approval of the Secretary of the Interior, promulgated certain rules for the government of this tribunal, defining offenses of which it was to take cognizance. It is believed that such a tribunal, composed as it is of Indians, will be a step in the direction of bringing the Indians under the civilizing influence of law.[34]

In *Ex parte Crow Dog*, the U.S. Supreme Court reversed the federal district court conviction of Brulé Sioux Chief Crow Dog, who was charged with the slaying of another Brulé chief, Spotted Tail. The Supreme Court based its reversal on the ground that the laws of the United States did not apply to acts of Indians in Indian country, a decision that challenged the basic foundation of federal justice in Indian country since 1825:

The petitioner is in the custody of the marshal of the United States for the Territory of Dakota, imprisoned in the jail of Lawrence County, in the First Judicial District of that Territory, under sentence of death, adjudged against him by the district court for that district, to be carried into execution January 14th, 1884. That judgment was rendered upon a conviction for the murder of an Indian of the Brulé Sioux band of the Sioux Nation of Indians, by the name of Sin-ta-ge-le-Scka, or in English, Spotted Tail, the prisoner also being an Indian, of the same band and nation, and the homicide having occurred as alleged in the indictment in Indian country, within a place and district of country under the exclusive jurisdiction of the United States and within the said judicial district. The judgment was affirmed, on a writ of error, by the Supreme Court of the Territory. It is claimed on behalf of the prisoner that the crime charged against him, and of which he stands convicted, is not an offence under the laws of the United States; that the district court had no jurisdiction to try him, and that its judgment and sentence are void. He therefore prays for a writ of habeas corpus, that he may be delivered from an imprisonment which he asserts to be illegal.

. . . To give to the clauses in the treaty of 1868 and the agreement of 1877 effect, so as to uphold the jurisdiction exercised in this case, would be to reverse in this instance the general policy of the government towards the Indians, as declared in many statutes and treaties, and recognized in many decisions of this court, from the beginning to the present time. To justify such a departure, in such a case, requires a clear expression of the intention of Congress, and that we have not been able to find.

It results that the First District Court of Dakota was without jurisdiction to find or try the indictment against the prisoner, that the conviction and sentence are void, and that his imprisonment is illegal.[35]

Enraged over the fact that one of the leading progovernment chiefs was murdered, Congress passed the Major Crimes Act in 1885. This act presented a major encroachment on tribal autonomy. Moreover, it provided overlapped jurisdiction with the Federal Enclaves Act by applying the Major Crimes Act to any offender, Indian or non-Indian, in Indian country. Moreover, American Indians were held to these standards even off the reservation:

That immediately upon and after the date of the passage of this act all Indians, committing against the person or property of another Indian or other person any of the following crimes, namely, murder, manslaughter, rape, assault with intent to kill, arson, burglary, and larceny within any Territory of the United States, and either within or without an Indian reservation, shall be subject therefor to the laws of such Territory relating to said crimes, and shall be tried therefor in the same courts and in the same manner and shall be subject to the same penalties as are all other persons charged with the commission of said crimes, respectively; and the said courts are hereby given jurisdiction in all such cases; and such Indians committing any of the above crimes against the person or property of another Indian or other persons within the boundaries of any State of the United States, and within the limits of any Indian reservation, shall be subject to the same laws, tried in the same courts and in the same manner, and subject to the same penalties as are all other persons committing any of the above crimes within the exclusive jurisdiction of the United States.[36]

J. Edgar Hoover, the former head of the Federal Bureau of Investigation, used the Major Crimes Act to expand the authority of the FBI throughout the United States. The original seven offenses became known as the Index Crimes and provided the basis of federal data collection in the yearly Department of Justice publication of the FBI's *Uniform Crime Reports: Crime in the United States.* Eventually the seven major crimes were expanded to thirteen offenses: (1) murder; (2) manslaughter; (3) rape; (4) carnal knowledge of any female, not his wife who has not attained the age of sixteen years (statutory rape); (5) assault with intent to commit rape; (6) incest; (7) assault with intent to kill; (8) assault with a dangerous weapon; (9) assault resulting in serious bodily injury; (10) arson; (11) burglary; (12) robbery; and (13) larceny. The FBI's presence in Indian country is due mainly to the exclusive federal jurisdiction of the Major Crimes Act (although exceptions to this rule are evident today and will be discussed in greater detail when we look at the Navajo criminal justice system). Following the Major Crimes Act, tribes still held exclusive jurisdiction over non–Index Crimes committed by Indians against Indians in Indian country, as specified by the Federal Enclaves Act; but, as noted earlier, this authority eroded as well due to modifications to the Assimilative Crimes Act and the introduction of Public Law 280 during the mid-1900s.[37]

Rules for the Courts of Indian Offenses were modified in 1892 following the end of the major Indian wars in the West. Now the appointed Indian judges needed to be men of intelligence, integrity, and of good moral character, with preference given to those who could read and write English and wore the clothes of a civilized person. Moreover, no Indian who was a polygamist could serve as a judge. Judges were now assigned districts, thus holding the title of district judge. They were still appointed by the commissioner of Indian affairs. The list of punishable offenses within the white-directed tribal jurisdiction included: (1) traditional dances, including the sun dance or any other similar celebration; (2) plural or polygamous marriages; (3) medicine men practices; (4) property destruction; (5) immorality (soliciting prostitution and cohabitation); (6) intoxication and the possession of alcohol; and (7) misdemeanors (all those crimes defined by the Assimilative Crimes Act).

These judges also had the responsibility of solemnizing marriages and keeping records of all legal marriages. They also were authorized to use the

Indian police to bring witnesses and defendants to the court. The court also held exclusive jurisdiction over appeals:

> The judges of the Indian court shall sit together at some convenient place on the reservation, to be designated by the Commissioner of Indian Affairs, at least once in every month, at which sitting they shall constitute the Indian court in general term. A majority of the judges appointed for the reservation shall constitute a quorum of the court and shall have power to try and finally determine any suit or charge that may be properly brought before it; but no judgment or decision by said court shall be valid unless it is concurred in by a majority of all the judges appointed for the reservation, and in case of a failure of a majority of the judges to agree in any cause, the same shall be continued, to be again tried at a subsequent term of the court. The court in general term shall be presided over by the senior judge in point of service on the reservation, and in case there be no such senior judge, the Commissioner of Indian Affairs shall designate one of the judges to preside.[38]

Allotment and the Destruction of the Five Civilized Tribes

The Five Civilized Tribes were termed such due to their adoption of the Euro-American legal and economic model during the early years of the republic, and they brought their U.S.-styled laws, courts, police, and corrections with them to Indian Territory (Oklahoma) during removal. Given that they had already accommodated the Western model of justice, they were generally exempt from the dictates of the Courts of Indian Offenses and other federally imposed judicial authority except for that which dealt with non-Indian offenders within Indian country. However, the Five Civilized Tribes fell out of favor with the federal government for their support of the Confederacy during the Civil War and suffered severe sanctions during Reconstruction. This set in motion plans to include them in the allotment plan—the foundation for cultural genocide at this time—which was already being imposed on other tribes.

Allotment represented the imposition of the Western Protestant ethic model of economic competition and individual responsibility, which was the diametrical opposite of the aboriginal communal, collective responsibility model. Moreover, the aboriginal traditional Indian cultural model reflected social communism. The 160-acre family allotments were comparable to the lands allotted to homesteaders who staked claims on federal public lands opened to settlers. This plan would free up so-called surplus lands held in common by the tribe through treaties. Some of this land was used to relocate other removed tribes in the past, but the plan now was to make this land available to non-Indian homesteaders. Initially, the allotted Indian land was to be held in trust by the U.S. government in order to prevent the land from being taxed or being taken illegally by non-Indians. Nonetheless, many Indians lost their allotment when challenged in court. Lastly, the Allotment Act was intended to have universal application within Indian country and was imposed without any requirement of consent of the tribes or Indians affected. The program was quite effective in that the total amount of treaty-granted, Indian-held land fell from 138 million acres in 1887 to 48 million acres in 1934, with much of this being desert or poor agricultural land. Besides, many Indian landowners eventually lost their allotments to the states for failure to pay property taxes. All told, allotment was a great success for proponents of Manifest Destiny and another dire failure for American Indians.[39]

General Allotment Act (Dawes Act): An act to provide for the allotment of lands in severalty to Indians on the various reservations, and to extend the protection of the laws of the United States and the Territories over the Indians, and for other purposes.

Section 1. That in all cases where any tribe or band of Indians has been, or shall hereafter be, located upon any reservation created for their use, either by treaty stipulation or by virtue of an act of Congress or executive order setting apart the same for their use, the President of the United States shall be, and he hereby is, authorized, wherever in his opinion any reservation or any part thereof of such Indians is advantageous for agricultural and grazing purposes, to cause said reservation, or any part thereof, to be surveyed, or resurveyed if necessary, and to allot the lands in said reservation in severalty to any Indian located thereon in quantities as follows:

To each head of a family, one-quarter of a section;

To each single person over eighteen years of age, one-eighth of a section. . . .

Section 6. That upon the completion of said allotments and the patenting of the lands to said allottees, each and every member of the respective bands or tribes of Indians to whom allotments have been made shall have the benefit of and be subject to the laws, both civil and criminal, of the State or Territory in which they may reside; and no Territory shall pass or enforce any law denying any such Indian within its jurisdiction the equal protection of the law. And every Indian born within the territorial limits of the United

States to whom allotments shall have been made under the provisions of this act, or under any law or treaty, and every Indian born within the territorial limits of the United States who has voluntarily taken up, within said limits, his residence separate and apart from any tribe of Indians therein, and has adopted the habits of civilized life, is hereby declared to be a citizen of the United States, and is entitled to all the rights, privileges, and immunities of such citizens, whether said Indian has been or not, by birth or otherwise, a member of any tribe of Indians within the territorial limits of the United States without in any manner impairing or otherwise affecting the right of any such Indian to tribal or other property. . . .

Section 8. That the provision of this act shall not extend to the territory occupied by the Cherokees, Creeks, Choctaws, Chickasaws, Seminoles, and Osage, Miamies and Peorias, and Sacs and Foxes, in the Indian Territory, nor to any of the reservations of the Seneca Nation of New York Indians in the State of New York, nor to that strip of territory in the State of Nebraska adjoining the Sioux Nation on the south added by executive order.[40]

Under allotment, special educational indoctrinations were imposed, including the use of English only in Indian schools (September 21, 1887) and the inculcation of patriotism in Indian schools (December 10, 1889). Allotment now made it convenient for the federal government to recognize the long neglected Mission Indians of California. And army officers were again established as Indian agents, but now served under the direction of the secretary of the interior (July 13, 1892). In early 1893, the author of the Allotment Acts, Henry L. Dawes, chaired the commission designed to apply the conditions of the act to the Five Civilized Tribes. This was known as the Dawes Commission. The Dawes Commission met with little support from the Five Civilized Tribes in this effort to further reduce their nations, especially since they already had a form of government that mimicked that of the larger U.S. society. This resistance led to congressional action known as the Curtis Act of June 28, 1898, which forced the dissolution of the Five Civilized Tribes, including land held in common and their tribal courts. This action abrogated all treaty promises for protected tribal lands west of the Mississippi River, making the trauma of forced removal even more painful.

Section 17. That it shall be unlawful for any citizen of any one of said tribes to enclose or in any manner, by himself or through another, directly or indirectly, to hold possession of any greater amount of lands or other property belonging to any such nation or tribe than that which would be his approximate share of the lands belonging to such nation or tribe and that of his wife and his minor children as per allotment herein provided; and any person found in such possession of lands or other property in excess of his share and that of his family, as aforesaid, or having the same in any manner enclosed, at the expiration of nine months after the passage of this Act, shall be deemed guilty of a misdemeanor. . . .

Section 26. That on and after the passage of this Act the laws of the various tribes or nations of Indians shall not be enforced at law or in equity by the courts of the United States in the Indian Territory. . . .

Section 28. That on the first day of July, eighteen hundred and ninety-eight, all tribal courts of Indian Territory shall be abolished, and no officer of said courts shall thereafter have any authority whatever to do or perform any act theretofore authorized by any law in connection with said courts, or to receive any pay for same; and all civil and criminal causes then pending in any such court shall be transferred to the United States court in said Territory by filing with the clerk of the court the original papers in the suit: *Provided*, That this section shall not be in force as to the Chickasaw, Choctaw, and Creek tribes or nations until the first day of October, eighteen hundred and ninety-eight. . . .[41]

Now that all tribes in Indian Territory (Oklahoma) fell under the allotment plan, Congress amended the Dawes Act on March 3, 1901, providing citizenship to all Indians in Oklahoma. However, this did not mean that an Indian's word held the same weight as that of a non-Indian in the white man's court.[42]

The conclusion of the Curtis (1898), Burke (1906), and Lacey (1907) Acts was statehood for Indian Territory, now called Oklahoma, the combination of two Choctaw words, *Okla* (people) and *humma* (red). Ironically, the red people's promised land was now opened to white settlers known as "boomers." Clearly, the policy of Manifest Destiny had struck a deadly blow to treaty rights and the integrity of federal policy. And the trend of cultural genocide continued with Indian allotments stolen by boomers, generally with the help of the white-run courts. In the final analysis, Oklahoma became the major Indian concentration camp for forcibly removed tribes, and once there, they were subjected to federal rules designed to destroy their aboriginal traditions, including their languages. Hence, in this steady process of deceit, thirty-two tribes were virtually destroyed: Cheyenne and Arapaho; Wichita and Caddo; Comanche, Kiowa, and Apache; Chickasaw; Potawatomi and Shawnee; Kickapoo; Iowa; Oto and Missouri; Ponca; Tonkawa; Kaw; Osage; Pawnee; Sac and Fox; Seminole; Choctaw; Creek;

Cherokee; Seneca, Wyandotte, Shawnee, Ottawa, Modoc, Peoria and Qua-paw (listed according to their designated settlements in Indian Territory, now known as Oklahoma). Following the conclusion of World War I, Indians outside of Oklahoma who served in the U.S. military could petition for U.S. citizenship. However, U.S. citizenship was not extended to all American Indians until 1924, when Congress passed the Indian Citizenship Act on June 2. Even then, the act carried a conditional provision, one which kept New Mexico from allowing American Indians to vote until 1967.[43]

The last section in this initial chapter of U.S.-sanctioned cultural geno-cide was directed against the Pueblo tribes of New Mexico (one tribe resides in Arizona—the Hopi). The nineteen Pueblo tribes were exempt from allot-ment until 1912 when New Mexico gained statehood. Now the Pueblos came under federal control. However, an unscrupulous local politician, Albert Bacon Fall, who later became President Warren G. Harding's secretary of the interior, devised a ploy designed to declare the Pueblo lands open to white settlement, doing so through Commissioner of Indian Affairs Charles H. Burke. Here, Indian lands, held in trust for the Pueblos, would be con-demned and forfeited because of the Pueblo's uncivilized practicing of their traditional religion, customs, and language. Fall and Burke had their plan presented to the U.S. Congress through Holm O. Bursum, U.S. Senator from New Mexico, in 1922. The Bursum Bill was passed by the Senate but was ultimately defeated due to strong opposition by American Indians and their allies. The notoriety associated with this blatant attack on the Pueblo Indians led to the resignation of Burke in 1923. Secretary of the Interior Fall was eventually arrested, convicted, and incarcerated in 1926 for the Tea Pot Dome scandal, one which tainted the short term (1921–23) of President Warren G. Harding.[44] And as a method of solidifying these legal procedures against American Indians, Title 25 of the United States Code was established in 1926. This entire title pertains specifically to Indians:

> The first official codification of the general and permanent laws of the United States was made in 1874 and followed by a perfected edition in 1878. From 1879 to 1907 a commission was engaged in an effort to codify the great mass of accumulating legislation. The work of the commission involved an expenditure of over $300,000, but was never carried to com-pletion. More recently the task of codification was undertaken by the late Hon. Edward C. Little as chairman of the Committee on the Revision of the Laws of the House of Representatives, who labored indefatigably from 1919 to the day of his death, June 24, 1924. The volumes which repre-sented the result of his labors were embodied in bills which passed the

House of Representatives in three successive Congresses unanimously but failed of action in the Senate. The Code now set forth has resulted from the hearty cooperation of the Committee of the House of Representatives on the Revision of the Laws, and the Select Committee of the United States Senate. . . .[45]

From the Ashes of Ethnic Cleansing—Indian Reorganization and Tribal Preservation

Four years following the granting of citizenship to all American Indians, the Meriam Report (*The Problem of Indian Administration*) was published in 1928 by the Institute for Government Research (Brookings Institute). Canby noted that the Meriam Report provided part of the impetus for a sweeping change in federal policy, which eventually led to passage of the Indian Reorganization Act of 1934 (also known as the Wheeler-Howard Act).[46]

The Meriam Report was a comprehensive review of Indian policy conducted by the Brookings Institute and chaired by Lewis Meriam. Commissioned by Secretary of the Interior Hubert Work, this study set the stage for Indian policy and Indian education for the next two decades. It addressed the dire failure of the federally mandated Indian boarding schools, which were instituted to destroy Native American cultural traditionalism and instead civilize and Christianize Indian children and youth. Meriam's report challenged these past methods of cultural genocide, thereby initiating education reform in Indian country.

Chapter 9 of the Meriam Report dealt exclusively with Indian education, arguing for cultural-specific progressive principles:

> The most fundamental need in Indian education is a change in point of view. Whatever may have been the official government attitude, education for the Indian in the past has proceeded largely on the theory that is is necessary to remove the Indian child as far away as possible from his home environment. . . . It is the task of education to help the Indian, not by assuming that he is fundamentally different, but that he is a human being very much like the rest of us, with a cultural background quite worthwhile for its own sake and as a basis for changes needed in adjusting to modern life.[47]

Meriam saw the restrictive boarding schools as being part of the Indian problem and suggested that, instead of isolating Indian students from both their own culture and that of the majority society, Indian students should be integrated into the existing public school system. The critical analysis that the Meriam Report provided contributed to passage of two Great Depression New Deal legislative actions, both enacted in 1934: the Johnson-O'Malley (J-O'M) Act and the Indian Reorganization (Wheeler-Howard) Act.

The Johnson-O'Malley Act provided congressional support for the changes proposed by John Collier, the first progressive commissioner of Indian affairs, who was appointed by President Franklin Delano Roosevelt. Collier first eliminated the Board of Indian Commissioners, the conservative group that initiated allotment and the harsh boarding schools. The idea now was to provide education for American Indians in regular public schools located near the reservation. J-O'M authorized the secretary of the interior to work in conjunction with state and territory school systems in arranging educational, medical, and other social welfare considerations relevant to American Indians attending these existing public day schools. This act established direct relationships between public schools and the Bureau of Indian Affairs (BIA), the relationship that continues to the present. Collier also established the Education Division within the Bureau of Indian Affairs, making it the primary agency responsible for Indian education, including public education (J-O'M schools). The BIA Education Division continued to exercise this authority until the termination era of the 1950s.[48]

The Johnson-O'Malley Act was augmented by the Wheeler-Howard Indian Reorganization Act, and both were passed within two months of each other. While the Indian Reorganization Act (IRA) provided for annual funding for special Indian education, its most significant aspect was the prohibition of allotment. The IRA also provided funds and government assistance for the purpose of expanding Indian trust lands as well as provisions relevant to tribal organization and incorporation. Clearly, it was the combined efforts of Collier's determination and John Dewey's progressive philosophy that made Indian education a unique integrative community program.

Collier's successes were considerable when compared to past Indian educational endeavors. He faced the same obstacles, including Indian resistance, that his predecessors had, yet Collier's programs were met with greater support from the Indian community. His Indian educational program included the closing of off-reservation boarding schools and the promotion of both reservation day schools and public school programs. These programs were strongly endorsed by Collier's education directors. The first, Carson Ryan, was a member of the Meriam Report team. He was replaced in 1936 by Willard Beatty, a progressive educator from Winnetka, Illinois. Beatty utilized holistic, progressive ideas, similar to those advocated by John Dewey, in his culturally relevant Indian education program. Instead of preparing Indian students for nonexisting urban jobs, Willard tailored Indian education to fit the indigenous rural environments within Indian country.

Collier's plan was successful during his tenure, with Indian school attendance at its highest up to that time. Moreover, allotment was abolished, and a considerable degree of tribal autonomy was returned to Indian groups. Unfortunately, his form of conditional cultural accommodation was undermined by both the Great Depression and the Second World War. While the Great Depression provided the vehicle for Collier's progressive Indian programs, its severity and duration plus the additional cost of the war effort served to make Indian programs a low priority where the practice of cultural genocide once again prevailed. Part of the problem was the demise of the Progressive Education Movement at the end of the Second World War. The result was an end, and in many instances a reversal, of the great experiment in progressive education and innovative, culturally relevant Indian programs initiated by Collier and his two Indian education directors, Ryan and Beatty.[49]

The Wheeler-Howard Act (IRA) was based on an assumption quite contrary to that of the Allotment Act. The IRA's premise was that tribes would be in existence for an indefinite period. Indian reorganization was designed to protect the land base of the tribes and to provide the tribes with some degree of self-government based on the Euro-American model. The federal trust was perhaps the single most significant element of the Indian Reorganization Act. It also restored to tribal ownership those lands and water rights proclaimed surplus under the Allotment Act that were not yet in non-Indian hands. Collier's *Annual Report of the Commissioner of Indian Affairs* articulated the benefits of the Wheeler-Howard Act (IRA):

> Through 50 years of "individualization," coupled with an ever-increasing amount of arbitrary supervision over the affairs of individuals and tribes so long as these individuals and tribes had any assets left, the Indians have been robbed of initiative, their spirit has been broken, their health undermined, and their native pride ground into the dust. The efforts at economic rehabilitation cannot and will not be more than partially successful unless they are accompanied by a determined simultaneous effort to rebuild the shattered morale of a subjugated people that has been taught to believe in its racial inferiority.
>
> The Wheeler-Howard Act provides the means of destroying this inferiority complex, through those features which authorize and legalize tribal organization and incorporation, which give these tribal organizations and corporations limited but real power, and authority over their own affairs, which

broaden the educational opportunities for Indians, and which give Indians a better chance to enter the Indian Service.

Even before the passage of the Wheeler-Howard bill a great spiritual stirring had become noticeable throughout the Indian country. That awakening of the racial spirit must be sustained, if the rehabilitation of the Indian people is to be successfully carried through. It is necessary to face the fact that pauperization, as the result of a century of spoliation, suppression, and paternalism, has made deep inroads. Of necessity it will take time, patience, and intelligent, sympathetic help to rebuild the Indian character where it has been broken down.[50]

The main problem with the IRA was the imposition of tribal organizations based on Western-style constitutions, much like that which occurred a century earlier among the Cherokee, Chickasaw, Choctaw, Creek, and Seminole—the so-called Five Civilized Tribes. Knowing the fate of the Five Civilized Tribes, many tribal leaders were reluctant to adopt a similar model, one with considerably more federal oversight and influence in Indian country. They feared the degree of federal paternalism being forced on tribes in exchange for the protection of their existing lands and resources. Sections 16, 17, and 18 of the IRA address the tribal government process:

Section 16. Any Indian tribe, or tribes, residing on the same reservation, shall have the right to organize for its common welfare, and may adopt an appropriate constitution and bylaws, which shall become effective when ratified by a majority vote of the adult members of the tribe, or of the adult Indians residing on such reservation, as the case may be, at a special election authorized and called by the Secretary of the Interior under such rules and regulations as he may prescribe. Such constitution and bylaws when ratified as aforesaid and approved by the Secretary of the Interior shall be revocable by an election open to the same voters, and conducted in the same manner as herein above provided. Amendments to the constitution and bylaws may be ratified and approved by the Secretary in the same manner as the original constitution and bylaws. In addition to all powers vested in any Indian tribe or tribal council by existing law, the constitution adopted by said tribe shall also vest in such tribe or its tribal council the following rights and power: To employ legal counsel, the choice of counsel and fixing of fees to be subject to the approval of the Secretary of the Interior; to prevent the sale, disposition, lease, or encumbrance of tribal lands, interests in lands, or other tribal assets without the consent of the tribe; and to negotiate with the Federal, State, and local Governments. The Secretary of the Interior shall advise such tribes or its tribal council of all appropriation estimates or Federal projects for the benefit of the tribe prior to the submission of such estimates to the Bureau of the Budget and the Congress.

Section 17. The Secretary of the Interior may, upon petition by at least one-third of the adult Indians, issue a charter of incorporation to such tribe: *Provided*, That such charter shall not become operative until ratified at a special election by a majority vote of the adult Indians living on the reservation. Such charter may convey to the incorporated tribe the power to purchase, take by gift, or bequest, or otherwise, own, hold, manage, operate, and dispose of property of every description, real and personal, including the power to purchase restrictive Indian lands and to issue in exchange therefor interest in corporate property, and such further powers as may be incidental to the conduct of corporate business, not inconsistent with law, but no authority shall be granted to sell, mortgage, or lease for a period exceeding ten years any of the land included in the limits of the reservation. Any charter so issued shall not be revoked or surrendered except by Act of Congress.

Section 18. This Act shall not apply to any reservation wherein a majority of the adult Indians, voting at a special election duly called by the Secretary of the Interior, shall vote against its application. It shall be the duty of the Secretary of the Interior, within one year after the passage and approval of this Act, to call such an election which election shall be held by secret ballot upon thirty days' notice.[51]

Wheeler-Howard (IRA) also defined who is an American Indian:

Section 19. The term "Indian" as used in this Act shall include all persons of Indian descent who are members of any recognized Indian tribe now under Federal jurisdiction, and all persons who are descendants of such members who were, on June 1, 1934, residing within the present boundaries of any Indian reservation and shall further include all other persons of one-half or more Indian blood. For the purpose of this Act, Eskimos and other aboriginal peoples of Alaska shall be considered Indians. The term "tribe" wherever used in this Act shall be construed to refer to any Indian tribe, organized band, pueblo, or the Indians residing on one reservation. The words "adult Indians" wherever used in this Act shall be construed to refer to Indians who have attained the age of twenty-one years.[52]

The Oklahoma tribes, those subjected to the worst elements of allotment and accounting for nearly one-third of the American Indians in the

United States, were exempt from the Wheeler-Howard Act. In June 1936, Congress extended the Wheeler-Howard Act to Indians residing in Oklahoma in the Oklahoma Indian Welfare Act.[53]

Although mentioned in the Wheeler-Howard Act, the nineteen Pueblo tribes of New Mexico were exempt due to Spanish land grant allotments that separated the Pueblos from other Spanish land grants. For centuries before white contact, the nineteen (Rio Grande) Pueblo tribes were organized into a loose confederation ruled by religious leaders. The Pueblo Indians were provided semi-autonomy from the Spanish following the 1680 uprising that temporarily drove the Spanish from what is now New Mexico. The Mexicans continued to respect this agreement, as did the U.S. territory, until 1912, when New Mexico achieved statehood, bringing the Pueblo tribes under federal regulation. The Pueblos became suspicious of the federal government following Albert Bacon Fall's and Charles H. Burke's ploy to steal their lands under the guise of allotment. While all but the Jemez Pueblo accepted the land protection offered by IRA, only three Pueblos (Laguna, Isleta, and Santa Clara) adopted tribal constitutions; however, in 1965, they coordinated a system based on their aboriginal confederation. Since then, Pueblos elect their own governor, while collectively a governor is elected by his peers to serve as the overall Pueblo president. Religious leaders continue to hold significant power in that in most Pueblos they elect the governor and serve as his or her advisory board.[54]

In blatant violation of Sections 16 and 17 of the conditions of tribal governance, as prescribed by the Wheeler-Howard Act, were the Hopi, a Pueblo tribe that resides on four mesas near both the Navajo and White Mountain Apache tribes in the northeastern portion of Arizona. Apparently, the aboriginal Hopi practices were too oppositional to Western beliefs for even the progressive Indian commissioner, John Collier, in that he elicited the assistance of the American Indian novelist Oliver LaFarge, who won a Pulitzer Prize for his study *Laughing Boy*, to help draft a tribal constitution that would both restrict the practice of Hopi traditional customs and reduce their Pueblo lands. The Hopi were suspicious of federal intervention, given that they were targets of President Harding's Secretary of the Interior Albert Bacon Fall and his schemes to defraud Indians of their land, oil, and mineral rights. Another element of Fall's scheme was to destroy religious freedom among these tribes, including the Hopi. The fabricated Hopi constitution was neither written nor adopted by vote by the Hopi people, and this resulted in a long-standing conflict between the Hopi and Navajo, which is still being bitterly fought in that region today. James explained this phenomenon in his book *Pages from Hopi History*.

The commissioner's office in Washington had been given to understand that the majority of the Hopi approved the plan (IRA). As a result, on December 14, 1936, Commissioner Collier signed his approval. Whereupon, whether the majority of the Hopi wished it or not, the Hopi "Tribe"—so far as the government of the United States was concerned—was officially established with a constitution and by-laws written for the most part by the distinguished author and anthropologist Oliver LaFarge. . . . It was in 1943 that in "Land Management District Six" the Bureau of Indian Affairs circumscribed a Hopi Reservation of 631,194 acres as opposed to the 2,499,588 acres in the Hopi Reservation decreed by President Arthur.[55]

This era of mixed progress in Indian country was soon reversed during the Eisenhower era of termination and relocation.

The Reemergence of Cultural Genocide and Anti-Indianism

A curt introduction to this section is provided by the 1999 Memorandum decision resulting from *Cobell v. Babbitt*, (30 F. Supp. 2d 24):

Less than two decades after the Reorganization Act was passed, in the early 1950s, congressional policy swung in a new direction. According to Assistant Secretary Gover, "this time the policy was called the 'termination policy.' Termination basically meant the severing of the relationship between the tribe and the United States, and, specifically, the severing of the trust relationship." Congress directed BIA to identify tribes that were said to be "ready for termination, ready to be released from federal supervision because by this point the conclusion had been reached that the real problem with Indian affairs, and the real reason the Indians are poor, is that they're under the thumb of the federal government." Following that direction, the United States withdrew recognition of the existence of certain tribes and forswore any responsibility to those tribes or their people as Indians. The tribal assets were gathered up and either administered by a corporate entity or distributed among the tribal members. Much like the allotment policy, this policy devastated the tribal communities. The termination policy ended quickly. After the 1960s, no further tribes were terminated.[56]

President Eisenhower appointed Dillon Myer, a former head of the Japanese-American Relocation Centers, to the position of commissioner of the Bureau of Indian Affairs during his administration. His dictatorial style set the stage for a combined executive and congressional endeavor to reverse the progress gained under the Wheeler-Howard and Johnson-O'Malley acts. The first act in this series was House Concurrent Resolution 108. On August 1, 1953, the Eighty-third Congress enacted a fundamental change in Indian policy, which again reinforced the concepts of cultural genocide and ethnic cleansing by attempting to abolish federal obligations to Indian groups and, by the swiftness of passing an "act of Congress," was ready to deny American Indians any special recognition and thereby relegate them as common members of the states within which their reservation was located:

> Whereas it is the policy of Congress, as rapidly as possible, to make the Indians within the territorial limits of the United States subject to the same laws and entitled to the same privileges and responsibilities as are applicable to other citizens of the United States, to end their status as wards of the United States, and to grant them all of the rights and prerogatives pertaining to American citizenship; and Whereas the Indians within the territorial limits of the United States should assume their full responsibilities as American citizens: Now, therefore, be it that it is declared to be the sense of Congress that, at the earliest possible time, all of the Indian tribes and the individual members thereof located within the States of California, Florida, New York, and Texas, and all of the following named Indian tribes and individual members thereof, should be freed from Federal supervision and control and from all disabilities and limitations specially applicable to Indians: The Flathead Tribe of Montana, the Klamath Tribe of Oregon, the Menominee Tribe of Wisconsin, the Potowatamie [sic] Tribe of Kansas and Nebraska, and those members of the Chippewa Tribe who are on the Turtle Mountain Reservation, North Dakota. It is further declared to be the sense of Congress that, upon the release of such tribes and individual members thereof from such disabilities and limitations, all offices of the Bureau of Indian Affairs in the States of California, Florida, New York, and Texas and all other offices of the Bureau of Indian Affairs whose primary purpose was to serve any Indian tribe or individual Indian freed from Federal supervision should be abolished. It is further declared to be the sense of Congress that the Secretary of the Interior should examine all existing legislation dealing with such Indians, and treaties between the Government of the United States and each such tribe, and report to Congress at the earliest practicable date, but not later than January 1, 1954, his recommendations for such legislation as, in his judgment, may be necessary to accomplish the purposes of this resolution.[57]

Two weeks later, Public Law 280 went into effect, which extended state jurisdiction over offenses committed by or against Indians in Indian country. A major problem with this legislation was the often hostile relationship between non-Indians and Indians in states where reservations existed. Now the non-Indians had their chance to further exploit their American Indian neighbors, who no longer had federal protection.

Section 2. Title 18, United States Code: (1162). State jurisdiction over offenses committed by or against Indians in the Indian country;

(a) Each of the States listed in the following table shall have jurisdiction over offenses committed by or against Indians in the areas of Indian country listed opposite the name of the State to the same extent that such State has jurisdiction over offenses committed elsewhere within the State, and the criminal laws of such State shall have the same force and effect within such Indian country as they have elsewhere within the State:

State of	Indian Country Affected
California	All Indian country within the State;
Minnesota	All Indian country within the State, except the Red Lake Reservation;
Nebraska	All Indian country within the State;
Oregon	All Indian country within the State, except the Warm Spring Reservation;
Wisconsin	All Indian country within the State, except the Menominee Reservation.

(b) Nothing in this section shall authorize the alienation, encumbrance, or taxation of any real or personal property, including water rights, belonging to any Indian or any Indian tribe, band, or community that is held in trust by the United States or subject to a restriction against alienation imposed by the United States; or shall authorize regulation of the use of such property in a manner inconsistent with any Federal treaty, agreement, or statute or with any regulation made pursuant thereto; or shall deprive any Indian or any Indian tribe, band, or community of any right, privilege, or immunity afforded under Federal treaty agreement, or statute with respect to hunting, trapping, or fishing or the control, licensing, or regulation thereof. . . .[58]

Less than a year later, in June 1954, the Menominee Indians of Wisconsin were added to the list by Congress.[59] They soon became the example of how devastating the policy of termination was in Indian country. Termination and Public Law 280 were unilateral policy decisions made by the U.S. Congress and forced upon Indian tribes. No tribe has ever accepted the terms of Public Law 280. Despite this fact, it continues in those so-designated states.

Another component of this plan to terminate federal obligations toward Indians included the transfer of Indian health care services from the Bureau of Indian Affairs (BIA) to the Public Health Service of the then U.S. Department of Health, Education, and Welfare. This new service under the Public Health Service became known as the Indian Health Service (IHS).[60] However, one of the most devastating aspects of termination was the twentieth-century method of Indian removal, the BIA's relocation program, where young Indians were enticed out of Indian country, away from their cultural and language base, to targeted urban settings. Relocation was operated by the Bureau of Indian Affairs, Branch of Relocation; grants were paid to Indians willing to leave Indian country for urban areas. A report on relocation was provided in the 1954 *Annual Report of the Commissioner of Indian Affairs*:

> Approximately 54 percent of the Indians assisted to relocate came from 3 northern areas (Aberdeen, Billings, and Minneapolis), and 46 percent came from 4 southern areas (Anadarko, Gallup, Muskogee, and Phoenix). They went to 20 different States. The Los Angeles and Chicago metropolitan areas continued to be the chief centers of relocation.[61]

The combination of termination and relocation contributed to a new social problem—psychocultural marginality—whereby American Indians were caught between two worlds without fully belonging to either. This represented the ultimate form of cultural genocide. Their culture and language again attacked by the combined effects of termination and relocation, a new generation of American Indians living off reservations and in urban Indian ghettos were socialized in a world of both psychological and cultural ambiguity—the foundation of marginality. With this process came increased social, health, and legal problems. Costo and Henry noted this process in their book, *Indian Treaties: Two Centuries of Dishonor*:

> Religious groups and white-controlled humanitarian organizations generally embodied the worst of the growing paternalism toward the Natives. Finally, the federal government, jockeying precariously between policies of assimilation and the growing recognition that the tribes simply would not

disappear together with their unique cultures, originated what has become known as the "Relocation Program." Indians were induced to go to the cities for training in the arts of the technological world. There they were dumped into housing that in most cases was ghetto-based, into jobs that were dead end, and training that failed to lead to professions and occupations. The litany of that period provides the crassest example of government ignorance of the Indian situation. The "Indian problem" did not go away. It worsened. The policies of the Eisenhower administration, which espoused the termination of federal-Indian relationships, was shown to be a failure, a gross injustice added to a history of injustice.[62]

Termination ended with the failed Menominee experience but did nothing to reverse the damage done by either relocation or Public Law 280. Wisconsin exemplified state hostility toward Indians within state boundaries. Indeed, the state went too far in its interpretation of the combined authority of termination and Public Law 280. Wisconsin felt that the law made all state statutes applicable to the dissolved reservations, including specified exemptions such as hunting and fishing rights. In 1964, the U.S. Supreme Court held that the Termination Act did not abrogate Indian treaty rights, since these rights were reserved by Public Law 280, which was passed by the same Congress. Continued poverty and exploitation eventually led to the Menominee Restoration Act in December 1973, which repealed the Termination Act of June 17, 1954, and restored tribal status and federal supervision.[63]

More problematic is the impact of Public Law 280. Attempts to impose state or territorial law in Indian country predated Public Law 280 by more than one hundred twenty years, with Georgia's attempt to extend state law within the Cherokee Nation. *Crow Dog* and other related cases in the 1880s reopened this debate with cases supported by the Departments of Interior (BIA) and Justice that were designed to challenge Chief Justice Marshall's recognition of tribal sovereignty in 1832 in *Worcester v. Georgia.*

Involvement by the Department of the Interior, in general, and the Bureau of Indian Affairs, in particular, was a blatant violation of the federal trust responsibility held by these agencies in their representation of their wards in Indian country. Collusion on the part of BIA Commissioner Henry Price with the U.S. Department of Justice in a number of cases during the 1880s, including *Crow Dog*, set the stage for passage of the Major Crimes Act and eventually Public Law 280. In many of these cases, the U.S. attorneys, who had legal responsibility to defend Indian wards, would join the states' attorneys in prosecuting Indian defendants in state courts using state statutes instead of allowing the tribes to adjudicate these cases involving Indian-versus-Indian offenses. The United States joined the states' attorneys in appealing rulings that upheld tribal sovereignty:

> While Crow Dog's case was in the process of trial and appeal, the BIA was involved in at least six parallel murder cases, each time attempting to extend some form of U.S. criminal law, either federal or state, to the tribes. The wide range of cases, which spanned the entire West, reveals that extension of criminal law to the tribes was a matter of BIA policy, and having been unable to induce the U.S. Congress to extend criminal jurisdiction over the tribes, the BIA was trying to induce state and territorial courts to do so in violation of its legal responsibility to defend the interests of the tribes. Moreover, the BIA prosecuted several of the cases simultaneously, using different approaches to gain criminal jurisdiction. Even if the agency was not certain of winning its desired result in *Crow Dog*, it had alternative cases ready for action.[64]

While Public Law 280 did serve to override Chief Justice Marshall's original conceptualization of Indian autonomy and sovereignty in Indian country, on the one hand, it did not completely obviate the federal trust relationship as many states hoped that it would. Nevertheless, Public Law 280 not only extended state laws and jurisdiction within Indian country, it also provided the states with power over the Indians in a way that contributed to a greater distance between the dominant Euro-American culture and that of Indian traditionalism. Intergroup friction increased under Public Law 280. Part of this friction stemmed from a number of factors: (1) the general hostility that non-Indians living near reservations learned within their enculturation; (2) the reciprocal antagonisms between two diametrically different social groups; (3) the fact that while the states had this new criminal authority, they could not tax tribal properties in order to pay for these services; and (4) the resentment that tribal leaders held toward both state and federal authorities for establishing these changes within the criminal justice system without their consent.

In 1968, Public Law 280 was amended to require tribal consent to state jurisdiction. No tribe has ever consented to this arrangement and, equally significant, no existing Public Law 280 jurisdiction has been revoked. Public Law 280 today involves 23 percent of Indian country in the lower forty-eight states as well as all Alaska Native communities, giving it an overall influence in over 75 percent of all U.S.-recognized Native American groups. Some of the optional states, like North Dakota, made their acceptance of Public Law 280 jurisdiction contingent on tribal consent and therefore never activated it, given that no tribe has yet consented. Other jurisdictions, like Arizona and South Dakota, exercise limited jurisdiction under Public Law 280. Arizona limits its jurisdiction to air and water pollution, while South Dakota limits its jurisdiction to state highways running through reservations.[65] Equally problematic are the quasi-Public Law 280 states whose jurisdictional authority over Indian country predated Public Law 280. Included here are New York, Maine, and North Carolina. New Mexico's jurisdictional agreements, some of which were enacted in the Spanish colonial era, are also complicated and appear to fall within the quasi-Public Law 280 category. Generally speaking, Public Law 280 and quasi-Public Law 280 states have treated their American Indian clients as second-class citizens, neglecting them at best and often abusing and exploiting them. This sentiment is still alive and well, especially in the western states.

CHAPTER TWO

CIVIL RIGHTS, SELF-DETERMINATION, AND THE NEW FEDERALISM

The pendulum of Indian policy and justice again moved from the extreme of cultural genocide toward tribal self-determination during the turbulent 1960s and 1970s. During this time, the federal government again overreacted to what they perceived as a contemporary Indian uprising, bringing in both federal law enforcement and the military at Wounded Knee, South Dakota, in their battle with the American Indian Movement.

The early 1960s witnessed a movement against the combined effects of termination and relocation, beginning with a Meriam-like study, initiated by the private Commission on the Rights, Liberties, and Responsibilities of the American Indian in 1961 and completed in 1966, entitled *The Indian: America's Unfinished Business.* In June 1961, notable tribal leaders met at the University of Chicago, forging a *Declaration of Indian Purpose* that outlined Indian-specific proposals and recommendations in the areas of development, education, health, housing, justice, and welfare. Part of this declaration was the Indian creed:

> WE BELIEVE in the inherent right of all people to retain spiritual and cultural values, and that the free exercise of these values is necessary to the normal development of any people. Indians exercised this inherent right to live their

own lives for thousands of years before the white man came and took their lands. It is a more complex world in which Indians live today, but the Indian people who first settled the New World and built the great civilizations which only now are being dug out of the past, long ago demonstrated that they could master complexity.

WE BELIEVE that the history and development of America show that the Indian has been subjected to duress, undue influence, unwarranted pressures, and policies that have produced uncertainty, frustration, and despair. Only when the public understands these conditions and is moved to take action toward the formulation and adoption of sound and consistent policies and programs will these destroying factors be removed and the Indian resume his normal growth and make his maximum contribution to modern society.[1]

The declaration also recommended specific legislative and regulatory proposals, which included abandonment of the termination and relocation elements of House Concurrent Resolution 108. It also called for an end to micromanagement by the Bureau of Indian Affairs, stating that American Indians were not looking for charity, paternalism, or even benevolence, but rather a recognition of, and a respect for, their culture and traditions.

During this same time, Secretary of the Interior Stewart Udall appointed a special Task Force on Indian Affairs,[2] which presented its report in July 1961. Because the task force was chaired by a "white Indian," W.W. Keeler, principal chief of the Oklahoma Cherokees (the Oklahoma Cherokee have the weakest requirements for enrollment—merely proof that a family member existed on the rolls during the time from removal to allotment), a dominant societal bias was inherent in this report. Keeler was an oil company executive and was phenotypically white. While the task force report called for a shift in policy from termination of federal trust relationships, the restoration of federal influence was qualified by a number of capitalistic endeavors and principles, including a withdrawal of federally mandated and often treaty-specific obligatory services to those tribes that it determined had substantial incomes and superior educational experiences. Also inherent in this report was the idea of forcing tribes to petition annually for federal monies from a number of sources where both Indians and non-Indians would compete.

During the late 1960s, the United States witnessed widespread civil unrest throughout the country, beginning with African-Americans fighting for their civil rights to middle- and upper-class white college students opposing the Vietnam war. Other underrepresented groups, such as gays and lesbians,

Hispanics/Chicanos, the elderly, and American Indians soon joined the mass protest that began with race riots in large metropolitan areas like New York City, Watts in Los Angeles, and Detroit. From this polarization emerged the American Indian Movement (AIM), a product of the urban relocation movement of the 1950s and, according to Vine Deloria, Jr., Public Law 280.[3] The American Indian Movement was an urban militant organization founded in Minneapolis in 1968. AIM was seen as a radical faction of the National Indian Youth Council (NIYC), a Pan-Indian organization founded in 1961. In this sense its radicalism was patterned after the Weatherman faction of Students for a Democratic Society (SDS), an Anglo-American college-level counterpart to NIYC and the Black Panthers, an African-American urban-ghetto militant group of the time.

This radicalism influenced the takeover of Alcatraz on November 9, 1969. On that date, seventy-eight American Indians made a dramatic predawn raid on Alcatraz Island, focusing worldwide attention on the new Indian protest movement. At its peak, on November 30, 1969, about six hundred Indians, representing some fifty tribes, occupied the island. These numbers declined after electricity, water, and telephones were shut off. All Indian occupants were forcefully removed a year and a half later. Clearly, this was a precursor to the occupation of the Bureau of Indian Affairs in Washington, D.C., in 1972 and the ill-fated ten-week takeover of Wounded Knee on the Pine Ridge Sioux Reservation in South Dakota in 1973. Vine Deloria, Jr., a popular media spokesperson for these radicalized Indians, contended that attempts by Public Law 280 states to tax the income and property of Indians in Indian country was another contributing element to this unrest. These radical actions resulted in numerous criminal offenses, including murder. The most controversial murder cases involved the deaths of two Federal Bureau of Investigation (FBI) agents, Jack R. Coler and Ronald A. Williams, and Joseph Stuntz, an American Indian, on June 16, 1975, during a firefight between members of AIM and the FBI on Pine Ridge, and the mysterious death of a Canadian Indian woman witness, Anna Mae Aquash, in early 1976. Leonard Peltier, an AIM leader, is currently serving a life sentence at Leavenworth Federal Penitentiary in Kansas for his alleged involvement in the killings of the FBI agents.[4]

Many reservation Indians did not side with AIM or its tactics. Others attempted to work within the existing political structure to bring about change within Indian country. This resulted in the creation of the Native American Rights Fund (NARF), the Indian Self-Determination and Education Assistance Act, the Indian Law Enforcement Improvement Act, and the Task Force Reports of the American Indian Policy Review Commission. The premise for all these actions was the Civil Rights Act of 1968. Titles II through VII of the Civil Rights Act of 1968 addressed expanding the Bill of Rights to Indians in Indian country, the authorization of a model code for Courts of Indian Offenses, and a provision that put the brakes on Public Law 280.

ICRA: Title II—Rights of Indians

Indian Rights

SEC. 202. No Indian tribe in exercising powers of self-government shall

1. make or enforce any law prohibiting the free exercise of religion, or abridging the freedom of speech, or of the press, or the right of the people peaceably to assemble and to petition for a redress of grievances;
2. violate the right of the people to be secure in their persons, houses, papers, and effects against unreasonable search and seizures, nor issue warrants, but upon probable cause, supported by oath or affirmation, and particularly describing the place to be searched and the person or thing to be seized;
3. subject any person for the same offense to be twice put in jeopardy;
4. compel any person in any criminal case to be a witness against himself;
5. take any private property for a public use without just compensation;
6. deny to any person in a criminal proceeding the right to a speedy and public trial, to be informed of the nature and cause of the accusation, to be confronted with the witnesses against him, to have compulsory process for obtaining witnesses in his favor, and at his own expense to have the assistance of counsel for this defense;
7. require excessive bail, impose excessive fines, inflict cruel and unusual punishments, and in no event impose for conviction of any one offense any penalty or punishment greater than imprisonment for a term of six months or a fine of $500, or both;
8. deny to any person within its jurisdiction the equal protection of its laws or deprive any person of liberty or property without due process of law;
9. pass any bill of attainder or ex post facto law; or
10. deny to any person accused of an offense punishable by imprisonment the right, upon request, to a trial by jury of not less than six persons.

Habeas Corpus

SEC. 203. The privilege of the writ of habeas corpus shall be available to any person, in a court of the United States, to test the legality of his detention by order of an Indian tribe.

ICRA: Title III—Model Code Governing Courts of Indian Offenses

SEC. 301. The Secretary of the Interior is authorized and directed to recommend to the Congress, on or before July 1, 1968, a model code to govern the administration of justice by courts of Indian offenses on Indian reservations. Such code shall include provisions which will (1) assure that any individual being tried for an offense by a court of Indian offenses shall have the same rights, privileges, and immunities under the United States Constitution as would be guaranteed any citizen of the United States being tried in a Federal court for any similar offense, (2) assure that any individual being tried for an offense by a court of Indian offenses will be advised and made aware of his rights under the United States Constitution, and under any tribal constitution applicable to such individual, (3) establish proper qualifications for the office of judge of the courts of Indian offenses, and (4) provide for the establishing of educational classes for the training of judges of courts of Indian offenses. In carrying out the provisions of this title, the Secretary of the Interior shall consult with the Indians, Indian tribes, and interested agencies of the United States.

SEC. 302. There is hereby authorized to be appropriated such sum as may be necessary to carry out the provisions of this title.

ICRA: Title IV—Jurisdiction over Criminal and Civil Actions

Assumption by State

SEC. 401. (a) The consent of the United States is hereby given to any State not having jurisdiction over criminal offenses committed by or against Indians in the areas of Indian country situated within such State to assume, with the consent of the Indian tribe occupying the particular

Indian country or part thereof which could be affected by such assumption, such measure of jurisdiction over any or all of such offenses committed within such Indian country or any part thereof as may be determined by such State to the same extent that such State has jurisdiction over any such offense committed elsewhere within the State, and the criminal laws of such State shall have the same force and effect within such Indian country or part thereof as they have elsewhere within that State.

(b) Nothing in this section shall authorize the alienation, encumbrance, or taxation of any real or personal property, including water rights, belonging to any Indian or any Indian tribe, band, or community that is held in trust by the United States or is subject to a restriction against alienation imposed by the United States; or shall authorize regulation of the use of such property in a manner inconsistent with any Federal treaty, agreement, or statute or with any regulation made pursuant thereto; or shall deprive any Indian or any Indian tribe, band, or community of any right, privilege, or immunity afforded under Federal treaty, agreement, or statute with respect to hunting, trapping, or fishing or the control, licensing, or regulation thereof.

Assumption by State of Civil Jurisdiction

SEC. 402. (a) The consent of the United States is hereby given to any State not having jurisdiction over criminal offenses committed by or against Indians in the areas of Indian country situated within such State to assume, with the consent of the Indian tribe occupying the particular Indian country or part thereof which could be affected by such assumption, such measure of jurisdiction over any or all of such offenses committed within such Indian country or any part thereof as may be determined by such State to the same extent that such State has jurisdiction over any such offense committed elsewhere within the State, and the criminal laws of such State shall have the same force and effect within such Indian country or part thereof as they have elsewhere within that State.

(b) Nothing in this section shall authorize the alienation, encumbrance, or taxation of any real or personal property, including water rights, belonging to any Indian or any Indian tribe, band, or community that is held in trust by the United States or is subject to a restriction against alienation imposed by the United States; or shall authorize regulation of the use of such property in a manner inconsistent with any Federal treaty, agreement, or statute or with any regulation made pursuant thereto; or shall deprive any Indian or any Indian tribe, band, or community of any right, privilege, or immunity afforded under Federal treaty, agreement, or statute with respect to hunting, trapping, or fishing or the control, licensing, or regulation thereof. . . .

Retrocession of Jurisdiction by State

SEC. 403 (a) The United States is authorized to accept a retrocession by any State of all or any measure of the criminal or civil jurisdiction, or both, acquired by such State pursuant to the provisions of section 1162 of title 18 of the United States Code, section 1360 of title 28 of the United States Code, or section 7 of the Act of August 15, 1953 (67 Stat. 588), as it was in effect prior to its repeal by subsection (b) of this section.

(b) Section 7 of the Act of August 15, 1953 (67 Stat. 588), is hereby repealed, but such repeal shall not affect any cession of jurisdiction made pursuant to such section prior to its repeal. . . .

Special Election

SEC. 406. State jurisdiction acquired pursuant to this title with respect to criminal offenses or civil causes of action, or with respect to both, shall be applicable in Indian country only where the enrolled Indians within the affected area of such Indian country accept such jurisdiction by a majority vote of the adult Indians voting at a special election held for that purpose. The Secretary of the Interior shall call such special election under such rules and regulations as he may prescribe, when requested to do so by the tribal council or other governing body, or by 20 per centum of such enrolled adults.

ICRA: Title VII—Materials Relating to Constitutional Rights of Indians

Secretary of Interior to Prepare

SEC. 701. (a) In order that the constitutional rights of Indians might be fully protected, the Secretary of the Interior is authorized and directed to—

(1) have the document entitled "Indian Affairs, Laws, and Treaties" (Senate Document Numbered 319, volumes 1 and 2, Fifty-eighth Congress), revised and extended to include all treaties, laws, Executive orders, and regulations relating to Indian affairs in force on September 1, 1967, and to have such revised document printed at the Government Printing Office;

(2) have revised and republished the treatise entitled "Federal Indian Law"; and

(3) have prepared, to the extent determined by the Secretary of the Interior to be feasible, an accurate compilation of the official opinions, published and unpublished, of the solicitor of the Department of the Interior relating to Indian affairs rendered by the Solicitor prior to September 1, 1967, and to have such compilation printed as a Government publication at the Government Printing Office.

(b) With respect to the document entitled "Indian Affairs, Laws, and Treaties" as revised and extended in accordance with paragraph (1) of subsection (a), and the compilation prepared in accordance with paragraph (3) of such subsection, the Secretary of the Interior shall take such action as may be necessary to keep such document and compilation current on an annual basis.

(c) There is authorized to be appropriated for carrying out the provisions of this title, with respect to the preparation but not including printing, such sum as may be necessary.[5]

The Civil Rights Act of 1968 was possible due to the influence of President Lyndon Johnson. A month prior to its passage he set the stage for the new era in Indian policy—that of self-determination. In his special message to Congress on March 6, 1968, Johnson proposed "a new goal for our Indian programs: A goal that ends the old debate about 'termination' of Indian programs and stresses self-determination; a goal that erases old attitudes of paternalism and promotes partnership self-help."[6] With its passage, the Civil Rights Act of 1968 finally extended to American Indians and Alaskan Natives the constitutional rights already granted to the general United States society and special classes: African-Americans, women, Puerto Ricans, and juveniles (*In re Gault, 1967*).

A significant provision ended the unilateral encroachment of jurisdiction by local and state agencies and authorities provided under Public Law 280. It also allowed Public Law 280 states to retrocede previous jurisdictions to the federal government. And it set the stage for a critical review of the anti-Indian policies established under House Concurrent Resolution 108, notably termination and relocation. Indeed, in his Special Message on Indian Affairs (July 8, 1970), President Richard Nixon continued his predecessors' lead, declaring termination a failure and calling on Congress to repudiate this policy. (Interestingly, these devastating policies were enacted and directed by President Eisenhower when Nixon served as his vice-president.) In 1973, Congress passed the Menominee Restoration Act, effectively ending the failed policy of "vulgar capitalism." President Nixon's influence on Congress included the Indian Education Act of 1972, extension of Indian preference in employment within the BIA, the Indian Financing Act of 1974, and the Indian Self-Determination and Education Assistance Act of 1975. The Indian component of the Civil Rights Act of 1968 also provided the impetus for the rise of Indian-interest legal and advocacy agencies such as the Native American Rights Fund (NARF) situated in Boulder, Colorado. Another stone in the foundation of Indian self-determination was laid when Senator Robert Kennedy (and following his assassination, Senator Edward Kennedy) hosted a Special Subcommittee on Indian Education in November 1969.[7] The subcommittee's report highlighted the marked discrepancies in Indian education, a significant social institution entrusted to the federal government. The report provided the following profile of Indian education at that time:

- Forty thousand Navajo Indians, nearly a third of the entire tribe, are functional illiterates in English.
- The average educational level for all Indians under Federal supervision is 5 school years.
- More than one out of every five Indian men has less than 5 years of schooling.
- Dropout rates for Indians are twice the national average.
- In New Mexico, some Indian high school students walk 2 miles to the bus every day and then ride 50 miles to school.
- The average age of top level BIA education administrators is 58 years.
- In 1953 the BIA began a crash program to improve education for Navajo children. Between then and 1967, supervisory positions in BIA headquarters increased 113 percent; supervisory positions in BIA schools increased 144 percent; administrative and clerical positions in the BIA schools increased 94 percent. Yet, teaching positions increased only 20 percent.
- In one school in Oklahoma the student body is 100 percent Indian; yet it is controlled by a three-man, non-Indian school board.
- Only 18 percent of the students in Federal Indian schools go on to college; the national average is 50 percent.
- Only 3 percent of Indian students who enroll in college graduate; the national average is 32 percent.
- The BIA spends only $18 per year per child on textbooks and supplies, compared to a national average of $40.
- Despite a Presidential directive 2 years ago, only one of the 226 BIA schools is governed by an elective school board.[8]

The Indian Self-Determination and Education Assistance Act was passed on January 4, 1975. Two days earlier, Senator James Abourezk of South Dakota established the American Indian Policy Review Commission, which led to task force reports published a year later on a number of aspects of the status of American Indians, including Indian health and alcohol and drug abuse. The Indian Self-Determination and Education Assistance Act provided avenues for native leaders in Indian country to contract with the federal government (Departments of the Interior and Health, Education and Welfare, now Health and Welfare and Education) to run their own programs guaranteed under U.S. trust obligations. The basis for this was the corruption and general ineptitude of the federal agencies mandated to provide quality services to American Indians and Alaskan Natives.

Congressional Findings

SEC. 2. (a) The Congress after careful review of the Federal Government's historical and special legal relationship with, and resulting responsibilities to, American Indian people, finds that:

(1) the prolonged Federal domination of Indian service programs has served to retard rather than enhance the progress of Indian people and their communities by depriving Indians of the full opportunity to develop leadership skills crucial to the realization of self-government, and has denied to the Indian people an effective voice in the planning and implementation of programs for the benefit of Indians which are responsive to the true needs of Indian communities; and

(2) the Indian people will never surrender their desire to control their relationships both among themselves and with non-Indian governments, organizations, and persons.

(b) The Congress further finds that:

(1) true self-determination in any society of people is dependent upon an educational process which will insure the development of qualified people to fulfill meaningful leadership roles.

(2) the Federal responsibility for and assistance to education of Indian children has not effected the desired level of educational achievement or created the diverse opportunities and personal satisfaction which education can and should provide; and

(3) parental and community control of the educational process is of crucial importance to the Indian people.

Declaration of Policy

SEC. 3. (a) The Congress hereby recognizes the obligation of the United States to respond to the strong expression of the Indian people for self-determination by assuring maximum Indian participation in the direction of educational as well as other Federal services to Indian communities so as to render such services more responsive to the needs and desires of those communities.

(b) The Congress declares its commitment to the maintenance of the Federal Government's unique and continuing relationship with and responsibility to the Indian people through the establishment of a meaningful Indian self-determination policy which will permit an orderly transition from Federal domination of programs for and services to Indians to effective and meaningful participation by the Indian people in the planning, conduct, and administration of those programs and services.

(c) The Congress declares that a major national goal of the United States is to provide the quantity and quality of educational services and opportunities which will permit Indian children to compete and excel in the life areas of their choice, and to achieve the measure of self-determination essential to their social and economic well-being . . . .[9]

A major outgrowth of self-determination was the Indian Law Enforcement Improvement Act of 1975. In his opening statement, Senator James Abourezk addressed the complexity of criminal jurisdiction within Indian country.

I know of no other problems in the Indian field today that are as complex and difficult to resolve as those found in the area of jurisdictional concern in Indian country. Contributing to this dilemma is the tangle of overlapping or mutually exclusive jurisdictions—Federal, State, and tribal—which govern law enforcement in Indian country. An outgrowth of the discredited "termination" policies of the 1950s resulted in congressional approval of Public Law 83-280, which served to exacerbate the problems emanating from law enforcement on Federal Indian reservations. Public Law 280 was adopted by the 83rd Congress and signed into law by President Eisenhower on August 15, 1953. The express purpose of that public law was to grant broad discretionary authority to the States to assume civil and criminal jurisdiction over Indian reservations within their borders.

Unfortunately, the Public Law 280 legislation was approved by Congress in the face of strenuous Indian opposition and denied consent of the Indian tribes which were affected by the act. In its final form the statute gave five States civil and criminal jurisdiction over all but three tribes within those States, and gave the United States authority to grant similar jurisdiction to all other States.

The Indian community has consistently opposed implementation of Public Law 280 since its enactment. Tribal leaders allege that Public Law 280 has failed to achieve the objective of improved law enforcement and justice on Indian reservations through the assumption of civil and criminal jurisdiction by the States. In the face of these circumstances, I can readily understand why major Indian organizations have established the repeal of Public Law 280 as a high priority on their legislative agenda.

Public Law 93-638: Title I—Determination of Civil and Criminal Jurisdiction and Law

SEC. 101. The Congress, after careful review of the Federal Government's historical and special legal relationship with the American Indian people, find that—

(a) the Federal Government has heretofore recognized the sovereignty of Indian tribes through treaties, agreements, executive orders, and statutes;

(b) Congress has heretofore declared it to be the policy of the United States to guarantee self-determination to American Indians and to preserve the Federal Government's relationship with and responsibility to Indian tribes;

(c) the lack of a consistent congressional Indian policy in the past has resulted in the unclear jurisdictional status of Indian country with varying patterns of jurisdictional checkerboarding, overlapping and inconsistencies which show little or no promise of clear and workable judicial determination;

(d) jurisdictional problems of increasing severity and magnitude in Indian country have demonstrated that subjecting Indians and Indian country to State or Federal civil and criminal jurisdiction and law without regard to the unique cultural, political, geographic, and social factors of each Indian tribe and reservation is unjust and unworkable;

(f) the Indian tribes will never surrender their rights to determine civil and criminal jurisdiction and law within the Indian country;

(g) true self-determination of Indian tribes and the solution of jurisdictional problems in Indian country require that Indian tribes design their own legal and judicial systems and determine how the exercise of civil and criminal jurisdiction and law in Indian country be shared by tribal, State, and Federal Governments and whether such jurisdiction and law be exclusive or concurrent; Indian tribal government and sovereignty must therefore be nurtured and strengthened by comprehensive Federal assistance in the improvement of law enforcement in Indian country.

Public Law 93-638: Title II—Improvement of Law Enforcement on Indian Reservations

SEC. 201. (a) The Secretary of the Interior is authorized and directed to establish and implement programs to improve law enforcement and the administration of justice within Indian reservations and Indian country.

(b) In implementing such programs the Secretary is authorized to make grants to, and contracts with, Indian tribes, to implement programs and projects to—

(1) determine the feasibility of Federal reacquisitions of jurisdiction and determination of jurisdiction over such Indian country or parts thereof occupied by such tribes, including preparation of law and order codes, substantive laws, codes of civil and criminal procedure, and establishment of plans for fulfilling tribal responsibilities under the jurisdiction sought to be reacquired or determined;

(2) establish and strengthening police forces of the tribes, including recruitment, training, compensation, fringe benefits, and the acquisition and maintenance of police equipment;

(3) establishing and improving tribal courts in order to assure speedy and just trials for offenders, the appointment, training and compensation of qualified judges, and the appointment, training and compensation of qualified Indian prosecution officers, and the establishment of competent legal defender programs;

(4) the establishment and maintenance of correctional facilities and the establishment and strengthening of correctional personnel departments, including recruitment, training, compensation, and fringe benefits.[10]

Part of the tribal testimony before the Senate Committee on Interior and Insular Affairs relevant to the Indian Law Enforcement Improvement Act addressed police and correctional abuses in Public Law 280 states. The statement of Ed Cline, then chairman of the Omaha Tribe in Nebraska, described the types of abuse and discrimination enacted under the auspices of Public Law 280 until the state retroceded criminal jurisdiction to the federal government following passage of the Civil Rights Bill of 1968. His testimony is critical, since he describes the complexities of criminal, civil, and juvenile justice in Indian country. Moreover, the Omaha Tribe was the first group to benefit from retrocession under the Civil Rights Act of 1968:

> Prior to retrocession, the tribe experienced harassment and unfair treatment at the hands of county law enforcement officials. Upon contact with county law enforcement officers, Omaha Indians were subject to physical abuse and discriminatory prosecution. Rehabilitation was nonexistent. Indians would be placed in jail upon arrest for minor offenses for which non-Indians would merely be told to appear in court.
>
> The county sheriff would refuse to set bail for an Indian, making him sit in jail until he could appear before the judge for arraignment. The final incident to precipitate retrocession was the birth of a baby in the county jail to an Indian girl who had pled to her jailer to believe that she was going to have the baby. The jailer's response was to give her an aspirin. As a result of this treatment, the baby died.
>
> On the Winnebago Reservation, located adjacent to the Omaha Reservation in the same county, ill-treatment of Indians by county law enforcement officers continues. The Winnebagos [sic] for like reasons of abuse and harassment are currently seeking retrocession of criminal jurisdiction by the State to the Federal Government.
>
> Following criminal retrocession, a court of Indian offenses was established, the Omaha Tribe being the first Indian tribe in the Nation to retrocede under Public Law 280. Under 18 United States Code, Section 1153, 13 major offenses committed by an Indian against either an Indian or non-Indian are prosecuted in Federal court. All crimes committed by non-Indians on the reservation are under State court jurisdiction. If an Indian commits a non-major crime on the reservation, he is subject to prosecution in the court of Indian offenses.
>
> The court of Indian offenses currently has one judge. A lay public defender practices before the court.
>
> The law enforcement officials on the Omaha Reservation are provided for by the Bureau of Indian Affairs. Police officers provide around the clock protection. After retrocession of PL 280 the state had only criminal jurisdic-

tion; it was unclear as to whether or not criminal jurisdiction included jurisdiction over juveniles. The county after retrocession failed to continue to exert jurisdiction over juveniles, so the tribe was forced to take up the slack. Although the tribe exercises juvenile jurisdiction out of necessity, the feeling is that the county neglects its civil responsibility to prosecute juveniles.

The Omaha Tribe runs a juvenile justice program under an LEAA [Law Enforcement Assistance Administration] grant but is handicapped in doing the kind of job that it would like to do, due to a lack of juvenile facilities.

Under retrogression, the State and county retain exclusive jurisdiction over the highways running through the Omaha Reservation. All traffic offenses committed by Indians on the reservation continue to be prosecuted in the State court system.

The Omaha Tribe approached the country sheriff's office to inquire about cross-deputizing of county law enforcement officers. The county refused to allow the tribe to cross-deputize any county officers.

Although problems do exist, the Omaha Tribe has been very content with its law and order system since retrocession of criminal jurisdiction. Located in a Public Law 280 State, retrocession of criminal jurisdiction and the maintenance of the law and order system has been the first step to self-determination for the Omaha Tribe.[11]

The next significant policy action relevant to the Civil Rights Act of 1968, self-determination, and Public Law 280 was the revision of the federal statutes established under the *Crow Dog* dilemma and the establishment of the Major Crimes Act in Indian country. The testimony before the Congressional Committee on the Judiciary—Criminal Jurisdiction in Indian Country session of March 10, 1976, included the May 20, 1975, remarks of Morris Thompson, commissioner of Indian Affairs. Thompson provided the following overview of what he considered serious defects of federal prosecution in Indian country:

The Major Crimes Act (18 U.S.C.-1153) provides that 13 enumerated offenses committed by Indians within Indian country (as defined by 18 U.S.C.-1151) shall be subject to the same laws and penalties applicable within the exclusive jurisdiction of the United States. However, in 1966 the Act was amended to provide that certain of these offenses—namely burglary, assault with a dangerous weapon, assault resulting in serious bodily harm, and incest—shall be defined and punished in accordance with the laws of the State in which such offenses were committed. This Act applies exclusively to

Indians whether the victim be Indian or non-Indian. A non-Indian committing these identical offenses against an Indian in Indian country is subject to the provisions of 18 U.S.C.–1152 which extends Federal criminal jurisdiction over such non-Indians, and provides that punishment will be defined by Federal Law. (A non-Indian who commits an offense against another non-Indian in Indian country is tried and punished in State court). State definition and punishment for these offenses often differ from Federal Law and, in many cases, State Law prescribes a more severe punishment than the Federal Law applicable within Indian country.

Because of the disparities between Indians and non-Indians in penalties given, both the Eighth and Ninth Circuits recently declared portions of the Major Crimes Act to be unconstitutional, specifically those regarding aggravated assault (*United States v. Cleveland*, 9th Cir., 1974; *United States v. Seth Henry Big Crow*, 8th Cir., 1975). Therefore, the Federal Government is now unable to prosecute Indians who commit assault resulting in serious bodily harm in Indian country in either of these two jurisdictions, which encompass a major portion of Indian country under Federal criminal jurisdiction. The problem is acute and leaves Indian communities without the protection not only of Federal law but of any law except in the sense that a person might be prosecuted for a lesser included offense. Tribal courts are restricted to jurisdiction over misdemeanors by the Indian Civil Rights Act of 1968 and except where a State has been granted criminal jurisdiction by Public Law 83-280 or other Acts of Congress, States do not ordinarily possess jurisdiction over offenses committed by Indians in Indian country. It is urgent that laws declared invalid be replaced as soon as possible.

H.R. 7592, a bill proposed by the Department of Justice, would restore the ability of the Federal Government to prosecute certain serious offenses by Indians under 18 U.S.C.–1153 which was lost as a consequence of the recent court decisions.[12]

The Indian Crimes Act of 1976 was an expansion of the Major Crimes Act of 1885 and extended the number of federally exclusive crimes to fourteen.

SEC. 2. Section 1153, title 18, United States Code, is amended to read as follows:

- Offenses committed within Indian country

Any Indian who commits against the person or property of another Indian or other person any of the following offenses, namely, murder, manslaughter, kidnapping, rape, carnal knowledge of any female not his wife, who has not attained the age of sixteen years, assault with intent to commit rape, incest, assault with intent to commit murder, assault with a dangerous weapon, assault resulting in serious bodily injury, arson, burglary, robbery, and larceny within the Indian country, shall be subject to the same laws and penalties as all other persons committing any of the above offenses, with the exclusive jurisdiction of the United States.

As used in this section, the offenses of burglary and incest shall be defined and punished in accordance with the laws of the State in which such offense was committed as are in force at the time of such offense.

In addition to the offenses of burglary and incest, any other of the above offenses which are not defined and punished by Federal law in force within the exclusive jurisdiction of the United States shall be defined and punished in accordance with the laws of the State in which such offense was committed as are in force at the time of such offense. . . .

SEC. 4. Section 342, title 18, United States Code, is amended as follows:

- Indians committing certain offenses; acts on reservations.

All Indians committing any offense listed in the first paragraph of and punishable under section 1153 (relating to offenses committed within Indian country) of this title shall be tried in the same courts and in the same manner as are all other persons committing such offenses within the exclusive jurisdiction of the United States.[13]

Landmark challenges to tribal law enforcement jurisdiction within Indian country included *Oliphant v. Suquamish Tribe* (1978); *Duro v. Reina* (1990); and *Supreme Court v. Navajo Nation* (1998). In the *Oliphant* case, Mark Oliphant, a non-Indian who resided on the Port Madison Reservation in Washington State, was arrested by tribal police and charged with resisting arrest and assaulting an officer. Oliphant claimed that he was not subject to tribal authority given that he was not an American Indian. His appeal was upheld by the U.S. Supreme Court, which cited the conditions of the Civil Rights Act of 1968, concluding that Indian tribes do not have inherent jurisdiction to try and to punish non-Indians.[14]

In 1990, the U.S. Supreme Court ostensibly extended the *Oliphant* decision to include not only non-Indians arrested in Indian country but nonenrolled Indians as well. On the Salt River Pima–Maricopa Indian Reservation in Arizona, in 1984, Albert Duro, then age fourteen, was implicated in a shooting murder on the reservation. Duro, an enrolled member of the

Torres-Martinez band of Cahuilla Mission Indians of California, was indicted for first degree murder in federal court under the Major Crimes Act. However, the case was dismissed at the federal level, and the Salt River tribe arrested and convicted Duro for lesser misdemeanor charges associated with the killing. Duro filed a habeas corpus writ to the United States District Court for the District of Arizona on the basis that he was a nonmember and that this violated his civil rights under the Civil Rights Act of 1968. The district court overturned his conviction, and the tribe appealed to the United States Court of Appeals for the Ninth Circuit, which reversed and upheld the tribe's misdemeanor jurisdiction over nonmember Indians, stating that, historically, tribes had exercised criminal jurisdiction over all Indians on reservations. It also noted that Duro's status as an Indian was a political and not a racial classification and therefore did not warrant considerations of discrimination. Duro appealed to the U.S. Supreme Court, which reversed the decision of the circuit court, doing so on the basis of common law rather than on constitutional grounds. This decision was seen by many as a further attempt by the High Court to erode tribal sovereignty. In *Duro*, the U.S. Supreme Court prohibited tribes from exercising those powers associated with autonomous states. It attempted to weaken tribal sovereignty and autonomy, thus increasing the dependency of tribes vis-à-vis their interpretation of tribes as domestic dependent nations.[15] Tribes were outraged by this decision and effectively petitioned Congress to intervene, leading to enactment of Public Law 102-137, which amended Section 1301 (Subpart 2) of the Civil Rights Act of 1968. Public Law 102-137, "Criminal Jurisdiction over Indians" (House Report No. 102-61), made permanent the legislative reinstatement of the power of Indian tribes to exercise misdemeanor criminal jurisdictions over all Indians within their jurisdiction.

> Pursuant to the testimony of several tribes, Congress needs to act because of the jurisdictional void the Supreme Court has created. Several states have passed resolutions recommending a permanent return to tribal jurisdiction, and the Justice Department has stated that the administration of justice in Indian country is better served by allowing tribes to exercise jurisdiction over all criminal misdemeanor cases involving Indians.

> The issue is one of public safety as well as tribal sovereignty. The Committee believes that the tribal court is the best forum to handle misdemeanor cases over non-member Indians. The Committee is concerned that chaos would result if tribes lose this long-held jurisdictional right.

The Committee asserts that Congressional power over Indian tribes permits recognition of the inherent right of tribes to retain misdemeanor criminal jurisdiction. The Committee assertion is based upon two fundamental maxims of Indian law enunciated by Mr. Justice Kennedy in the *Duro* decision that (1) Congress determines Indian policy and (2) tribes retain all rights not expressly taken by Congress.

The Committee notes that Congress has the power to acknowledge, recognize, and affirm the inherent powers of tribes. The Committee notes that tribes have retained the criminal jurisdiction over non-member Indians and this legislation is not a federal delegation of this jurisdiction but a clarification of the status of tribes as domestic dependent nations. Hence, the constitutional status of tribes as it existed prior to the *Duro* decision remains intact.[16]

Despite this legislative action, in 1998, Russell Means, one of the AIM (American Indian Movement) leaders challenged three criminal charges filed against him by the District Court of the Chinle Judicial District of the Navajo Nation. Means was charged with threatening and battering his father-in-law, Leon Grant, a member of the Omaha tribe, and battering Jeremiah Bitsui, a Navajo. Means claimed that being a member of the Oglala Sioux Nation, he was exempt from Navajo jurisdiction even though he was residing on the Navajo reservation at the time of these alleged assaults. In his petition to the Navajo Nation Supreme Court, Means contended that the Navajo Nation has no jurisdiction over nonmember Indians. In its May 11, 1999, decision, the Navajo Nation Supreme Court moved against Russell Means, holding that the Navajo Nation has criminal jurisdiction over all Indians who enter the Navajo Nation. Moreover, individuals, regardless of race or ethnicity, who assume tribal relations with Navajos by intermarriage (*hadane*), residence, and other activities are subject to the criminal jurisdiction of the Navajo Nation. Means's petition was dismissed, and his case was remanded to the Chinle district court for trial. The in-law, or hadane, interpretation of Navajo jurisdiction goes beyond what Congress articulated in Public Law 102-137. However, being an American Indian, Means could not challenge this element of the Navajo Supreme Court decision in a higher U.S. court. The Navajo Supreme Court cited the June 1, 1868, treaty with the United States and not Public Law 102-137 in reaching their decision. [17]

Other legal issues within Indian country associated with Indian self-determination include (1) Indian health, notably substance abuse; (2) religious freedom; (3) child abuse; and (4) gaming. The American Indian Policy Review Commission, an outgrowth of Indian self-determination, provided their final reports in 1976 and 1977. The commission made 206 specific recommendations overall but was considered too favorable toward American Indians, especially in regard to Indian sovereignty and expanded federal trust responsibilities, and therefore was largely ineffective. However, the chairman of Task Force Eleven: Alcohol and Drug Abuse, Reuben Snake, a Winnebago-Sioux, was a contributing factor in the passage of the American Indian Religious Freedom Act of 1978 and the Anti-Drug Abuse Act of 1986, which provided needed Indian youth intervention programs in Indian country. Chairman Snake's elegant words gave notice that not much had been done since the ravages of substance abuse was investigated and published in the Synder Act of 1921.

The American Indians and Alaska Natives are some of the most deprived, isolated, and misunderstood people in the United States. Before the advent of the European settlers, the Native Americans were proud and culturally secure people and were at peace with themselves and the land on which they lived. They were rich in every sense of the word. Historically, their causative factors were positive, limiting alcohol and drug usage (such as peyote) to ceremonies and spiritual rituals. It permitted their "spirits to soar," gave them "visions." Deviance from this controlled usage was not permitted.

The steamrolling effect of the "civilized society" upon the Indian people has wreaked a havoc which extends far beyond that of loss of material possessions. The American Indian and Alaska Native are caught in a world wherein they are trying to find out who they are and where they are, and where they fit in. The land which was once their "mother," giving them food and clothing, was taken. Their spiritual strengths were decried as pagan, and familial ties were broken. Their own forms of education, i.e., that of legends, how to live, how to respect themselves and others, were torn asunder by the "white society's reading, writing, and arithmetic." No culture could, or can, be expected to be thrust into a world different from its own and adapt without problems of cultural shock. Also, the Indian people were not even given citizenship until 1924. An 1832 federal Indian law prohibiting the sale of liquor to Indian people remained in effect until 1953 and could have been instrumental in the formation of the "hidden group," "drink until it's gone," and "quick" drinking patterns that Native American people exhibit. The Indian people of today are proud of their heritage and are fighting to maximize its influence upon their lives in a dominant white world. Many have succeeded. Many have not.[18]

As part of Public Law 99-570, the Anti-Drug Abuse Act of 1986, Subtitle C addressed Indians and Alaska Natives. This became known as the

Indian Alcohol and Substance Abuse Prevention and Treatment Act of 1986. Under the findings of the general provisions the significance of substance abuse prevention and treatment was articulated.

SEC. 4202. Findings.

The Congress finds and declares that:

(1) the Federal Government has a historical relationship and unique legal and moral responsibility to Indian tribes and their members,

(2) included in this responsibility is the treaty, statutory, and historical obligation to assist the Indian tribes in meeting the health and social needs of their members,

(3) alcoholism and alcohol and substance abuse is the severe health and social problem facing Indian tribes and people today, and nothing is more costly to Indian people than the consequences of alcohol and substance abuse measured in physical, mental, social, and economic terms,

(4) alcohol and substance abuse is the leading generic risk factor among Indians, and Indians die from alcoholism at over 4 times the age-adjusted rates for the United States population, and alcohol and substance misuse results in a rate of years of potential life lost nearly 5 times that of the United States,

(5) 4 of the top 10 causes of death among Indians are alcohol and drug related injuries (18 percent of all deaths), chronic liver disease and cirrhosis (5 percent), suicide (3 percent), and homicide (3 percent),

(6) primarily because deaths from unintentional injuries and violence occur disproportionately among young people, the age-specific death rate for Indians is approximately double the United States rate for the 15 to 45 age group,

(7) Indians between the ages of 15 and 24 years of age are more than 2 times as likely to commit suicide as the general population, and approximately 80 percent of those suicides are alcohol-related,

(8) Indians between the ages of 15 and 24 years of age are twice as likely as the general population to die in automobile accidents, 75 percent of which are alcohol-related,

(9) the Indian Health Service, which is charged with treatment and rehabilitation efforts, has directed only 1 percent of its budget for alcohol and substance abuse problems,

(10) the Bureau of Indian Affairs, which has responsibility for programs in education, social services, law enforcement, and other areas, has assumed little responsibility for coordinating its various efforts to focus on the epidemic of alcohol and substance abuse among Indian people,

(11) this lack of emphasis and priority continues despite the fact that Bureau of Indian Affairs and Indian Health Service officials publicly acknowledge that alcohol and substance abuse among Indians is the most serious health and social problem facing the Indian people, and

(12) the Indian tribes have the primary responsibility for protecting and ensuring the well-being of their members, and the resources made available under this subtitle will assist Indian tribes in meeting that responsibility.

SEC. 4203. Purpose.

It is the purpose of this subtitle to:

(1) authorize and develop a comprehensive, coordinated attack upon the illegal narcotics traffic in Indian country and the deleterious impact of alcohol and substance abuse upon Indian tribes and their members.

(2) provide needed direction and guidance to those Federal agencies responsible for Indian programs to identify and focus existing programs and resources, including those made available by this subtitle, upon this problem,

(3) provide authority and opportunities for Indian tribes to develop and implement a coordinated program for the prevention and treatment of alcohol and substance abuse at the local level, and

(4) to modify or supplement existing programs and authorities in the areas of education, family and social services, law enforcement and judicial services, and health services to further the purposes of this subtitle.[19]

Public Law 99-570 provided for Indian youth programs under Part III, including a "Tribal Action Plan" designed to address juvenile justice within Indian country. Training for law enforcement and juvenile training was assigned to the Bureau of Indian Affairs (BIA) law enforcement component. Areas addressed include: (1) medical assessment and treatment of juvenile offenders; (2) juvenile detention centers; (3) development of a Model Indian Juvenile Code; and (4) uniform law enforcement data collection.

Section 4227 (Indian Health Youth Programs) established tribal detoxification and rehabilitation programs for Indian youth as well as the creation of Youth Regional Treatment Centers (YRTC) to service each Indian Health Service (IHS) area. Today, there are ten Indian Health Service YRTCs located in eight states: Alaska (2); Arizona (1); California (1); New Mexico (2); North Carolina (1); Oklahoma (1); Oregon (1); and Washington (1). Enrolled tribal youth, ages twelve to nineteen, are referred to these inpatient facilities by their respective tribes for substance abuse treatment. Individual, group, and family therapy are integrated components of the treatment plan. Those who complete these programs receive additional outpatient services when back home. These YRTCs are designed to track clients once they leave a facility and to report aggregate outcome studies to their funding source— the Indian Health Service.[20]

Indian religious freedom is another area addressed by Indian self-determination. Historically, the denial of traditional practices and the forced imposition of the Christian way was seen as a significant component of the U.S. policy of cultural genocide. With Indian self-determination, efforts were made to identify those traditional practices that would no longer bring criminal sanctions. The American Indian Religious Freedom Act was passed on August 11, 1978, as part of a joint congressional resolution providing, for the first time, support for Indian cultural autonomy—the same deficits in U.S./Indian policy that Reuben Snake addressed two years earlier in his task force report on alcohol and drug abuse in Indian country. It also articulated Indian First Amendment rights, spelled out by the Civil Rights Act of 1968.

> Whereas the freedom of religion for all people is an inherent right, fundamental to the democratic structure of the United States, and is guaranteed by the First Amendment of the United States Constitution;
>
> Whereas the United States has traditionally rejected the concept of a government denying individuals the right to practice their religion and, as a result, has benefited from a rich variety of religious heritages in this country;
>
> Whereas the religious practices of the American Indian (as well as Native Alaskan and Hawaiian) are an integral part of their culture, tradition, and heritage, such practices forming the basis of Indian identity and value systems;
>
> Whereas the traditional American Indian religions, as an integral part of Indian life, are indispensable and irreplaceable;
>
> Whereas the lack of a clear, comprehensive, and consistent Federal policy has often resulted in the abridgment of religious freedom for traditional American Indians;
>
> Whereas such religious infringements result from the lack of knowledge or the insensitive and inflexible enforcement of federal policies and regulations premised on a variety of laws;
>
> Whereas such laws were designed for such worthwhile purposes as conservation and preservation of natural species and resources but were never intended to relate to Indian religious practices and, therefore, were passed without consideration of their effect on traditional American Indian religions;

Whereas such laws and policies often deny American Indians access to sacred sites required in their religions, including cemeteries;

Whereas such laws at times prohibit the use and possession of sacred objects necessary to the exercise of religious rites and ceremonies;

Whereas traditional American Indian ceremonies have been intruded upon, interfered with, and in a few instances banned:

Resolved by the Senate and House of Representatives of the United States of America in Congress assembled, That henceforth it shall be the policy of the United States to protect and preserve for American Indians their inherent right of freedom to believe, express, and exercise the traditional religions of the American Indian, Eskimo, Aleut, and Native Hawaiians, including but not limited to access to sites, use and possession of sacred objects, and the freedom to worship through ceremonials and traditional rites.

SEC. 2. The President shall direct the various Federal departments, agencies, and other instrumentalities responsible for administering relevant laws to evaluate their policies and procedures in consultation with native traditional religious leaders in order to determine appropriate changes necessary to protect and preserve Native American religious cultural rights and practices. Twelve months after approval of this resolution, the President shall report back to Congress the results of his evaluation, including any changes which were made in administrative policies and procedures, and any recommendations he may have for legislative action.[21]

These words did not in themselves end the Indian religious wars. Peyote use among the Native American Church (NAC) became a heated legal debate resulting in continued criminalization in Indian country. The peyote religious war was particularly intense within the Navajo Nation, where the Christianized Navajo, especially the Mormon Navajo, fought to greatly restrict the Native American Church (NAC) on the "Big Res." This pushed the Native American Church closer to the American Indian Movement (AIM) radicals, causing an internal schism and intratribal conflict like that which existed among the Plains Sioux earlier in the 1970s. The Indian religious freedom and peyote use issue came to the U.S. Supreme Court in 1988 in *Employment Division, Department of Human Resources of the State of Oregon, et al. v. Smith*. Here, Alfred Smith and Galen Black, two substance abuse counselors employed by a county alcohol and drug prevention and treatment center, were fired for taking peyote during Native American Church ceremonies. Their appeal was based on their rights to draw unemployment benefits subsequent to their termination by the county. The U.S. Supreme Court upheld their denial of benefits on administrative procedures but avoided the peyote issue, determining that this lay within the authority of the U.S. Congress relevant to legislation augmenting the 1978 Native American Religious Freedom Act.[22]

Reuben A. Snake, Jr., the tireless Winnebago Indian and lifelong member of the Native American Church, dedicated the last years of his life to an effort to amend the American Indian Religious Freedom Act to protect the religious use of peyote by American Indians. Toward this end he established the Native American Religious Freedom (NAFR) project in conjunction with the Native American Rights Fund. NAFR is an all-Indian legal services organization that emerged in 1970 as part of the California Indian Legal Services. In 1971, NARF became an independent organization, located in Boulder, Colorado, that expanded in 1984 to include a second branch in Anchorage, Alaska, in order to address legal issues facing Native Alaskans. Reuben Snake, Peterson Zah, president of the Navajo Nation, Senator Daniel K. Inouye, chairman of the Senate Committee on Indian Affairs, and NARF, through the joint efforts of the Religious Freedom Restoration Act Coalition and the American Indian Religious Freedom Coalition and twelve congressional hearings, were instrumental in getting the American Indian Religious Freedom Act of 1978 amended in 1994. President George Bush had refused to sign any bill that would expand the 1978 act, but in 1993, President Clinton signed into law the Religious Freedom Restoration Act (RFRA), which reversed the Supreme Court's ruling in *Smith* but did little to fully protect the free exercise of traditional Native American religious rites. Efforts were again taken to amend the American Indian Religious Freedom Act. On October 6, 1994, with President Clinton's signature, House Resolution 4230 then became Public Law 103-344. This bill amended the 1978 act to provide for the legal protection for the use, possession, or transportation of the sacrament peyote and also provided protection against discrimination for such use, possession, or transportation in all fifty states and the District of Columbia. It overturned previous U.S. and state laws against the use of peyote for American Indians when this use was for religious purposes. However, it did not require prison authorities to permit the use of peyote by Indian inmates.

The other American Indian religious issue pertains to the use of eagle feathers. President Clinton signed a government directive addressing this issue on April 29, 1994. The directive provides for the distribution of eagle feathers for Native American religious purposes. It authorizes the Department of the Interior to maintain an adequate refrigerated repository for the distribution of eagle feathers to qualified American Indians.[23]

An expansion of Indian self-determination relevant to child abuse in Indian country came with the New Federalism concept initiated in 1989. Congressional findings of chronic child abuse in Indian country, especially those abuses committed by non-Indian BIA teachers, provided a new impetus for tribal control of Indian education. It also expanded child protection laws to include Indian country. The *Final Report and Legislative Recommendations* of the U.S. Senate's Special Committee on Investigations of the Select Committee of Indian Affairs also reviewed the potential for corruption and fraud in Indian country.

Paternalistic federal control over American Indians has created a federal bureaucracy ensnarled in red tape and riddled with fraud, mismanagement, and waste. Worse, the Committee found that federal officials in every agency knew of the abuses but did little or nothing to stop them.

Federal agencies knew, for example, that hundreds of millions spent on the government's program to promote Indian economic development were largely drained by shell companies posing as legitimate Indian-owned firms. The Bureau of Indian Affairs (BIA) did not need the Committee to discover that 19 of the largest so-called Indian companies that garnered federal contracts were frauds: a BIA Division Chief warned his superiors in an internal memo before the Committee's hearings that the entire program was a "massive fraud (and) financial scandal." Yet, in 31 years, the BIA only discovered two minor instances of possible fraud.

In federally run schools for Indians, BIA officials knew that school administrators had hired teachers with prior offenses for child molestation. Moreover, BIA knew its employees had failed to report or investigate repeated allegations of sexual abuse by teachers, in one case for 14 years. Yet BIA promoted negligent school administrators and, unlike all 50 states, never fully adopted a system that required employees to report and investigate child abuse.

Federal agencies responsible for protecting natural resources also neglected known problems. For instance, federal officials in Oklahoma admitted that Indian land was "wide open" to oil theft, yet for the past three years they uncovered none. They even ignored specific allegations against the nation's largest purchaser of Indian oil, which Committee investigators later caught repeatedly stealing from Indians.

The federal budget for Indian programs equals $3.3 billion annually. Yet, surprisingly little of these funds reach the Indian people. In fact, the total household income for American Indians from all sources, including the federal government, is actually less than the entire federal budget of $3.3 billion.

Not only do American Indians suffer from this extreme waste. Year after year, all American taxpayers must foot the bill for a negligent and unresponsive bureaucracy from a limited budget.

The Committee found that the BIA also permitted a pattern of child abuse by its teachers to fester throughout BIA schools nationwide. For almost 15 years, while child abuse reporting standards were being adopted by all 50 states, the Bureau failed to issue any reporting guidelines for its own teachers. Incredibly, the BIA did not require even a minimal background check into potential school employees. As a result, BIA employed teachers who actually admitted past child molestation, including at least one Arizona teacher who explicitly listed a prior criminal offense for child abuse on his employment form.

At a Cherokee Reservation elementary school in North Carolina, the BIA employed Paul Price, another confessed child molester—even after his previous principal, who had fired him for molesting seventh grade boys, warned BIA officials that Price was an admitted pedophile. Shocked to learn several years later from teachers at the Cherokee school that Price continued to teach despite the warning, Price's former principal told several Cherokee teachers of Price's pedophilia and notified the highest BIA official at Cherokee. Instead of dismissing Price or conducting an inquiry, BIA administrators lectured an assembly of Cherokee teachers on the unforeseen consequences of slander.

The Committee found that during his 14 years at Cherokee, Price molested at least 25 students, while the BIA continued to ignore repeated allegations—including an eyewitness account by a teacher's aide. Even after Price was finally caught and the negligence of BIA supervisors came to light, not a single official was ever disciplined for tolerating the abuse of countless students for 14 years. Indeed, the negligent Cherokee principal who received the eyewitness report was actually promoted to the BIA Central Office in Washington—the same office which, despite the Price case, failed for years to institute background checks for potential teachers or reporting requirements for instances of suspected abuse. Another BIA Cherokee school official was promoted to the Hopi Reservation in Arizona, without any inquiry into his handling of the Price fiasco.

Meanwhile at Hopi, a distraught mother reported to the local BIA principal a possible instance of child sexual abuse by the remedial reading teacher, John Boone. Even though five years earlier the principal had received police reports of alleged child sexual abuse by Boone, the principal failed to investigate the mother's report or contact law enforcement authorities. He simply notified his superior, who also took no action. A year later, the same mother eventually reported the teacher to the FBI, which found that he had abused 142 Hopi children, most during the years of BIA's neglect. Again, no discipline or censure of school officials followed: the BIA simply provided the abused children with one counselor who compounded their distress by intimately interviewing them for a book he wished to write on the case.

Sadly, these wrongs were not isolated incidents. While in the past year the Bureau has finally promulgated some internal child abuse reporting guidelines, it has taken the Special Committee's public hearings for the BIA to fully acknowledge its failure.[24]

In 1990, the federal government for the first time established an Indian child protection statute. Title IV of Public Law 101–630 (Miscellaneous Indian Legislation) provided the Indian Child Protection and Family Violence Prevention Act. The major elements of this act are to:

1. require that reports of abused Indian children are made to the appropriate authorities in an effort to prevent further abuse;
2. authorize such actions as are necessary to ensure effective child protection in Indian country;
3. establish the Indian Child Abuse Prevention and Treatment Grant Program to provide funds for the establishment on Indian reservations of treatment programs for victims of child sexual abuse;
4. provide for the treatment and prevention of incidents of family violence; and
5. authorize other actions necessary to ensure effective child protection on Indian reservations.[25]

Another self-determination issue is Indian gaming. Tribes felt that they had the authority to offer on-reservation gaming under the conditions of self-determination even if the state where the reservation was located did not approve of gaming. Tribal leaders had an unusual supporter in President Ronald Reagan, who felt that tribe-initiated funding sources, like gaming, would help justify his administration's cuts in federal treaty obligation monies to tribes for program support. The test case for Indian gaming came from a Public Law 280 state in 1981. The U.S. Fifth Circuit Court ruled that Florida's bingo laws did not apply to the Seminole Indians despite its Public Law 280 status. Here, the court held that reservation gaming is immune from state regulation due to tribes' unique status as sovereign nations within the United States.

By 1984 there was widespread support for Indian gaming in Indian country. That year, at the National Congress of American Indians (NCAI), it was noted that one-third of the tribes offered bingo and felt that this was an economic godsend for them given their history of limited resources, minimal capital, high unemployment, and the severe cutbacks being imposed by the Reagan administration. However, tribes soon attempted to expand to casino gambling and met with strong resistance not only from states but also from the established gaming industry in places such as Las Vegas and Atlantic City. The potential for corruption both internally and from organized crime also raised concerns at the tribe, state, and federal levels. These concerns led to congressional action in October 1988 with passage of Public Law 100-497: The Indian Gaming Regulatory Act (IGRA).

The IGRA provided federal standards for gaming on Indian lands and established the National Indian Gaming Commission. President Reagan appointed Tony Hope (actor Bob Hope's son) as the first chairman of the commission. The IGRA also distinguished between three classes of Indian gaming and provided corresponding regulations for each class. Class I gaming on Indian lands pertains to traditional Indian games of chance that would most likely involve only intra-Indian participation. These games are to be within the exclusive jurisdiction of the tribe and do not require external oversight. Class II gaming pertains to games of chance such as bingo, which most likely would involve non-Indian and/or nonresident participation. For Class II gaming, the tribe must adopt a tribal ordinance regulating these activities. However, this level of Indian gaming can be conducted only in Indian country if the state in which the tribe is located approves any form of games of chance. Currently, only Utah and Hawaii do not approve any form of such games. Class III pertains to casino-style gambling and has the strictest regulatory obstacles for participating tribes. Class III gaming in Indian country requires a tribal-state compact along with federal approval.

Today, most of the controversy concerning Indian gaming involves Class III gaming. Numerous states have politicized this issue, and some, like New Mexico, have attempted to exploit Indian gaming revenues for their own benefit, this despite their long history of exploitation of their American Indian neighbors. Indeed, New Mexico was the last state to allow Indians residing in Indian country (Navajos, Apaches, and nineteen Pueblo groups) to vote, doing so in 1948 but for male Indians only. In 1967, female Indians of voting age who resided in Indian country were also finally allowed to vote in the state. New Mexico now holds its tribes (certain Pueblos and the two Apache tribes) hostage for 16 percent of the gross receipts from their Class III gaming enterprises. In 1989 the Red Lake band of Chippewa Indians and the Mescalero Apache in New Mexico filed suit challenging the constitutionality of the Indian Gaming Regulatory Act on the grounds that the tribe-state compact undermined both tribal sovereignty and federal responsibility to Indian tribes. In 1992, seven more tribes joined the class-action suit, including the Eastern band of Cherokee Indians of North Carolina and the Isleta Pueblo Indians of New Mexico. These suits and similar gaming conflicts are forcing both the U.S. Congress and the federal courts to reexamine the Indian gaming issue.[26]

Changes in Indian law enforcement, tribal jurisdiction, and punishment in Indian country also occurred in the 1990s during this era of modifying the Indian self-determination policy. Public Law 101-379, the Indian Law Enforcement Reform Act, was enacted on August 18, 1990. This act established the separate BIA federal police in Indian country. The Department of the Interior established a separate Branch of Criminal Investigation under the Division of Law Enforcement Services in Indian country. This agency is separate from the Department of Justice's Federal Bureau of Investigation (FBI), which historically has had exclusive jurisdiction in investigating federal (felony) crimes in Indian country. The BIA police can now enforce and investigate infringements of federal law and, with the consent of the tribe, tribal law. Moreover, this BIA police agency operates independently of the BIA agency superintendent or the BIA area office director. BIA police carry firearms; execute or serve warrants; enforce tribal law if authorized by the tribe; make felony arrests; and assist, when requested, any federal, tribal, state, or local law enforcement agency in the enforcement or carrying out of laws in Indian country.[27]

In late 1993, Congress passed Public Law 103-176, the Indian Tribal Justice Act. This was an expansion of Public Law 102-137, which overturned *Duro v. Reina* in 1991. Here, the Bureau of Indian Affairs changed the Branch of Judicial Services to the Office of Tribal Justice Support. In terms of Indian self-determination, this effort was designed to provide technical assistance and training to tribes for the development of:

1. tribal codes and rules of procedure;
2. tribal court administrative procedures and court records management systems;
3. methods of reducing case delays;
4. methods of alternative dispute resolution;
5. tribal standards for judicial administration and conduct; and
6. long-range planning for the enhancement of tribal justice systems.[28]

In 1994, passage of Public Law 103-322, the Violent Crime Control and Law Enforcement Act of 1994, brought the death penalty back to Indian country. The influence of the Indian Self-Determination and Education

Assistance Act of 1975 and opposition to the Public Law 280 unilateral imposition of federal or state jurisdiction in Indian country is evident in Section 60002, paragraph 3598: "Special provisions for Indian country."

> Notwithstanding sections 1152 and 1153, no person subject to the criminal jurisdiction of an Indian tribal government shall be subject to a capital sentence under this chapter for any offense the Federal jurisdiction for which is predicated solely on Indian country (as defined in section 1151 of this title) and which has occurred within the boundaries of Indian country, unless the governing body of the tribe has elected that this chapter have effect over land and persons subject to its criminal jurisdiction.[29]

The last area of Indian justice we will look at in this overview is that of white-collar crime and the exploitation of Indian resources by big businesses, often in collusion with the BIA, the federal agency responsible for protecting the Indian trust status. Federal trust responsibilities were articulated in the Synder Act of 1921.[30] The act directed the BIA, under the supervision of the secretary of the interior, to provide inspectors, supervisors, superintendents, clerks, field matrons, farmers, physicians, Indian police, Indian judges, and other employees. The dismal failure of the BIA in this charge was spelled out by the U.S. Senate, Select Committee on Indian Affairs, in their final report, which was issued in 1989, sixty-eight years to the month after the passage of the Synder Act.

> BIA's mismanagement is manifest in almost every area the Committee examined. Although the consequences are far less severe than those suffered by innocent children, in road construction, facilities management, procurement, loan programs, financial management of Indian trust funds, computer services, and realty management, among others, the Committee found a pattern of callously ignoring known problems, defending and promoting incompetent staff, and ostracizing the few capable employees who dared to speak out against the institutional incompetence that surrounded them. . . .
>
> The Interior Department's Bureau of Land Management (BLM) is charged with detecting and preventing the theft of oil and gas on Indian lands. Since 1981 in Oklahoma alone, BLM has assigned at least nine experts to inspect Indian wells and report possible incidents of theft. Yet, these experts admitted to the Committee that they spent 75 percent of their time in their offices, not working in the field where theft could be detected. They simply waited for some companies to report insignificant instances of theft— for a total of nine thefts of $20,490 in nine years. At that, they confessed

that they did not even properly report these thefts to law enforcement authorities.

While these officials were waiting for the phone to ring, Koch Oil, the largest purchaser of Indian oil in the country, was engaged in a widespread and sophisticated scheme to steal crude oil from Indians and others through fraudulent mismeasuring and reporting. The Committee sent its investigators into the field to conduct covert surveillance and caught Koch stealing from Indians on six separate occasions. By further investigation, the Committee determined that Koch was engaged in systematic theft, stealing millions in Oklahoma alone. . . .

Principal Recommendations of the Special Committee on Investigations

"We must put a stop to the monopolistic greed and commercial tyranny which has characterized the acts of certain oil companies on Indian land in Oklahoma, whose conduct in shamefully disregarding the rules and regulations of the Department of the Interior has cost both the Indian lessor and the independent operator millions of dollars."

Those words are not ours. The Secretary of the Interior wrote them in a letter to President Theodore Roosevelt in 1907. That they so uncannily mirror our findings testifies to the repeated failure of the federal government to serve American Indians. At least 42 congressional investigations have recommended federal reorganization, restructuring, re-tinkering. And in one nine-year period alone, the BIA was actually reorganized ten times. The time for tinkering is over. The time for bold leadership is now. Working together with tribal officials on a government-to-government basis, we must create a blueprint for a New Federalism for American Indians. The time has come for a federal policy that, by negotiated agreements with tribes, abolishes paternalism and, while providing the requisite federal funds, allows tribal governments to stand free—independent, responsible, and accountable. . . .

The empowerment of tribal self-governance through formal, voluntary agreements must rest on mutual acceptance of four indispensable conditions:

1. The federal government must relinquish its current paternalistic controls over tribal affairs; in turn, the tribes must assume the full responsibilities of self-government;
2. Federal assets and annual appropriations must be transferred *in toto* to the tribes;

3. Formal agreements must be negotiated by tribal governments with written constitutions that have been democratically approved by each tribe; and

4. Tribal governmental officials must be held fully accountable and subject to fundamental federal laws against corruption.[31]

This led to passage of the Trust Fund Management Reform Act of 1994. Nonetheless, this resulted in little change, and in February 1999, U.S. District Judge Royce Lambert, in response to a multi-million-dollar lawsuit by American Indians against the U.S. government, held both the secretary of the interior and the secretary of the treasury in contempt of court for the destruction of thousands of records relevant to the mismanagement of millions of dollars allocated for American Indians in Indian country. This was the result of a class-action lawsuit filed on June 10, 1996, with the assistance of the Native American Rights Fund (NARF). The lawsuit was filed on behalf of 300,000 Indians seeking redress for government mismanagement of billions of dollars of trust funds. In 1996, NARF provided the following overview of the problem:

> Over 300,000 individual Indians and 200 tribes and their members are the direct victims of this continuing scandalous government wrongdoing. The price for this government negligence and malfeasance is being paid by some of the poorest citizens of this great country. And each day this mismanagement continues, these individuals and their families lose more and more of their money to the open, outstretched hands of the federal government—which by law is required as a fiduciary to protect their assets and interests.[32]

On September 8, 2000, while the class-action suit was still being contested, the only American Indian cited in the suit, Kevin Gover, assistant secretary of the interior and director of the BIA, offered a formal apology for the BIA's legacy of racism and inhumanity, including massacres, forced relocations, and attempts to destroy Indian languages and cultures. Gover offered this apology at the BIA's 175th anniversary celebration. While speaking only for the BIA, Gover is the highest-ranking U.S. official to apologize for these abuses.

PART II

INDIAN JUSTICE

CHAPTER THREE

ABORIGINAL JUSTICE: CHEROKEE BLOOD VENGEANCE

Pre-Columbian American Indian justice was based on a system of harmony between both man and nature. Traditional American Indian justice was part of the overall folk culture based on the "Harmony Ethos." This system is in marked contrast to the Euro-American system of justice of individual culpability, *mens rea*, and due process, based upon the Protestant ethic. The Cherokees best reflect both the aboriginal Harmony Ethos and its contrast with the Euro-American system in that the early Cherokee society was better studied than any other American Indian group at the time of white contact in what is now the United States. Moreover, the Cherokees, in their attempt to adapt to the demands of their new white neighbors, transformed their traditional culture so that it better conformed with that of the British-American system. In doing so, they and their smaller Muskhogean trading neighbors, the Choctaws, Chickasaws, Creeks, and Seminoles, successfully adopted elements of the Euro-American society into their cultures, thus becoming known as the Five Civilized Tribes. Clearly, a look at the Cherokees' aboriginal justice of blood vengeance and their subsequent adaptations to the dictates of the Euro-American form of justice best illustrates the contrasts between Harmony Ethos and Protestant ethic justice models as well as providing insight into the nature of U.S.-Indian policy, notably the administration of justice.

The Protestant Ethic and the Genesis of U.S. Justice

The ideals of any viable society are rooted in a social philosophy that provides a collective worldview and answers to the nature of existence. Social philosophies provide relevant metaphysical constructs of social realities, which are then transformed into political, social, and moral norms that, when institutionalized, are perpetuated and enforced by the social order through a variety of sanctions. The society's particular values and ideals are presented to the collectivity via the group's epistemological methodology— the main vehicle for socialization and enculturation. Perhaps Erich Goode stated this process best:

> All civilizations set rules concerning what is real and what is not, what is true and what false. All societies select out of the data before them a world, one world, the world taken for granted, and declare that the real world. Each one of these artificially constructed worlds is to some degree idiosyncratic, unique. No individual views reality directly, in the raw, so to speak. Our perceptions are narrowly channeled through concepts and interpretations. What is commonly thought of as reality, that which exists, or simply is, is a set of supposition, rationalizations, justifications, defenses, all generally collectively agreed-upon, which guide and channel each individual's perceptions in a specific and distinct direction. The specific rules governing the perception of the universe which man inhabits are more or less arbitrary, a matter of convention. Every society establishes a kind of epistemological methodology.[1]

Regardless of great differences in cultures, social prescriptions and sanctions always exit. Emile Durkheim drew attention to this nearly a century ago when he posited that crime is present not only in societies of one particular type but in all societies. Accordingly, he asserted that no society is exempt from the problem of criminality and that a major difference across societies is in the form of the acts that are considered deviant.[2]

The U.S. justice system is clearly based upon the Protestant ethic worldview. Weber, in *The Protestant Ethic and the Spirit of Capitalism*, articulated a philosophical debate concerning the emergence of capitalism. According to this thesis, asceticism promoted by certain Protestant religions, notably the Calvinists, Pietists, Methodists, Baptists, Quakers, and

Puritans, in their theological dogma helped develop a psychological condition among their members that was conducive to, and supportive of, capitalism. The Protestant ethic of "predestination," or calling, set the stage for social achievement based upon an ascetic way of life. Within this scheme, the combination of the greatest possible productivity in work coupled with the rejection of luxury led to a lifestyle that influenced the spirit of capitalism. Here wealth was a clear indication of one's superiority and evidence that one was predestined by God for this success.[3]

Weber drew on the writings of the English Puritans of the latter part of the seventeenth century, wherein the pious bourgeois were viewed as being justified in their differential business and social success since this was a calling to which Providence had predetermined their superiority. This ethic was first brought to the New England colonies by the Puritans and later, in what is now the United States, by the Quakers and Baptists. Western capitalism, however, came about when business was separated from the extended family, and the availability of a labor pool emerged. Out of this new model, society changed as one's occupational status, mainly the male head-of-household status, now determined one's family's social position vis-à-vis the new stratified social order. Work became an end in itself, leading to the work ethic. Within this perspective, the individual was separated from the primary group associated with folk cultures. Individual responsibility emerged as well as the corresponding psychological concept of guilt. In folk cultures responsibility was shared through the primary collectivity such as the extended family or clan, while the psychological response was one of shame.

With the work ethic came the foundations of justice and the belief that enfranchised members of society, mainly adult free white males, were responsible for their actions and, consequently, their successes and failures. Hence, from the Puritan ethic emerged a more pervasive, secular morality currently known as the Protestant ethic, wherein social position is determined by one's occupational status and material wealth. The Americanized version of the Protestant ethic germinated another unique element—that of a moral imperative to expand and dominate the United States even at the expense of others, especially those considered to be morally and biologically inferior, such as blacks, Asians, Hispanics, and American Indians. This ethnocentric moral imperative became known as Manifest Destiny—the ultimate form of materialism. From this perspective, the ideals of justice, the adversarial system with the assurance of due process and the presumption of innocence until proven guilty beyond a reasonable doubt, applied only to those enfranchised by the dominant society. This concept of selective admission into the acceptable in-group and the exclusion of those considered to be from the inferior out-groups justified the exploitation of women and children in the mills of New England, Chinese as railroad workers, African black and American Indian slavery, armed conflict initiated with Mexico and Spain, and the long history of physical and cultural genocide toward American Indians. Wolfgang Mieder assessed the impact of the Protestant ethic on American Indians:

> As people look back at the colonization of the Americas by Europeans in the year when the world commemorates the quincentenary of Columbus's discovery of America, it is becoming even more obvious that the native population suffered terribly in the name of expansion and progress. Native Americans were deprived of their homelands, killed mercilessly, or placed on reservations where many continue their marginalized existence today. Early concepts of the "good Indian" or "noble savage" quickly were replaced by attitudes and policies that reduced the native inhabitants to "wild savages" who were standing in the way of expansionism in the name of "manifest destiny."[4]

Manifest Destiny, or the belief that the white Protestant American society had the calling to dominate what is now the United States, allowed the dominant society to denigrate those who did not belong to their selective in-group so much so that the truth was not necessary in dealing with these lesser humans. Hence, the long history of broken treaties and contravening federal policies when dealing with American Indians. These policies were pervasive, involving all three branches of the federal government, and continue to the present.

The American Indian Harmony Ethos

The Harmony Ethos provided a similar belief system for North American Indians prior to European influence. Many elements of this aboriginal worldview have survived to the present. Common tenets of the Harmony Ethos transcend the hundreds of American Indian and Native Alaskan groups residing in North America (northern Mexico, the United States except the Pacific islands, and Canada) despite variations in their creation myths—the justifying epistemological methodology for subscribing to the Harmony Ethos. Basic to this worldview is the superiority of nature as it is represented by Father Sky and Mother Earth. Within this scheme of things, humans are a dependent component reliant on all elements of life, organic and inorganic, for their survival. Rocks, sand, soil, and minerals are important components within this wholistic perspective, as are trees, grass, plants, and everything that crawls, walks, swims, and flies. Water is the life blood of

Mother Earth, while rain, wind, and lightning reflect the intimate interactions between Mother Earth and Father Sky. This symbiotic relationship between Mother Earth and Father Sky is what sustains life itself. And like human relations, this relationship can be stormy at times. The particular American Indian or Native Alaskan creation myth signifies the role of the group vis-à-vis other humans and special elements of nature. For instance, the snake and the owl play diametrically opposed roles within various American Indian groups, representing either evil or good omens, depending on the creation myth.

The role of humans is to live in harmony with nature regardless of nature's course. Prayers are made to Mother Earth and all the particular elements represented by her as well as to Father Sky, the giver of the sun, moon, wind, rain, and temperature. Order is provided by nature, and in this respect, the number four is significant within the Harmony Ethos. The four seasons determine the horticultural process and hence the tribal rites, rituals, customs and ceremonies. The four directions, like the sign of the cross among Roman Catholics, hold sacred connotations. Here, the world is sliced into four quadrants, with the east being the most sacred direction. Indeed, the east-west direction represents the red road, or power road, among many tribes. What differs is the rotations of these quadrants. In some tribes, it is clockwise, as among the Sioux, while in others it is counterclockwise, as among the Cherokees. The four colors also differ according to tribes. However, red, blue, and black are common colors, with the fourth color being either white or yellow.

Accordingly, prescribed human customs and corresponding behaviors were established in these folk cultures in order for these groups to live in harmony with nature. Tribal status and role expectations were dictated according to the basic four aboriginal life stages: infancy, childhood, adulthood, and old age. Education was a lifelong process occurring *in vivo*, that is, in real life, requiring taking chances and experiencing life in the raw and not so much from others' experiences. Infants were often nourished using operant conditioning, whereby positive reinforcements for undesirable behaviors such as crying were ignored. Childhood received family, clan, and community indulgence and a maximum of social stimulation. Possessiveness by the biological parents was discouraged. Instead, children received attention from all of their relatives. This process limited the psychological impact of separation or divorce of their parents. Children were encouraged to engage in gender-specific play, which prepared them for their adult roles. Guidance was provided by the elders, often referred to as the grandparents—those considered to have the greatest wisdom in the group.

Adulthood was attained through a marked *rite de passage* that brought the individual from childhood into adulthood. Adolescence was avoided during aboriginal times in that the indulged child, along with a group of same-sex peers, would undergo a public, and often painful, transformation from dependent children into their new status of productive adults. Adults had considerable freedom but needed to abide by the customs of the group. A common taboo was not directly drawing attention to one's self. Honor had to be bestowed by others who witnessed your admirable deeds.

Another constraint on personal behavior was the collective sharing of both positive and negative behaviors. While an individual's honor and successes were shared by his family and clan, so was any crime or dishonor. Clan honor was earned through the acts of its members, while wisdom was gained by experiences in life. The give-away was, and still is, the family's or clan's way of recognizing and honoring successful members of their group. In the give-away, the honored person does not receive these gifts. Instead, the family or clan of the honoree distributes their personal possessions to others in the tribe in recognition of the honored member. Hence, the more a family or clan organizes give-aways, the greater the respect this family or clan has in the tribe. The final life-state is that of respected elder. These people have experienced life (counting coup) and now have the wisdom to assist others within the tribe who have questions about life. They are also the teachers of the children passing on the oral tradition of the family, clan, and tribe, including the group's rites, customs, rituals, taboos, and sanctions.

The Harmony Ethos stressed the importance of individual independence and the avoidance of overt aggressiveness. Third persons or objects were often used to convey dissatisfaction in intratribal interactions. Other characteristics of the Harmony Ethos include: resentment of authority; hesitancy to command others; reluctance to refuse requests made by others in their group; obligatory hospitality and sharing with kinfolk; impassivity regarding greetings and exchanges; refusal, or unwillingness, to contradict others; and the absence of gestures in public speaking.[5] These attributes differ considerably from those spelled out in the Protestant ethic, which stresses competition, personal aggressiveness, and individual accountability. The Harmony Ethos called for group cooperation and not individual competition. Indian children and adults sat in a circle for a couple of reasons. One is so that the circle of harmony would be maintained and the other is so that individual statuses could not be determined as in more hierarchical arrangements.

Individual achievements were tempered by the belief that any success, whether in hunting, fishing, farming, gathering, human or animal reproduction, or warfare, was due to the blessings of Father Sky and Mother Earth. Indeed, the plants, fish, and animals were prayed to and thanked for providing the lowly humans with continued sustenance for life. Aboriginal life was replete with purification rituals preparing the American Indian for his or her chores in life. These were followed by rituals of thanks for any successes. Most significantly, balance had to be restored when natural resources were used. This was evident in the rules governing both domestic and inter-tribal conflict.

The Cherokee Example of the Harmony Ethos

The Cherokee worldview is based on their creation myth. In their aboriginal worldview, Mother Earth is seen as a great floating island suspended by four cords attaching it to Father Sky, viewed as constituted of solid rock. These anchor cords kept Mother Earth from sinking into the water surrounding it. Insects and animals were credited with discovering Mother Earth, notably Beaver's grandchild, the little Water-Beetle. Before Water-Beetle discovered Mother Earth lying below the water, all living things lived in the sky vault, Galunlati. But conditions were crowded on Galunlati, and a new home needed to be found. Once Water-Beetle discovered the mud below the water, this mud was brought to the surface and attached at the four corners by the cords to the sky vault.

At first the mud was too wet to settle on, and Great Buzzard was asked to fly down from Galunlati and check if Mother Earth was dry enough for the insects and animals to come down. Great Buzzard got tired surveying Mother Earth, and where his wings hit the mud, valleys were created, and on the up-swing of his wings he created the mountains (which exist where the aboriginal Cherokees resided in the Appalachian Mountains of western North Carolina, eastern Tennessee, and north Georgia). Once the mud was dry, the insects, animals, and humans left Galunlati to reside on Mother Earth. They then got the sun to track daily from east to west over Mother Earth. According to the Cherokee creation myth, the sun is female while the moon, her brother, is male. Hence, the sun is called "Nunda that dwells in the day" and the moon is called "Nunda that dwells in the night."

A major component of this creation myth is the need to cooperate with one another, producing harmony. From this myth came the role of insects, plants, animals, and minerals. The Cherokees believe in "little people" who reside in the forest and assist the Cherokees when they are in need. Two of these little people were transformed into poisonous snakes (Copperhead and Rattlesnake), hence the Cherokees' reverence for these reptiles. Moreover, all animals, except the Bear, who is considered a lower human form, are respected and thanked whenever they allow humans to kill them for food, tools, and skins. Essentially, this is the Cherokee creation myth.[6]

The aboriginal Cherokees called themselves *Ani-yun-wiya*, translated to mean either the "real people" or the "principal people." The term "Cherokee" emerged only after white contact. Hernando de Soto, the Spanish explorer, referred to these people as Chelaque Indians, while later they were referred to as Chalaque (1557), Cheraqui (1699), and eventually as Cherokees during the late 1700s. John Reid claimed, on the other hand, that Cherokee is the name assigned these people by neighboring tribes, a term signifying "cave people." Linguistically, the Cherokees belong to the Iroquoian groups, although their separation from the Iroquois in northeastern United States and southern Quebec, Canada, apparently happened quite a long time ago, since the Cherokees' history indicated wars with the Iroquois. Another group, the Tuscarora Indians of eastern North Carolina, also belonged to this linguistic family, and many of the Tuscarora joined the Cherokees once their lands were taken by whites. The Cherokees were the largest southeastern tribe at the time of European contact, while their cousins, the Iroquois, were the largest group in the Northeast. Archaeological evidence indicates that the Iroquoian linguistic family spread from what is now southeastern Canada to Florida. The only other linguistic family with a wider distribution is the Athapascans, who ranged from Alaska to northern Mexico. Both the Apache and Navajo belong to the Athapascan linguistic family.[7]

Although the aboriginal Cherokees had access to considerable territory, estimated to include all or part of the present states of Virginia, Tennessee, North and South Carolina, Georgia, and Alabama, other tribes shared this region as well. Neighboring tribes included the Powhatan, Monacan, Tuscarora, Catawba, Saure, Cherawa, Creek, and Chickasaw Indians. Numerous other tribes lived in what is now North Carolina, the current home of the eastern band of Cherokee Indians, or the Qualla Cherokees. Among these were the Algonquian, Hatteras, Chowan, Weapomeiok, Woccon, Cape Fear, Coosa, Shawnee, Saure, Chickamauga, Occaneechee, Kayauwee, Ano, Saxapahaw, and Siouan tribes.[8] The Cherokees had considerable mobility until the advent of white contact, when they were compelled to forfeit much of their land through treaties. Indeed, forty-three thousand square miles of Cherokee territory was taken by whites within a fifty-year period (1785–1835), culminating with removal and the Trail of Tears.

The Cherokee social structure was unique even among southeastern Indian groups. They seemed to manifest a fierce sense of pride, and this tradition continued after white contact. At the time of white contact, the clan was the strongest structural unit in their culture. There were seven clans among the

Cherokees. Traditionally, the clan was the most significant regulatory unit; within the Cherokee social structure, both lineage (matrilineal) and residence (matrilocal) were determined by the female's clan affiliation. This system placed considerable importance on the female in the family, village, and clan structures. The seven clans were the Wolf Clan (*Ani-Waya*), Deer Clan (*Ani-Kawi*), Bird Clan (*Ani-Tsiskwa*), Paint Clan (*Ani-Wadi*), Long Hair or Blue Clan (*Ani-Sahani*), Blind Savannah or Wild Potato Clan (*Ani-Gatage*), and Holly or Twisters Clan (*Ani-Gilahi*).[9]

Secondary to the clan structure were the villages. These were mostly autonomous political entities, although four discernible clusters were found to exist at the time of European contact. It was these seven clans and sixty horticultural villages that comprised the Cherokees' traditional homeland. Evidence of a larger tribal government is lacking. For all practical purposes, the aboriginal Cherokees had a rural community structure comprised of autonomous villages linked only through sentiment, clan lineage, and folk obligations. Intravillage wars and altercations were rare, and seemingly every effort was made to settle disputes peaceably in order to bring harmony back to the people. This was quite an endeavor considering that these villages were distributed over a vast territory accommodating an estimated twenty thousand Cherokees.

A certain degree of regionalism did exist, since certain Cherokee dialects were associated with at least four basic village clusters: the Overhill, Lower Towns, Middle Settlement, and Valley Towns. Each of these village clusters shared a particular geographical area in addition to a dialect. During the pre-Columbian era, regional leaders emerged to represent their districts in national crises. Equally significant were the seven Mother Villages, representing the headquarters of the respective seven clans. The early Cherokee civil, juvenile, and criminal justice system focused on vengeance and balance at the clan level, not at the individual and tribal levels.

The early Cherokees lived in permanently located villages where they farmed, fished, and hunted. A village's location was important, since level land was needed for farming, and water sources, such as rivers, ponds, lakes, springs, and brooks, were desired for crops, fishing, travel, and drinking water. Size was also an important factor in that each village housed between three hundred and six hundred people. Some early writers compared these villages with medieval European villages, which had similar fields and gardens. This arrangement facilitated both mutual help in the division of labor and better protection from hostile groups. These pre-Columbian villages were surrounded by a stockade fence designed to protect the village perimeter.

Within the village, the central structure was the Town House, later named the Council House. This was a seven-sided building, large in size, and elevated from the rest of the village structures. This structure and the unique form of Cherokee democracy were responsible for maintaining harmony during aboriginal times. The seven sides of the building represented each of the Cherokee clans. All important public activity took place within the Town House. This alone suggests the size of this structure, since it had to accommodate all of the village adults. The Town House represented the heart of the village, and there a symbolic flame was kept burning year-round, signifying the village's vitality. Other village structures consisted of private homes. These were long dwelling buildings with a reed infrastructure covered with mud and straw adobe and roofed with bark shingles; they were usually windowless and had only a single entrance in order to avoid sneak attacks. These family structures had a single hole in the roof for the smoke from the cooking fire to escape. It is estimated that an average of ten people, a typical extended clan family unit, occupied each home, with newly married couples residing with the bride's mother (matrilocal arrangement).

The two legal institutions governing the aboriginal Cherokees were the village council and the clan, which was more powerful since it transcended the village structure. The governing body of each village was the council, an assembly of all the adult men and women. Each adult had a vote. The rules were that no weapons were allowed in the Town House. Everyone was permitted to speak, and custom required that everyone be heard. Village policy was determined in the Town House through democratic deliberation; all adults, both men and women, participated in these discussions. During these deliberations the Cherokees sought a consensus as to what was best for the village. The council did not legislate or adjudicate; its role was to seek consensus and compromise in order to maintain harmony within the group. Once a consensus was reached, dissenters were ignored and never chastised. This collective will, that of collective responsibility, represented the regulatory force at the village level and was superseded only by clan obligations. Conspicuously absent were formal control agencies such as police, courts, and jails. Serious transgressions involved the clan, not the village structure; the latter intervened only when no viable solution seemed readily available. Accordingly, the village council's function was primarily advisory; the ultimate decision was left to the respective clans arbitrating the issue.

Blood vengeance was the traditional vehicle used in resolving serious transgressions, the most serious involving violation of marriage taboos and murder. Here, the clans acted as corporate individuals, each representing the parties involved in a fashion similar to our civil court procedures. Other matters were regulated by the village council, which was presided over by either the white chief or the red chief. The white chief regulated domestic affairs, which were especially important from spring planting until the fall harvest. The red chief, or priest warrior, was more important during the winter season, which was the time for war. Women played an important role in both domestic and war councils; evidence indicates that on occasion they even served as white chiefs. They had considerable authority in the domestic council by virtue of the existing matrilineal kinship structure that linked the Cherokees as a people. To be recognized as a Cherokee one had to be either born or adopted into one of the seven clans. Even in the war council an assemblage of war women, known as pretty women, was present and consulted regarding strategy, time of attack, and other important matters.

Accordingly, justice was linked to the Cherokees' horticultural lifestyle. Their year was divided into two seasons, summer and winter; the white chief and the domestic council were most critical during the summer months and the red chief and war council were more active during the winter months. Overall, six festivals punctuated the year, all relating to the harvest and village purification. These festivals were: First New Moon of Spring, New Green Corn, Green Corn, First Appearance of the October New Moon, Establishment of Friendship and Brotherhood, and Bouncing Bush. These festivals portrayed the cycle of life, which began each year with the spring planting and ended with the autumn harvest, which signified the success of the year's effort. Together, these festivals and ceremonies celebrated the balance and harmony between Mother Earth and Father Sky—the entities that provided sustenance for the Cherokee people.

The year's end was celebrated with a communal cleansing festival when old clothing, furniture, and other artifacts representative of the past year were discarded and burned in a large village bonfire. Next, the sacred fire in the Town House was extinguished, and the Town House and all village dwellings were swept clean, thereby symbolically purging the village and its people of all past errors, sins, and transgressions. A new sacred fire was then ignited, and the Town House was whitewashed. All personal transgressions were now forgiven, including unresolved murders. Everyone in the village purified themselves by drinking the "black drink," which induced vomiting and hence internal cleansing, preparing themselves for a new year.[10]

The unique aspect of the early Cherokee social structure was its high degree of local autonomy and decentralized control. A crisis seemed to dictate the emergence of a temporary tribal headman, with his selection contingent upon the collective will of the Cherokee people as a whole. The early Cherokees were a collection of independent villages linked by their clan identification and a shifting, changing leadership, which arose to meet each individual crisis, and which adapted to meet the problems at hand. Rule by consensus instead of law and the emergence of a leader who ruled only when needed are the bases of the aboriginal Cherokee Harmony Ethos.

Domestic relationships were governed through clan obligations that permeated all villages and behaviors. These customs were regulated through folkways, mores, and laws involving all levels of interaction, from the most intimate to the tribal level. Clearly, the clan represented the highest civil authority during aboriginal times. At the same time, the informal clan regulatory network allowed for considerable individual freedom on the part of the adult Cherokee, so much so that the aboriginal female was allowed much more discretion in her behavior than was experienced by her Euro-American counterpart. In many respects, the aboriginal Cherokee female had far more autonomy and authority than her contemporary white counterpart has today.

The female stages of development were infancy, childhood, and womanhood; for a few, the higher statuses of clan matriarch and of pretty woman (council to the red chief) were possible for mature elders (beyond menopause). The Cherokee male's developmental stages included infancy, childhood, manhood, and, again for a few, the highest status of beloved man, and of village or regional red or white chief. Elders of both genders were revered as grandparents, those with wisdom.

Mate selection, family size, and the duration of the marriage were all matters where women had considerable voice. Tribal custom merely dictated that a Cherokee male could not marry into his own or into his biological father's clan. Other major taboos concerned mourning and the remarriage of surviving relatives. Men were encouraged to marry their dead wife's sister. Men often married women from appropriate clans outside their villages. A man lived in the village and household of his wife. Marriages were regulated by the women in the village. They punished both male and female offenders, including widows or widowers who violated mourning regulations and even publicly fell upon a male who neglected his wife or children. Otherwise, there was considerable freedom within the marriage.[11]

The Cherokees had no word for adultery or promiscuity, and contractual marriages and dowries were not part of the Cherokee way. A female gave her consent to the marriage and had the ultimate say regarding most aspects of family life. Cherokee women divorced their husbands by simply putting them out of the house or by taking in another man. The children stayed with their mother in her village, while the ex-husband moved back into his mother's village and home. Apparently, little hostility emerged from these situations, especially between males, since brothers were not obligated to defend a sister's honor, and any redress surrounding neglect was managed by fellow clan women. A woman even possessed license to kill her baby at, or soon after, birth. A similar act committed by the father constituted murder.

From our cultural perspective, many of the early Cherokee behavioral patterns may seem perplexing. One of the most difficult aspects of behavior to comprehend is the Cherokee concept of the individual and how this relates to the traditional Cherokee Harmony Ethos. Avoidance and harmony are the most important elements of this ethos. Elaborated networks of avoidance provided the needed regulatory sanctions, minimizing the need for and use of formal controls such as police power, courts, and corporal punishment. Ostracism, often referred to as social death, was the ultimate control mechanism; this represented but one aspect of avoidance. Disapproval, ridicule, and vengeance, administered through the clan structure, provided the necessary negative sanctions. Within this perspective the individual was seen as an autonomous entity free to regulate his or her life within the confines of clan obligations. The individual was not subordinate to the village, hence physical coercion as such was virtually lacking during pre-Columbian times.

Marked differences exist between the Cherokee Harmony Ethos and the Euro-American Protestant ethic. Individual achievement, competitiveness, and culpability, although crucial to the Protestant ethic, are alien to the Cherokee Harmony Ethos. Individual status within the Cherokee traditional culture was determined through clan affiliation and role performance within the village setting. By the same token, the Cherokees had greater latitude in personal behavior, since they were not subjected to numerous secondary controls like those evident under societies that subscribed to the Protestant ethic.

Problems occurred when these two ethics clashed. The Harmony Ethos manifests certain traits conducive to the maintenance of harmonious internal relationships. Foremost, overt hostilities were avoided; when they did occur, causation was often projected to a neutral third person or object. Hence, the Cherokees in early times (as well as today) were more apt to speak sparsely, to be devoid of gestures while speaking, to look away from the person addressing them, and to avoid voicing an opinion publicly regardless of how deeply they felt about the issue.

Group cooperation, not individual competitiveness, was the basic social value associated with aboriginal life. In order to insulate the individual from the internalization of excessive guilt or frustration resulting from these complex avoidance networks, stressful conflict situations were conveniently resolved through the use of real or imaginary third persons or objects. To illustrate how this process operated, early white trappers brought rum to the Cherokees in order to placate them, and when they became intoxicated, the blame was placed on the rum and not on the Cherokees under the influence.

Similarly, if a woman was annoyed by another woman's child, she calmly solicited the use of a neutral third person, usually a woman not related to anyone involved in the altercation, to discretely inform the child's mother of her offspring's behavior. Many of these avoidance networks were quite complex, requiring considerable restraint on the part of those involved. Perhaps this is why the early Cherokees relied so heavily on expressive activities such as stick ball and wars. These subtle tensions also emphasize the significance of the yearly purification rituals where all offenses were forgiven.[12]

Still, sporadic aggression did occur within the domestic domain, and in these instances, the law of clan vengeance prevailed. Serious transgressions involved either abusive treatment of women and children by males, violation of mourning taboos, and homicide. These were clan matters and not village or personal issues. Clan obligations, and not emotions or morality, prevailed, making Cherokee justice a rational process often resulting in methodical planning and execution. Individual shame most often sufficed in detaining the wrongdoer until his fate was determined and implemented. A few did manage to evade justice by escaping to towns of refuge, villages occupied by clans other than those involved in the altercation. This was not a popular recourse, since this action tended to shame the offender's clan. Offenders were allowed to return to their own village following the purification ritual and the beginning of the new year, at which time all wrongdoers, even murderers and other capital offenders, were exonerated. Apparently, this reentry process was not accompanied by any bitterness or negative stigma on behalf of the parties involved, although it weakened the status of the offender within his or her primary group, the clan.

The warrior role represents yet another aspect of early Cherokee behavior. War provided the most substantial release mechanism for the Cherokees. It was during war celebrations that most restraints were relaxed and total emotional expression prevailed. The warrior role clearly was the most important facet of the male's status. The young Cherokee male was conditioned for war. War, like domestic relations, was based on vengeance and was more a village than a clan matter. The cause of most wars involved encounters with other (non-Cherokee) Indian groups within the vast territory claimed by the Cherokees. Harmony, or balance, was the rule of Cherokee battles. The Cherokee Harmony Ethos dictated that all Cherokee deaths had to be avenged, necessitating retaliatory raids.

Cherokee wars, like all everything else in Cherokee culture, were highly regulated by custom. Ideally, the enemy killed should equal the number of Cherokees killed in previous encounters. In this sense wholesale massacres were not condoned. Yet the frenzy and enthusiasm that accompanied Cherokee war parties and their celebrations frightened white observers, and some whites felt that the Cherokees deliberately sought excuses for war, especially during the winter season. War obviously provided an important release for the otherwise deferential situation demanded by the avoidance ethic dominating tribal relationships. It also follows that the village purification ritual also occurring during the winter season, provided the necessary license for the Cherokee males to purge themselves of the year's tension and frustration.

Nonetheless, wars were not free-for-alls. The killing was limited, and excess victims were brought back as captives. If the Cherokee death toll exceeded the enemy killed, then captives, especially adult males, would be slain to balance the tally. Women and children captives were often adopted into their captor's clan, gaining all the rights and privileges of their adopted clan. These adoptions were often necessary in order to compensate for the clan's decimated rank due to war casualties.

Wars and stickball games not only allowed for legitimate expression of tension release but also provided a competitive arena within the otherwise harmonious Cherokee culture. This competition allowed the male Cherokee to distinguish himself as a warrior and/or ball player and maintain high status and prestige, while passively adhering to the dictates of the avoidance ethos. The warrior image provided these individuals with a monumental psychological advantage over less distinguished village members.

The ball play was an interclan domestic activity with as many as fifty males on each team. The objective was to take a stuffed animal-skin ball from the center of the ball field to the team's goal line. No holds were barred, making it a violent game where death was not uncommon. Sometimes the death of a player was by design, since the ball game represented one of the acceptable, and honorable, vehicles used in resolving interclan blood vengeance. War parties were also used in this fashion, with the marked man occupying a vulnerable position prior to the attack. These types of death were the most honorable for the offender and his clan. A more humiliating death was to be hunted down, caught, bound hand and foot, cast off a cliff, and left to be devoured by wild animals and birds. Accordingly, the aboriginal Cherokee behavioral patterns were accommodated through a complex interplay between domestic and war activities, controlled avoidance and emotional expressions, group compliance, and individual discretion. This was the essence of Cherokee justice under the traditional Harmony Ethos.

Euro-American Influence on Cherokee Justice

In the late 1700s, increased white contact and pressure from the U.S. government for a treaty (Hopewell Treaty of 1785) created a situation of perpetual crisis among the Cherokee people. This brought a demand for permanent he sixty villages throughout the Cherokee territory. Little nali village, emerged as the tribe's beloved man, or most nguished warrior (red chief). Subsequently, a Grand ......onal Council was developed in 1792 to deal specifically with the issues of national leadership, centralized government, and a new political philosophy sufficient to prepare the Cherokees for continuous Indian-white relationships. Little Turkey was selected as the first principal chief of the Cherokees and the leader when the Cherokee Nation emerged.

At this time, many of the traditional elements found in the village domestic and war councils were incorporated into the Grand Cherokee National Council. Council members ruled by consensus, not by law. However, a hierarchy of authority did emerge, with recognition given to a principal spokesperson, referred to officially as the chief speaker, or beloved man, of the whole nation. There was also the establishment of regional chiefs, one for each of the four territorial areas (Overhills, Lower Towns, Middle Settlement, and Valley Towns), as well as recognition of the village chiefs representing their own autonomous constituency. This complex arrangement made rule by consensus difficult to say the least. The weak and tenuous position of the principal chief only made matters worse, yet Little Turkey held this system together until his death in 1807.

Formal controls soon replaced the traditional rule of consensus, and as early as 1795, a tribal police force was created to curb horse theft (horse theft was not a problem during pre-European times since the horse was introduced to America by Europeans). The first Cherokee police force was known as the Regulating Companies, and eventually a more permanent police structure, the Light Horse Guard, emerged in 1808. The year 1808 also marked the official beginning of the Cherokee Republic, later known as the Cherokee Nation. In addition to the establishment of a tribal police force, laws were written down for the first time. The Grand Cherokee National Council now selected the principal and vice chiefs, and this body along with these leaders were empowered to enact and enforce laws. In 1810, the Grand Cherokee National Council weakened clan control and specifically outlawed the traditional process of clan vengeance.[13]

In 1817, a national bicameral legislature consisting of an upper house, the Standing Committee, and a lower house, the National Council (later renamed the General Council), replaced the Grand Cherokee National Council comprised of area and village chiefs. The upper house members were selected from the National Council, while all the council members were elected at large for two-year terms. Accordingly, the tribal territory was apportioned into eight districts (Coosawatee, Anchee, Etowee, Hickory Log, Chatooga, Chiokamaugah, Aquohee, and Tawquohee), each with its own district judge and marshal. Tribal control was maintained through four circuit judges and a company of Light Horse Guard, each serving a double district jurisdiction.

By 1822, the mold for the Cherokee Nation was set. Path Killer was principal chief, Charles Hicks was vice chief, John Ross was president of the National Committee, and The Ridge was speaker of the National Council. Hicks, Ross, and The Ridge later played crucial roles within the Cherokee Nation. A year later, the Cherokee Nation developed a Supreme Court consisting of a bench of circuit judges, who heard twenty-one cases during the first term. These Euro-American adaptations earned the Cherokees, and their neighbors who made similar changes (Choctaw, Chickasaw, Creek, and Seminole), the title "The Five Civilized Tribes."

Paradoxically, Western-style democracy was also the root of cultural regression regarding certain aspects of the Cherokee lifestyle. Females, who were once the political peers of male Cherokees, were now disenfranchised, like their white counterparts. Now, only male descendants of Cherokee females, with the exception of black mixed-bloods, were eligible candidates for any elective or appointed office, if they were at least twenty-five years of age. All eighteen-year-old males, except those of black mixed-blood, could vote. Accordingly, the principal and vice chiefs, the treasurer, the three Supreme Court justices, and national marshals were elected by the General Council for four-year terms. The General Council could override the chief's veto with at least a two-thirds margin. Due process, a Bill of Rights, trial by jury, and religious freedom were also incorporated into the new Cherokee constitution.

The success of the Cherokee Nation was remarkable by any standard. By 1825, the Cherokees were successful farmers, herdsmen, and merchants. There were large crops of cotton, tobacco, wheat, and corn. Cherokee merchants had a favorable trade balance, with international exports extending as far west as New Orleans. The Cherokee Nation operated in the black. However, part of their conversion to a Western-style civilization required them to own black African slaves. Nonetheless, eastern white liberals were proud of the Cherokees' progress, and there certainly was little doubt that the Cherokees had successfully adopted a separate, yet equal, cultural lifestyle paralleling that of the dominant United States society.

Ironically, the seeds of destruction were being sown as the Cherokee Nation emerged. The ratification of the United States Constitution by the southern states totally disregarded the Cherokee Nation and, in effect, sliced up the Cherokee Nation and other southern tribal reservations into their respective states. The 1802 Georgia Compact provided the United States with all western lands formerly claimed by Georgia in exchange for President

Jefferson's promise to transport all Indians from the state's borders. The 1803 Louisiana Purchase provided the land for the forced removal of all American Indian groups east of the Mississippi River to lands west of the river, known as Indian Territory. Soon after the Louisiana Purchase, Jefferson made a concerted effort to encourage the southeastern Indians to exchange their traditional lands for new homes in Indian Territory. The Cherokees were among the most reluctant to accept this proposal. Federal agents then sought out the most susceptible Cherokee leaders, enticing them to make territorial concessions in exchange for personal wealth. These actions led to greater distrust of the U.S. government by the Cherokees and led to the National Council's policy of prohibiting the sale of Cherokee land to non-Cherokees, making such transactions a capital offense.

Nevertheless, the U.S. government was successful in getting a few Cherokee leaders, against the opposition of the principal chief, both councils, and the vast majority of the Cherokee people, to secretly sign the 1835 New Echota Treaty, and by 1838 all but a thousand Cherokees, those residing in the rugged mountains of North Carolina, were forcefully removed to Indian Territory, or Oklahoma. Nearly one-fifth of the entire Cherokee population perished during this brutal roundup and process, which has been recorded for history as the Trail of Tears. The Cherokees were rounded up by the U.S. Army, under General Winfield Scott, and placed in stockades while whites unceremoniously took over their farms, homes, and businesses. Removal left many, both Americans and foreigners, shocked. Yet, President Van Buren, in a message to both houses of Congress, praised the Cherokee removal as a good event for all parties involved.

The Cherokees rebuilt their nation in Oklahoma, only to have it destroyed once again when Indian Territory was opened up to whites and, subsequently, statehood. The Cherokee Nation did, however, carry out its law against selling Cherokee lands, executing the signers of the 1835 Removal (New Echota) Treaty. The Ridge, his son, John, and Elias Boudinot were executed in June 1839 in Indian Territory for the role they played as U.S. government agents in the removal debacle.[14]

This chapter is presented as an illustration of not only the differences between American Indians' traditional ways and those of the Western societies. It highlights the events that American Indians have had to endure over the years in what can best be labeled corrupt and deceptive U.S.-Indian policy. Criminal justice has been equally impacted by these policies, since Indian country falls under congressional oversight and federal jurisdiction for all felony crimes.

AMERICAN INDIAN RELIGIOUS FREEDOM WITHIN THE CRIMINAL JUSTICE CONTEXT: HISTORY, CURRENT STATUS, AND PROSPECTS FOR THE FUTURE[1]

By Little Rock Reed

Preface

By Laurence Armand French

Timothy "Little Rock" Reed, a mixed-blood of Sioux ancestry, was a strong and articulate advocate for the contemporary Indian warrior, especially for those Indian warriors whose coup counting and dog soldiering included long prison terms. While in prison in Ohio in the 1980s and 1990s, Little Rock wrote articles for the *Journal of Prisoner on Prison,* a Canadian periodical from the critical sociology perspective. The journal editor, Brian MacLean, a noted North American criminologist and ex-convict who had served prison time, helped to develop this forum for the inmate's perspective. Little Rock made valuable contributions to this journal while incarcerated.

After a decade in prison in Ohio for armed robberies and drug theft, Little Rock fled to New Mexico in 1993, six weeks before the completion of his parole. Little Rock was picked up in Taos, New Mexico, in 1994, and while he was awaiting extradition back to Ohio and prison, District Judge Peggy Nelson ruled that Little Rock fled under duress and under a reasonable fear for his safety and life, effectively giving Little Rock protected fugitive status in New Mexico. The New Mexico Supreme Court concurred with this decision in 1997. In his ruling, the chief justice stated that Little Rock was not a fugitive from justice but rather a refugee from injustice. Ohio then petitioned Little Rock's case to the U.S. Supreme Court. While awaiting the U.S. Supreme Court's decision Little Rock had the opportunity to participate in the 1998 Academy of Criminal Justice (ACJS) annual convention. The president of the ACJS at this time, Gennaro F. Vito, broke precedence by holding these meetings in Albuquerque, New Mexico. Not only was this site a first for the ACJS, the Native American theme was a first as well. President Vito, along with Program Chair Michael Blankenship and Local Arrangements Chair Larry French, produced an unprecedented sixteen presentations on Native American justice issues and had an all-Indian welcoming panel, of which Little Rock was a participant.

Little Rock eventually lost his fight before the U.S. Supreme Court and was returned to Ohio. However, the publicity surrounding his case forced Ohio officials to reinstate only the six weeks that remained on his parole instead of charging him with the more serious offense of parole violation that could have resulted in years of additional incarceration. Little Rock returned to New Mexico and his Navajo wife and child and continued in his effort to bring tribal-centric religious freedom to the prisons. Unfortunately, he died on January 16, 2000, from injuries resulting from an automobile accident. This chapter reflects Little Rock's work-in-progress on this important criminal and social justice issue.

Introduction

The primary purpose of this [chapter] is to analyze the legal status and future prospects of Native American prisoners' free exercise claims. However, as [Allison] Dussias has suggested, when discussing current Native American free exercise issues, it is important to examine the history of Native American free exercise claims in general as well as the United States government's treatment of traditional Native American religious practices. "'History plays an absolutely central role in the enterprise of Indian law because much of the field rests on construing and interpreting the legacy of time.' . . . [I]n Indian law, history 'provides more than context: because of the discernable impact of past events, it is an important element in Indians' everyday life and an unavoidable component in litigation.'"[2] Thus this chapter begins with a discussion of U.S. policy regarding traditional Native religious practices, as well as an explanation of the spiritual significance of certain traditional Native religious practices that are commonly at issue in Native American free exercise litigation.

Before the first white man appeared on this continent, now known as "America," there were well over a thousand tribes, each having its own language and dialect, but none of which contained a word for "religion." However, the indigenous peoples of this continent did have—and continue to have—profound religious belief systems, which dictate[d] their ways of life and were/are indeed the fabric of their cultures. While their distinct tribal traditions, beliefs, and practices vary, they all contain a common understanding, and that is that all aspects of the Creation are related. I can best explain this by describing the spiritual significance of the *canunpa wakan*, or the "sacred pipe," which is commonly known by non-Indians as the "peace pipe." This description is based on my own understanding as a sun dancer and pipe carrier in the Lakota traditional way of life.

Long ago, the sacred pipe was brought to the Lakota people by a spirit woman sent by the Creator. When she brought the pipe, she instructed the people in its meaning and use. Much like Jesus was brought to the people on another continent, the pipe came swaddled in a bundle, with blessings of peace, and teachings of love and respect for the sanctity of all life.

The pipe consists of a bowl made of a certain stone that is the blood of the people. It represents the people and the earth. It represents the female side of Creation. The pipe also consists of a stem, which, when used in ceremony, is placed into the bowl. It represents the male side of Creation. It is made of wood, and represents everything that grows and lives upon the earth: the trees, the grasses, the flowers. The pipe also contains items that represent the waters and all the life that lives in and under the waters. And it contains items that represent all that reside above the earth: the sky, the air we breathe, the sun, the clouds, the moon, the planets, and so on. So when the pipe is taken out of its bundle and used in ceremony, it represents virtually every aspect of God's creation. When the tobacco—which is generally the inner bark of the red willow—is placed into the bowl of the pipe, it is offered to the four cardinal directions and to the sky and to the earth, from whom we invoke the spiritual powers of the universe. The tobacco itself represents every aspect of the Creation: all the people, all the animals, birds, and insects, all the plants, the rocks, the waters, the sky, and all that is a part of God's Creation. When we place the tobacco into the pipe, our prayers bring together all of the Creation, and our prayers are for harmony and peace, and healing. The smoke carries our prayers to the Creator and out to the four directions, the sky, and the earth. And when we complete our prayers, we say "*Mitakuye oyasin,*" or "All my relations," so that all of God's creation (all our relations) will receive blessings. But the sacred pipe is much more than a mere item that represents the Creation. It is a powerful instrument, which many Native people can attest does actually facilitate physical healing.

There are many tribal instruments and ceremonies that, though different than the pipe ceremony, generate the same results and have the same significance to Native people, on both individual and collective levels. One thing all Native American ceremonies have in common is that they were given to the people by the Creator with specific instructions as to their use and meaning, and they are integral to the ways of life and to the spiritual and physical welfare of the indigenous peoples of this land. As will become apparent in the forthcoming discussion, the disruption of or interference with the free exercise of Native American religion is detrimental to the physical, spiritual, and psychological well-being of the people indigenous to this land. Because their religious beliefs and practices are, in fact, integral to the ways of life of the indigenous peoples, their destruction by the United States government does in fact constitute genocide.[3]

It is also important for the reader to understand the spiritual significance of sacred sites to Native Americans.[4] Michael Simpson, an Indian law attorney, identified some points on the subject:

Although substantial differences exist between the various tribal religions, some generalizations about traditional Native American religions are possible. First, traditional Native American religions are pervasive, giving all aspects of Indian life a spiritual significance. See, e.g., 25 U.S.C. 1302 (1988)(the Indian Civil Rights Act, while imposing most of the provisions of the Bill of Rights upon tribes, makes an exception for the Establishment Clause due to a conscious recognition that government and religion are inextricably interwoven in some tribes). . . .

Second, Native American religions differ profoundly from most major world religions in their attitudes toward history. Most major world religions are "commemorative," as a substantial portion of their religion deals with commemorating sacred events of the past. . . . Native American religions, however, are "continuing" as their ceremonies and rituals deal with the ongoing interaction between the tribe and the natural world it inhabits. . . .

Finally, Native American religions are fundamentally inconsistent with at least one major world religion, Christianity, in their conceptualization of the relationship between mankind and the environment. Native American religions have a more profound appreciation of the interdependence of all living things. Further, Indian rituals and ceremonies are seen as necessary to ensure the continuing health of "Mother Earth." . . . In contrast, Christianity generally distinguishes between mankind and the natural environment. For example, Genesis 1:26–28 states that man should "have dominion over" and "subdue" the earth.[5]

United States Policy of Christianization

There was no idea of interfering with the Indians' personal liberty any more than civilized society interferes with the personal liberty of its citizens. It was not that long hair, paint, blankets, etc., are objectionable in and of themselves—that is largely a question of taste—but that they are a badge of servitude to savage ways and traditions which are effectual barriers to the uplifting of the race.

—*Annual Report of the U.S. Department of Interior*, Report, Commissioner of
Indian Affairs, H.R. Doc. No. 5, 57th Congress, 2nd Session, 1902

I have plans to burn my drum, move out and civilize this hair. See my nose? I smash it straight for you. These teeth? I scrub my teeth away with stones. I know you help me now I matter. And I—I come to you, head down, bleeding from my smile, happy for the snow clean hands of you, my friend.

—J. Welch, *Riding the Earthboy*, 1976

In the latter nineteenth century, it was apparent to political and Christian leaders of the United States that the political and religious forms of tribal life were so closely intertwined as to be inseparable. It was apparent that tribal political resistance to the theft of Indian lands was premised not on a concept of ownership of the lands, but rather on a profound spiritual obligation, as stewards of the land, to protect it. It was apparent to U.S. leaders that, in order to successfully suppress tribal political resistance, it was imperative that tribal religious activities be suppressed as well.[6] Accordingly, it became the policy of the United States government to virtually criminalize American Indian religion. By the mid-1880s, nearly every form of Indian religion was banned on the reservations, and very extreme measures were taken to discourage Indians from maintaining their tribal customs and religious practices.

This discouragement usually came in the form of imprisonment of ceremonial participants or starvation through the withholding of food, although more extreme efforts at suppressing Native American religious freedom included the threat of military intervention.[7,8] This threat became a horrible reality when, in December 1890, the Seventh Cavalry slaughtered approximately three hundred unarmed Lakota men, women, and children (mostly women and children) associated with the Ghost Dance, which was a dance brought to the people by a Native prophet, who had told the people when explaining the dance to them: "I went up to heaven and saw God and all the people who had died a long time ago. God told me to come back and tell my people they must be good and love one another, and not fight, or steal, or lie. He gave me this dance to give to my people."[9]

As a matter of government policy, traditional Native American religious dances were deemed to be the product of "gross heathenism," as reflected in the August 31, 1882, report of one agent: "The great evils in the way of their ultimate civilization lie in these dances. The great superstitions and unhallowed rites of a heathenism as gross as that of India or Central Africa still infects them with its insidious poison, which, unless replaced by Christian civilization, must sap their very life blood."[10]

In a December 2, 1882, letter to the commissioner of Indian affairs, Secretary of Interior Henry Teller argued that the dances should be discontinued, by force if necessary.[11] As a result, in April 1883, the commissioner established a set of "Rules for Indian Courts," which identified a number of "Indian Offenses," including ceremonial dances, the destruction or distribution of property, and mourning rituals.[12,13] As observed by Matthiessen, "on pain of imprisonment, the Lakota were forbidden the spiritual renewal of traditional ceremonies; even the ritual purification ceremony of the sweat lodge was forbidden. They were not permitted to wear Indian dress or sew beadwork. . . ."[14]

Even Indian funeral ceremonies were declared to be illegal, and drumming and any form of dancing had to be held for the most artificial of reasons. The Lummi Indians from western Washington, for example, continued some of their tribal dances under the guise of celebrating the signing of their treaty. The Plains Indians eagerly celebrated the Fourth of July, for it meant that they could perform Indian dances and ceremonies by pretending to celebrate the signing of the Declaration of Independence.[15]

As Robert Burnette and John Koster noted, "There are on file orders from the Department of the Army and the Department of Interior authorizing soldiers and [Bureau of Indian Affairs] (BIA) agents to destroy every vestige of Indian religion, that is, to destroy the Indian's whole view of the world and his place in the universe."[16] The sacred Sun Dance was discontinued or held in secret until the 1950s, and even when it was brought back into the open in the 1950s, it was not conducted entirely in accordance with tradition because certain aspects of the ceremony were deemed by non-Indians to be barbaric and unacceptable[17]; medicine bundles and sacred pipes were confiscated, broken, and burned; medicine men were jailed for practicing traditional healing or holding ceremonies. As late as the 1930s, the BIA had openly promulgated a law called the "Indian Offenses Act" forbidding the practice of "[Indian] religion and . . . the rites of the Native American Church . . . which is a fusion of Christian and Indian beliefs. Any Indian who practiced either could be sentenced up to six months in jail or fined $360, more than most Indians' yearly incomes in those times."[18]

As Steven Tullberg, Robert Coulter, and Curtis Burkey have pointed out, Indian names, which have spiritual significance, were replaced by English names and even traditional hairstyles were forbidden under penalty of criminal law[19]: "Those [Indians] who resisted this colonial rule were labeled as 'hostiles' and were subjected to arbitrary criminal punishment, including imprisonment and forced labor, as determined by the [BIA] agent. Mass arrests of 'hostile' leaders were ordered and many served lengthy sentences at Alcatraz and elsewhere."[20]

Throughout the mid-nineteenth century, the government negotiated with various Christian sects and divided the Indians up between them in order to Christianize the Indians. As some authorities have observed, the missionaries worked diligently at stomping out Indian religion and at separating young Indians from their "heathen" parents and relatives and at "raising" Indian people up from their "savage" state of existence to the level of the "civilized" Christian society.[21] However, this process was a bit slow, and as more and more Europeans immigrated to this new land, the need for new lands [on which to settle] increased. The Americans became impatient. They wanted instantaneous conversions of Indians to an agrarian "civilized" life.[22]

Thus, in 1878, the government established the first BIA boarding school at Carlisle Barracks in Pennsylvania, which marked the beginning of a systematic attack on Indian religions and cultures through the de-Indianization of the children. Over the next couple of years there were a dozen such schools established. To ensure attendance at the schools, Indian children, unlike their Anglo counterparts, "were captured at gunpoint by the U.S. military and taken to distant BIA boarding schools."[23] BIA employees' kidnapping of the children was also a fairly popular method of ensuring attendance.[24] For those parents who were reluctant to let their children be taken away and placed into the boarding schools, rations and annuities were withheld.[25] The purpose of these boarding schools was adequately stated by U.S. Supreme Court Justice Douglas in 1973:

> The express policy [of the schools was that of] stripping the Indian child of his cultural heritage and identity: Such schools were run in a rigid military fashion, with heavy emphasis on rustic vocational education. They were designed to separate a child from his reservation and family, strip him of his tribal lore and mores, force the complete abandonment of his native language, and prepare him for never again returning to his people.[26]

This "Americanization" of Indian children was thought to be most effective if they were removed from all tribal influence at the earliest age possible, "before the traditional tribal way of life could make an indelible stamp on them."[27] Thus, they were taken to boarding schools at such great distances that the [children's] contact with family was virtually impossible. For example, "Indian children were . . . shipped from South Dakota or New Mexico to Carlisle Barracks in Pennsylvania where the death rate of students sometimes [exceeded] that of children on disease ridden, malnourished reservations."[28] Even as recently as the "enlightened" era of the 1960s and 1970s, Indian children in Alaska were shipped as far away as Oklahoma, "6,000 miles from their parents."[29] All of these same techniques and practices were utilized by the Canadian government against Native Americans as well.

The Indian boarding school experience is best characterized as an American horror story. The speaking of tribal languages was a physically punishable offense in the boarding schools.[30] For most of the children, this amounted to having one's mouth washed out with lye soap and a wire brush every time [one] was caught communicating with other children in the only language [one] knew. Until one could learn the English language, oral human communication was virtually illegal.

Christianity was forced upon the children and continues to this day to be stressed over tribal religions at the boarding schools.[31] I have listened to many personal accounts of the boarding school experience. They all carry themes not unlike one boarding school graduate who recalled: "One of the bad tastes it leaves in my mouth is that when we were there . . . they cut our hair, and shaved our heads, and forced us to go to Sunday School where they showed us pictures of this man with long hair and a beard and told us he loved us."[32]

Absolutely everything that was even remotely identifiable as being Indian was uncompromisingly prohibited at the boarding schools, and the students were constantly reminded that they should be ashamed of their heritage, their culture, and their religion, and that Indians who fail to simulate the white man's values, dress, customs, mannerisms, and even points of view are filthy, dirty, stupid, disgusting, and less than human. Many children would climb out the windows of the boarding schools in an attempt to return to the warmth of their families. Many died of exposure during their attempts. Punishment for recurrent runaways commonly included being placed in dark, locked closets, or having balls and chains attached to their ankles so as to humiliate them in front of other children and to discourage others from running away. The runaways—and consequently the deaths from exposure—became so numerous that many of the schools barred their windows to keep the children in.[33] The greatest impression on the children was the overwhelming brutality, both physical and psychological. The staff member vested with the task of keeping the children in line was known as the "disciplinarian," whose title was changed to "boy's adviser" or "girl's adviser" around World War II; and shortly before that, the brass-studded harness strap that went with the job was replaced by a rubber hose, which leaves no marks, although some children beaten on their hands [were] crippled for life.[34] Up into the 1960s and 1970s, "unmanageable" children were regularly handcuffed and beaten in at least some of the schools.[35] The handcuffing itself is a discipline that has permanently scarred some of the students, and the most controversial practice at the Intermountain Boarding School near Brigham City, Utah, was the use of Thorazine, a powerful tranquilizer. Boarding School authorities maintain that Thorazine is used only when the student is a danger to himself or people around him, usually because of drunkenness. The *Physician's Desk Reference*, a pharmaceutical guide used by doctors, states that Thorazine is a dangerous drug if misused and that use in the presence of alcohol is inadvisable.[36]

"Running the belt line" was a common form of punishment for those caught practicing their tribal religions, which meant that the "guilty" student was to crawl between the legs of other students who were forced to lash at [him or her] with belt buckles. Other common punishments included standing on tiptoes with arms outstretched for long periods; paddlings; being locked in dark closets (known as going to "jail") for extended periods; lifted dress spankings to humiliate little girls; the wearing of dresses to humiliate little boys; and having hands whacked with sharp-edged rulers. One school employee at Intermountain was notorious among the students for dunking their heads into the toilet whenever he suspected them of drinking.[37] The tone of the boarding school is brought to light in Burnette and Koster's description of the Intermountain School in Utah:

> A massive institution surrounded by a chain link fence, it looks very much like the military installation it once was. The school is seven hundred miles from the Navajo reservation it was created to serve. Many of the staff members are Mormons, whose religion teaches them that the American Indians are Lamanites, the remnants of the Ten Lost Tribes of Israel, condemned to wear dark skins and to wander for their sins against God. The Mormons, of course, are entitled to their beliefs, but anyone except the BIA might pause [to ask] believers in this sort of racist myth to exercise a sensitive control over Indian destinies.
>
> The BIA does not pause, because like Pratt [the designer and founder of the BIA boarding school system], they want to feed the Indians to America. A pamphlet issued by the Intermountain school information office spells this out:
>
> "The essential difference [between Intermountain and public schools] is that public schools have the task of *preserving* the prevailing customs of our society, namely the same language, the same costume, same diet, housing, social customs and civic responsibilities. The task of the Intermountain School is to *change* language, *change* diet, costume, housing, manners, customs, vocations, and civic duties" [emphasis added].
>
> "Changing people's habits and outlooks is one of the most complex tasks in human affairs," the pamphlet concludes. Indeed. Particularly when the people don't want to be changed, at least at the expense of their dignity and mental health.[38]

Cahn quoted quite a few of the students in his work, but none of those quoted, I think, are as illustrative of the mental state of the average student as the one who proclaimed after graduating: "Education. . . . It has separated you from your family, your heritage. . . . What more sickening life do you want? So god help me I didn't ask for this!"[39]

Despite these kinds of attempts to destroy American Indian religion and culture, there are those who have maintained their traditions in secrecy, and most of the ceremonies and traditional teachings have survived to some extent, at least where the people have survived. However, the struggle for Native American religious freedom continues, for as one authority has observed[40]:

> By the second half of the twentieth century, the overt attempts by Congress and the Commissioner of Indian Affairs to destroy Native American religions and replace them with Christianity had ended, and in recent years, federal courts have considered a number of cases involving Native American free exercise rights. In these cases, the plaintiffs have generally fared no better than their ancestors in their efforts to vindicate their right to practice traditional Native American religions. In considering these plaintiffs' rights under the Free Exercise Clause, federal courts have relied on a number of theories to reject the claims, such as treating them as involving cultural rather than religious interests, and elevating other concerns, such as property rights and penological objectives, above free exercise rights.[41,42]

The Continuing Struggle

> The injustice and genocide [have] not ceased, for it is our belief that without our religion and traditional practices, the spirit of our people shall slowly die and wither away.[43]
>
> —Laughing Coyote, North Fork Mono Tribe, California, 1992

Religious freedom is one of the fundamental rights upon which the American government was founded. Indeed, it was religious persecution and intolerance in their own countries that brought many Europeans to this continent in the first place. This fundamental right was expressed in the Establishment and Free Exercise Clauses of the First Amendment to the United States Constitution: "Congress shall make no law respecting an establishment of religion, or prohibiting the free exercise thereof." This right is made applicable to the states through the Fourteenth Amendment. The fundamental right of religious freedom has been reaffirmed in many court decisions and congressional acts. In 1963, the United States Supreme Court held that the Free Exercise Clause of the First Amendment mandated that when the government or its agents burdened the free exercise of religion, such burden must be justified by a "compelling state interest," which cannot be served by "less restrictive means."[44] Between 1963 and 1990, the Court had stated this rule in different but very clear ways. In one case, the Court held that "only those interests of the highest order and those not otherwise served can overbalance legitimate claims to the free exercise of religion."[45] And in another, the Court ruled that state laws burdening the practice of religion "must be subjected to strict scrutiny and could be justified only by proof by the State of a compelling interest."[46] Even when a compelling government interest was present, however, the Court had ruled that the regulation infringing on the free practice of religion must be the least restrictive alternative to achieve that interest.[47]

It would be two American Indian cases that impelled the High Court, after a quarter century, to modify the law it had established in 1963.[48] The Court's modifications of the law ultimately tossed American Indian religion into the legal wastebasket and placed other minority religions at great risk.[49] In these cases, the Supreme Court held that a government action that creates an incidental burden on religious freedom, or which may even have "devastating effects" on the religion itself, need not be justified by a compelling state interest which cannot be served by less restrictive means. These cases will be discussed [in the following section], for even before they were decided, Indians received very little First Amendment protection in the courts.

For example, in the 1970s, Congress investigated claims that Indians were being denied the use of certain sacred objects, that they were being prohibited from worshipping in traditional ways, and that the federal [government] and state governments were severely disrupting Indian religious practices and ceremonies and desecrating sacred sites. In response, Congress passed a joint resolution in 1978, the American Indian Religious Freedom Act, which declared it a policy of the United States: "To protect and preserve for American Indians their inherent right of freedom to believe, express and exercise the traditional religions of the American Indian, Eskimo, Aleut and Native Hawaiians, including but not limited to access to sites, use and possession of sacred objects, and the freedom to worship through ceremonies and traditional rites."[50]

However, the act, as with most resolutions, contained no enforcement provisions, and has thus been entirely ineffective at protecting and preserving Native religious rights.[51] In fact, a task force established by the Carter administration to evaluate government policies and procedures pursuant to the Act, identified 522 instances where federal agencies were violating Indian religious practices in 1978 and 1979.[52] The report cited, for example, the

U.S. Navy's bombing of Native Hawaiian sacred sites (entire islands) for target practice; the denial of access to traditional sacred sites to many Indians of various tribes; and the drilling of oil wells through sacred grounds. In many cases, the lands referred to in the task force's report were lands expressly reserved by treaty to the Indian nations and tribes involved. Although the task force made recommendations that would put an end to many of these atrocities, to this day not one of those recommendations has been adopted. And thus many of those atrocities continue, some of which are described [here]. It is necessary, first, for the reader to understand that certain sites are held profoundly sacred to Native Americans, whether . . . burial grounds, the points from which they emerged in their creation stories, or places they have been instructed by the Creator to perform certain ceremonies to ensure the continuing well-being of the people and the earth.

The significance of sacred sites is illustrated in a case involving the Navajos and Hopis.[53] In Hopi religious tradition, it is believed that the Creator destroyed the world for its evil. Those who remained faithful to the Creator's will were chosen to survive. They were protected inside the earth, which is believed to be the Mother—the "Womb" from which the faithful emerged. They were then sent out on four migrations until they came to Oraibi (located in what is now known as Arizona) and settled. Oraibi is considered to be the crossroads of these four migrations and was the first of several Hopi villages that were settled after the emergence. These villages are guarded by the spirits of the four main clans of the Hopi. These spirits reside at four high points that surround the area, which are believed to be the home of the Kachina Clan. The Kachinas are the spirits sent by the Creator to guide the other clans down the road of life according to the will of the Creator. It is vital to the Hopi way of life, the Hopi religion, and indeed the very well-being of the Hopi as a people that these four high points wherein the Kachinas dwell, and from whence the Kachinas guard and guide the people, be protected and respected. What non-Indians know today as the San Francisco Peaks are where these Kachinas reside. These peaks are also held sacred to the Navajos for very similar reasons. The Navajos and Hopis have been struggling long and hard to preserve and protect the San Francisco Peaks and other sacred sites, such as Mount Taylor, Big Mountain, and Mount Eldon, from corporate development.

In 1981, the courts decided that the American Indian Religious Freedom Act provided no protection to the Indians and that the development and expansion of a ski resort was more important than Hopi religion. It was decided that the Navajos and Hopis should find another place to practice their religion.[54]

Many similar religious deprivations have occurred and continue to occur because the courts have refused to provide any protection to Indian religious rights where sacred sites are involved. The courts have allowed the federal [government] and state governments to construct dams that have flooded sacred sites[55]; they have allowed sacred sites and ceremonies to be disrupted and exploited by the government in order to promote tourism, which the courts have found to be of greater public interest than the religious rights of Indians[56]; they have allowed the government to dump highly toxic uranium tailings onto sacred sites[57]; they have allowed the government to deny Indians access to sacred sites for ceremonial purposes on their own lands.[58] And they have allowed the construction of logging roads and the destruction of forests on sacred ground, including burial sites.[59] It is very unlikely that these kinds of government actions would receive the courts' blessings if the sacred sites at issue were Anglo cemeteries or Christian churches.

One judge who recognized the intolerable potential of destroying Indian sacred sites was Northern California's District Court Judge Stanley A. Weigel, who issued an order enjoining the construction of a logging road through the Six Rivers National Forest, a project of the Forest Service. Judge Weigel ruled that the road, running from Gasquet to Orleans (also known as the "G-O Road"), would desecrate traditional sacred sites that are central to the religion of several tribes, including the Karuk, Yurok, Tolowa, and Hupa Indians.

In April 1988, the United States Supreme Court reversed Judge Weigel's decision. While acknowledging that the G-O Road "would have devastating effects on traditional Indian religious practices," the Court nevertheless ruled that the economic "needs and desires" of commercial exploiters must necessarily take precedence over the religious rights of American Indians. The Court ruled that governmental actions which infringe upon or destroy American Indian religions are permissible so long as: "(1) the government's purpose is secular and not specifically aimed at infringing upon or destroying the religion; and (2) the government's action does not coerce individuals to act contrary to their religious beliefs."[60]

The Association on American Indian Affairs addressed the significance of the G-O Road decision in the following excerpt from testimony it submitted to the Senate Select Committee on Indian Affairs:

> This decision greatly threatens the free exercise of Indian religions and, in many cases, the ability of the religions themselves to survive. Congress must take action to ensure that Indian religions are accorded the same respect and protections provided to other religions. American Indian religions are based on the natural world. Religion, social organization, political life, the eco-

nomic system and spatial order are interconnected and subject to the forces of nature and the spirits of the universe. From one generation to the next, continuity is maintained through the natural world. In essence, Indian religions are land-based theologies which entail site-specific worship. Sacred places of power can be thought of as amplification points for human, psychic, and spiritual energy. This type of worship is indispensable to the practice and preservation of Native religions. The survival of a religion may be threatened by man-made changes to or an outsider's use of a particular site.

Many sacred sites can be found on federal lands. It is for that reason that the G-O Road decision is so dangerous. We believe that once a site is established as sacred, the burden should then be placed on the government to show that its management practices are appropriate. Because of the site-specific nature of American Indian religious belief and practice, such protection is essential for the free exercise of American Indian religions.[61]

The Supreme Court again rendered a decision that devastated the entire Native American community in 1990. In *Oregon v. Smith*,[62] the respondents, two members of the Native American Church, were fired by a private drug rehabilitation program because they had ingested peyote for sacramental purposes at a Native American Church ceremony. Their applications for unemployment compensation were denied by the state of Oregon under a law disqualifying employees discharged for work-related "misconduct." The respondents challenged the denial of their applications as a violation of their free exercise rights. The United States Supreme Court held that the Free Exercise Clause permits states to prohibit sacramental peyote use and thus to deny unemployment benefits to persons discharged for such use. The *Smith* Court said that the Supreme Court has "never held that an individual's religious beliefs excuse him from compliance with an otherwise valid law prohibiting conduct that the State is free to regulate. On the contrary, the record of more than a century of our free exercise jurisprudence contradicts that proposition."[63] The *Smith* decision effectively overruled the standard established in earlier jurisprudence that required the states to show a "compelling interest," which could not be achieved by "less restrictive means." Had the Court been willing to reasonably apply that standard to the *Smith* case, it would probably have arrived at a decision to exempt the sacramental use of peyote from laws proscribing the use of peyote as a drug, for the very purpose of those laws—that is, to eliminate illegal drug use and abuse—is undermined by applying such laws to Indians.[64]

Many authorities have concluded, and many studies have demonstrated, that the Native American Church and its sacramental use of peyote has been more successful at curing Indians of alcoholism and drug abuse than any therapeutic program in existence.[65] This research supports the proposition that the states have a compelling interest in encouraging the sacramental use of peyote and the Native American Church for Indians, as such practice promotes the interest in maintaining laws proscribing the use of illegal drugs.

As a result of the *Smith* decision, Congress enacted the Religious Freedom Restoration Act in 1993,[66] the stated purposes of which were "to restore the compelling interest test[67] . . . to guarantee its application in all cases where free exercise of religion is substantially burdened . . . [and] to provide a claim or defense to persons whose religious exercise is substantially burdened by government.[68] However, the Supreme Court held the Religious Freedom Restoration Act to be unconstitutional.[69]

After years of attempts by the American Indian community to have the American Indian Religious Freedom Act of 1978 amended so as to contain some enforcement provisions, Congress amended the act in 1994. The amendments addressed several specific areas of interest to the Native community, including the following:

1. sacred sites
2. eagle feathers and animal parts
3. peyote use
4. prisoners' rights[70]

American Indian Religious Freedom within the Prison Context

> That the question of religious freedom in prison is raised in this case by a Native American simply compounds the lamentable character of cases of this nature, since it cannot be gainsaid that the destruction of American Indian culture and religious life was for many years a conscious policy of this nation. . . . Moreover, . . . it is a terrible comment upon our society that a serious question exists as to whether the security of a prison is compromised by permitting inmates to engage in legitimate religious practices.
>
> —Judge Karlton[71]

In 1992–93, while serving as director of the Native American Prisoners' Rehabilitation Research Project (NAPRRP), I conducted a survey of the religious programming and policies affecting Native American religious practices within the United States Bureau of Prisons, the fifty state prison systems, and the federal prison system in Canada.[72] The survey involved a lengthy questionnaire that federal and state prison officials responded to, as well as an examination of all existing administrative regulations and state statutes relating to grooming standards and the practice of American Indian religious freedom. The results of that survey, as it applied to the federal prison systems in Canada and the United States, indicated that:

1. In Canada, the first sweat lodge was constructed for use by Native American prisoners in 1972.[73] At the time of the survey, every major prison in Canada had a sweat lodge, allowed all prisoners to wear long hair regardless of religious affiliation, and allowed Native American prisoners, at a minimum, to have either frequent or full-time access to headbands, medicine bags, sage, cedar, sweet grass, tobacco ties, drums, beading materials, the sacred pipe, gourd rattles, and eagle feathers.[74,75] In response to the survey, the Canadian prison officials indicated that the ceremonies and practices associated with these sacred objects, instruments, and herbs have never caused any problems beyond those associated with any other activity allowed in the prisons, including Christian religious activities and recreational activities. The officials also indicated that the religious practices of Native American prisoners served a very positive rehabilitative function.

2. The United States Bureau of Prisons responded to the survey by indicating that "the procedures followed by the Chaplaincy Services . . . for American Indian inmates to practice their religion in the various institutions throughout the Bureau . . . include sweat lodges, pipe ceremonies, pow wows, and talking circles and the availability and use of all the items you listed in . . . your questionnaire."[76]

Although the Bureau of Prisons' response to the survey indicated that these practices were permitted in all the federal prisons in the United States, at that time, the NAPRRP was aware of at least one pending lawsuit in which Indian prisoners in the Bureau of Prisons were alleging denial of access to these sacred objects.[77] Moreover, the NAPRRP, based on its communications with American Indian prisoners, was aware at that time of instances in which Indian prisoners requesting access to sweat lodge ceremonies were transferred to different federal prisons, because the wardens at some federal prisons did not want to be burdened with accommodating the religious needs of Indian prisoners.[78] Additionally, although the Bureau of Prisons made no reference to the wearing of long hair by male prisoners in its response to the survey, it was and is the policy of the Bureau of Prisons to allow the wearing of long hair by all prisoners regardless of religious affiliation.

Of the fifty state prison systems contacted in the NAPRRP survey, thirty-four states (64%) responded.[79] Those that responded revealed the following:

1. Eighteen states indicated that they allow sweat lodges at their prisons and that accommodation of sweat lodge ceremonies had caused no problems with penological objectives, with the exception that: (a) South Dakota officials stated that there "have been instances when the inmates have not been willing to stop service at count time"[80]; (b) Arizona prison officials indicated that in 1987 a prisoner was raped in a sweat lodge, and in 1990 a sweat lodge was used to make/store alcohol products.[81]

2. Twenty-seven states indicated that they allow male prisoners to wear long hair regardless of religious affiliation; one state indicated that it allows exemptions from short-hair rules for those prisoners whose sincerely held religious beliefs require the wearing of long hair; five states indicated that they forbid all male prisoners to wear long hair regardless of religious affiliation; and one state (Indiana) indicated that it had no uniform statewide policy, so that some prisons allowed all prisoners to wear long hair while others prohibited all male prisoners [from wearing] long hair.

3. Five states that allow the wearing of long hair indicated that there were a few isolated incidents in which long hair was used to conceal contraband.[82]

4. All of the states indicated that there had been no other breaches of security as a result of the wearing of long hair, although South Dakota officials commented that they "have had problems with injuries in the industry shop," a problem that can be alleviated by the mandatory wearing of hair nets or ponytails around dangerous machinery.

5. Twenty-one states indicated that they allow prisoners to hold pipe ceremonies.

6. Seventeen states indicated that they allow the religious wearing of headbands.

7. Twenty-one states indicated that they allow the wearing of medicine bags.

8. Twenty states indicated that they allow the prisoners access to sage.

9. Eighteen states indicated that they allow prisoners access to cedar.

10. Nineteen states indicated that they allow prisoners access to sweet grass.

11. Ten states indicated that they allow prisoners access to tobacco ties.

12. Twenty states indicated that they allow prisoners access to the ceremonial drum.

13. Thirteen states indicated that they allow prisoners access to beading materials.

14. Twenty states indicated that they allow prisoners access to the sacred pipe.

15. Ten states indicated that they allow prisoners access to gourd rattles.

16. Twenty-one states indicated that they allow prisoners access to eagle feathers.

17. All of the states that have allowed the practices identified above indicated that they had experienced no problems with allowing prisoners to have access to any of the sacred objects, with the exception of Arizona, who identified one incident that was caused by a prison guard.[83]

The NAPRRP was familiar with the prison policies and practices in a number of the states that did not respond to the survey, and provided comments regarding those states:

ALABAMA: We are aware of at least two lawsuits currently pending against the prison officials in Alabama because they will not allow Native Americans to practice traditional religious beliefs.

FLORIDA: At least one Florida prison has allowed a Native American prisoner to carry a pipe bundle, including the sacred pipe, sage, cedar, sweet grass and tobacco, and to go pray by himself out-of-doors, without incident. However, Florida prison officials forcibly cut prisoners' hair in violation of religious beliefs.

IDAHO: The Idaho prison system allows Native American prisoners to have sweat lodge ceremonies, pipe ceremonies, and access to all of the items identified in our survey questionnaire, as well as long hair.

IOWA: The state of Iowa allows Native American prisoners to participate in sweat ceremonies and to wear long hair.

MISSOURI: Native American prisoners in Missouri's maximum security prison are allowed to wear long hair, but when they are transferred to some lesser security prisons they have it cut off by brute force. Sweat lodges and pipe ceremonies are forbidden in the Missouri prison system.

MONTANA: The wearing of long hair and all of the religious practices referred to in our survey questionnaire are allowed by some Montana state Native American prisoners. However, the prisoners claim that all of these practices, including the burning of tobacco, are prohibited for some of the Native Americans for punitive reasons.

NEVADA: Native American prisoners in Nevada are allowed to wear long hair and have pipe ceremonies, sweat lodge ceremonies and medicine bags.

NEW YORK: Prisoners in New York are allowed to wear long hair. Pow wows are allowed in some prisons, but we are unsure of the extent of religious practices allowed in all the prisons. Some New York prisons do forbid congregate worship services for Native Americans.

OHIO: Ohio prison officials cut some prisoners' hair by force while
             allowing other prisoners to wear long hair, notwithstanding
             sincerely held religious beliefs. Pipe ceremonies are allowed in
             some prisons, provided an outside spiritual leader conducts
             the ceremony, while the wardens of other prisons refuse to
             allow any Native American spiritual leader to enter the prison.
             Native American religious requests in Ohio have long been
             denied.

OKLAHOMA: Some lesser security prisons in Oklahoma allow sweat lodges
             while they are denied to prisoners in other prisons. The same
             is true with respect to all of the religious practices and objects
             identified in our survey questionnaire. Some prisoners may
             wear long hair while others have it forcibly cut notwithstand-
             ing religious belief. The attorney for the Oklahoma Depart-
             ment of Corrections has informed us that contraband has
             never been found in any prisoner's hair in Oklahoma
             although all Oklahoma prisoners were allowed to wear long
             hair up until 1986.

OREGON: The wearing of long hair and all of the religious ceremonies
             and objects referred to in our survey questionnaire [are]
             allowed in the Oregon prisons.

TENNESSEE: We are aware that an Apache prisoner on death row in Ten-
             nessee has had access to a sweat lodge, and that there were no
             problems with it. We are also aware that he and other Ten-
             nessee prisoners have long hair. However, we were recently
             informed by the prison chaplain that he could not discuss any
             Native American religious practices or policies in the Ten-
             nessee prison system because of pending litigation concerning
             the subject matter.

WYOMING: The Native American prisoners in the state of Wyoming are
             allowed sweat ceremonies, pipe ceremonies, and all the reli-
             gious items identified in our survey questionnaire, as well as
             long hair.[84]

The results of the NAPRRP's survey are relevant to this discussion
because, as the United States Supreme Court has observed on occasion,
"[w]hile not necessarily controlling, the policies followed at other well-run
institutions would be relevant to a determination of the need for a particular

type of restriction."[85] Indeed, the practices allowed at many of the prisons in North America over the past quarter century appear to demonstrate that the religious practices most commonly at issue in Native American prisoners' free exercise cases can be accommodated without jeopardizing legitimate penological objectives and, in fact, promote some recognized penological objectives such as rehabilitation of prisoners.[86] Unfortunately for Native American prisoners, the courts have seldom considered the rehabilitative value of the free exercise of Native American religion, although this rehabilitative value has long been established. For example, one authority has pointed out that in the mid-1970s, culture-specific programs, the central components of which are sweat lodges, were established in the state of Washington's four major prisons.[87] Within four years after these programs were established, the proportion of Indian prisoners in the state's prisons had dropped from 5 percent to 3.5 percent.[88] "Prison wardens in other states have discovered that allowing Native Americans to practice their religion has lowered rates of disciplinary action [i.e., prisoner misconduct], improved prisoner attitude, and advanced the rehabilitation process."[89]

As observed by Seven: "For prison officials, the [sweat] lodge and other religious programs are ways to reduce the high rate at which released inmates commit crimes. Robert Lynn, religious program manager for the Department of Corrections, says inmates in Oregon's prisons who were actively involved in religious programs over several years in the late seventies had a recidivism rate of 5 percent, compared to the national rate of close to 75 percent at the time."[90]

In the same way that the rehabilitative value of Native American religious practices has been ignored by the courts, when considering the practices at "other well-run institutions" in determining the need for restrictions, the courts have generally focused only on those institutions that have barred Native American practices, as discussed below.[91] However, there have been some exceptions to this. For example, in *Roybal v. DeLand*,[92] the U.S. District Court for the District of Utah concluded that the Utah Department of Corrections' ban on the use of sweat lodges was arbitrary, noting that "nineteen [state] prison systems as well as the Federal system have concluded that the sweat lodges are a manageable accommodation and [that they present] no significant infringement on any legitimate penological interest."[93]

Unlike most Native prisoner cases, which generally go unnoticed by the public, the *Roybal* case attracted an unusual amount of publicity as a result of the relatively large Native American population in Utah and the involvement of the Native American Rights Fund based in Boulder, Colorado. The *Salt Lake Tribune*, which followed the ongoing legal battle between the Native

American prisoners and the Utah Department of Corrections, published stories in which prison officials from various parts of the country expressed their expert opinions, based on their experience with accommodating Native American religious practices within the prison context. For example, George Sullivan, the warden of the maximum security New Mexico State Penitentiary and a thirty-year veteran of the prison system in Oregon, was quoted, when asked if the sweat lodge poses a threat to the security or other penological objectives:

> I can't believe you're asking me this question. Fifteen years ago in Oregon we allowed our first [sweat lodge] and it was the most valuable, least offensive problem for administrators of anything we do. . . . There is no problem and everything is to be gained. . . . If Utah is talking about drugs being used in the ceremony, I can guarantee you that they have conjured ghosts in closets. There's no merit, no substance to it. All they have to do is contact their fellow professionals across the country to learn that. Their imagined torment is simply that. . . . [94]

When the prison officials failed to relent or to consult with their "fellow professionals across the country," the court ultimately granted summary judgment in favor of the prisoners, noting that:

> Warden Robert Tansy of the New Mexico Penitentiary; Warden Robert D. Goldsmith of the Arizona State Prison, Florence; former Nebraska Correction Director and Warden Joseph Vitek all stated [that] in their experience sweat lodges impose no additional cost, staff, safety and security problems associated with any other prison activity. . . . Actually, the only evidence indicating otherwise consists of speculative, self-serving statements regarding unfocused fears of the Utah prison officials. Accordingly, this court finds that there is no rational, valid connection between the regulation banning sweat lodges altogether and any legitimate penological interest.[95]

Another reason that the practices at other prison facilities are relevant is that the Supreme Court has admonished the lower courts to "defer to the informed discretion of prison officials."[96] However, the courts have overwhelmingly used this admonishment as a basis for dismissing Native American prisoners' claims and deferring to the discretion of *uninformed* prison officials who have barred Native American religious practices while ignoring the opinions of those officials who have experience from which to draw their conclusions that the practices are not a threat to legitimate penological objectives.[97] In many of these cases, the officials' affidavits or testimony in support of banning religious practices were mere reproductions of the testimony of other state officials who lacked any personal knowledge or evidence with which to substantiate their fears justifying the bans.[98]

In an exceptional case in which a Native American prisoner's free exercise claims were actually considered by the district court,[99] U.S. District Court Judge Karlton stated that "[w]hatever the deference owed prison officials, it must be accorded only 'the *informed* discretion of corrections officials.'"[100] Judge Karlton reasoned:

> The [Supreme] Court's resolution requiring [the lower courts to defer to the discretion of prison officials] is premised, in substantial part, on the assertion that "courts are ill equipped to deal with the increasingly urgent problems of prison administration and reform." Assuming the observation is relevant, it hardly seems sufficient to justify the kind of deference both explicitly and implicitly required by the cases. Examining the problem from the limited perspective of competence to administer a prison fails to recognize the obverse, which is that prison officials, preoccupied as they must be with matters such as security concerns, are ill equipped to make judgments about the exercise of constitutional rights. For assuredly, just as a court decree intrudes on judgments made by prison administrators concerning the area of their responsibility, a failure of the court to act, premised on undue deference, permits the prison authorities to make judgments of a constitutional character.[101]

Unfortunately, Judge Karlton's decision was overturned by the Ninth Circuit Court of Appeals.[102]

The free exercise of prisoners' religious freedom is governed by the principles enunciated by the United States Supreme Court in *Turner v. Safely*.[103] In *Turner*, the Court held that prison regulations infringing on prisoners' constitutional rights are valid if they are reasonably related to legitimate penological interests. The Court outlined four factors that the courts should consider in determining whether a regulation is reasonable:

(1) whether the regulation infringing on the prisoner's rights has a logical connection to the penological interests invoked to justify it;

(2) whether reasonable alternative means of exercising the asserted right remain open to the prisoner;

(3) whether the accommodation of the asserted right will have an adverse impact on guards, other prisoners, and the allocation of prison resources; and

(4) whether ready alternatives that fully accommodate the prisoner's rights could be implemented at *de minimus* cost to valid penological interests.

Since the establishment of these criteria in *Turner*, there have been few cases in which the courts have actually applied these four factors to their analysis of the issues involved. Those courts which have done so have ruled in favor of the prisoners.[104] For example, in *Roybal*, the court applied the *Turner* analysis and concluded that:

(1) there was no valid connection between the policies that prohibited the sweat lodge and any legitimate penological interests asserted to justify the policies;

(2) there were/are no alternative means for the Indians to adequately practice their religious beliefs;

(3) there would be very little, if any, adverse impact on prison staff, other prisoners and prison resources and that there may, in fact, be a positive influence on other prisoners because of the positive impact and rehabilitative effect on the Native American prisoners; and

(4) the fourth *Turner* factor was no problem because the prison officials may reasonably regulate how, when, where and who may participate in the religious ceremonies involved.[105]

Another case in which the four *Turner* factors were applied by a court was *Sample v. Borg*, in which the court considered the reasonableness of policies prohibiting a Native American prisoner in segregation from having access to tobacco ties and medicine bags, and prohibiting Native American spiritual leaders from conducting pipe ceremonies with the prisoner during the course of regular religious visits to the segregation block[106]:

The plaintiff in this case is a sincere adherent of his [Native American] religion, and seeks the right to celebrate various religious rites and possess various religious artifacts, all of which are deeply rooted in the Native American religious experience. . . . [The] plaintiff seeks to participate in a pipe ceremony when visited by a medicine man at his cell door. The plaintiff suggests that the pipe could be passed between the participants through the food port in the door. The defendants' objection to the pipe ceremony as proposed by plaintiff appears to be twofold: first, a fear that the pipe could be used as a weapon, and second, a fear of the ripple effect caused by granting

Native Americans this opportunity. Although defendants have had difficulty articulating both concerns, the court cannot find that the concerns are completely irrational. Thus one can imagine that allowing the pipe to be passed through the port would in theory provide the worshipper in the cell with a weapon to employ against his cell mate, at least for the period of time until it was returned to the medicine man. Moreover, permitting the ceremony might well lead to demands by Catholics, for instance, that they be given Communion.[107] I have suggested above that the relationship between the rule prohibiting the pipe ceremony and common sense is not wholly absent; nonetheless, the question remains as to whether it is unreasonably related to legitimate penological interests. . . . To determine the answer to that question, I turn to the four-factor test articulated in *Turner*.

First, is there a "valid, rational connection" between the prison regulation and the legitimate governmental interest put forward to justify it? . . . Of course, security and the safety of a cellmate are legitimate governmental interests. Yet, upon analysis, the relationship between that interest and the regulation is so remote as to make it difficult to find it "valid." Surely, if a prisoner wishes to attack his cellmate, he can use another homemade weapon, or use his bare hands.[108] Moreover, permitting the adherents of other religions to participate in such religious rites as may be conducted at the cell door through the food port does not appear to represent any more significant burden to the staff than does permitting the religious visit in the first place. While I cannot say that the relationship between the rule and its purported justification is wholly irrational, I find it is so "remote" as to be "arbitrary."

Second, I must determine whether there is an "alternative means of exercising the right [which] remains open to the prison inmates." . . . The exact dimension of this factor is uncertain. As the [Supreme] Court has since explained, "[i]n *Turner* we examined whether the inmates were deprived of 'all means of expression.' We think it appropriate to see under these regulations whether [prisoners] retain the ability to participate in other . . . religious ceremonies."[109] . . . As I noted above, under the regulation plaintiff is deprived of all outward manifestations of his religious commitment. While it is true that he may engage in solitary and inward religious conduct such as prayer and meditation, to hold that the availability of such practices is sufficient to uphold the ban [on pipe ceremonies] would render the second factor meaningless. Put another way, since the state cannot deprive the plaintiff of his ability to pray alone and in silence, it is meaningless to ask whether the state's failure to deprive the plaintiff of that opportunity supports a finding that its deprivation of other religious rites is reasonable. I have noted above that the state has deprived the plaintiff of the sweat lodge ceremony [by virtue of placing him in segregation], thus making the spiritual need for participation in the pipe ceremony more urgent. The state argues, however, that an alternative means of purification, namely fasting, demonstrates that there are available alternatives. This court must reject that argument. "Permitting" fasting is not evidence of the reasonableness of the state's rules because, like solitary silent prayer, the plaintiff can engage in fasting without the state's permission.[110] Given the state's ban on all religious ceremony it can prohibit, I conclude that consideration of the second factor suggests that the state's rule is an exaggerated response to its real security concerns.

The third factor to be considered is "the impact accommodation [of the religious practice] . . . will have on guards and other inmates, and on the allocation of prison resources generally." . . . Because the prison already allows visits by clergy, it is difficult to see that permitting the pipe ceremony will have any significant direct impact upon guards, other inmates . . . or other resources.[111] On the other hand, as I have noted above, it may well be that inmate adherents of other faiths will demand that they be permitted to engage in such religious rights as may be practiced through the food port. Nonetheless, there is no evidence of what burdens such demands would have on the resources of the institution. Surely, fundamental constitutional rights cannot be curtailed on the basis of unsubstantiated and, indeed, unfocused fears.[112]

The final factor to be considered relates to whether alternatives to the rule, in this case a complete ban, exist. "(T)his absence of ready alternatives is evidence of the reasonableness of a prison regulation," while the existence of "an alternative that fully accommodates the prisoner's right at *de minimus* cost to valid penological interests" may be "evidence that the regulation is not reasonable, but is an 'exaggerated response' to prison concerns." As noted above, plaintiff's proposal to permit the pipe ceremony at the door is an alternative to the total ban and from all that appears of record will have a *de minimus* impact on the prison personnel, other inmates, or the budget of the prison. For all of the above reasons, it does not appear to this court that the state has struck a constitutionally appropriate balance between the plaintiff's First Amendment rights and prison administrative needs concerning its rule banning celebration of a pipe ceremony at the door of the plaintiff's cell. . . . [113]

In addition to the pipe ceremony issue, the court in *Sample v. Borg* found that the total ban on American Indian prisoners' possession of tobacco ties while incarcerated in segregation violated free exercise rights, and that the "burden on prison personnel to inspect ties could be made *de minimus* by limiting [the] number of ties: [L]imiting tensile strength of [the] string minimized danger of [the] tie being used as [a] weapon[114]; and requiring [the] tie to be kept in [the] inmate's cell minimized [the] potential for conflict between staff and [the] ripple effect as to other prisoners."[115]

The plaintiff in *Sample v. Borg* also sought the right to possess a medicine bag, which was confiscated upon transfer from general population to segregation. With regard to this issue, the court stated:

> [Prison officials] object because of fear that the bag may be used to contain the makings of weapons (pebbles, dried berries and the like), and for fear that inspections by guards to insure the contents were not contraband could result in violent confrontation. Defendants also assert fears that disputes concerning such items could lead to violence between cellmates. I noted above that at trial Defendants proved the remarkable ability of prisoners to turn the most innocent of objects into weapons.[116] While I must confess a suspicion that Defendants' response is exaggerated, I cannot say in light of the evidence that such is the case. Given the deference [to the discretion of prison officials] I am enjoined to apply, I must find against plaintiff's claim in regard to medicine bags.[117]

Unfortunately for the Native American prisoners, the court's decision in *Sample v. Borg* was reversed because of the failure of the court to appropriately "defer" to the judgment of prison officials.[118]

The trial courts' decisions in *Sample v. Borg* and *Roybal v. DeLand* were indeed unique. The case of *Kemp v. Moore* provides a glaring example of the treatment most Native American prisoners' free exercise claims receive in the courts.[119] In *Kemp*, a Chickasaw prisoner in Missouri challenged policies banning the sweat lodge and the wearing of long hair in accordance with sincerely held religious beliefs. The prisoner had been confined in a maximum security prison in Missouri for four years, during which time he was allowed to wear his hair long in accordance with his beliefs. After four years, however, his security level was reduced, and he was transferred to a less secure prison. At the time he was transferred, the Missouri Department of Corrections' short hair regulations, which contained an exemption for American Indians, was disregarded by the prison officials at the prison to which he was transferred. Upon arrival at the minimum security prison, the prisoner was ordered to get his hair cut. He refused and presented verification of his exemption from the statewide policy, which was disregarded by the prison officials. The prison superintendent ordered prison guards to shear the hair off of the prisoner's head, which they did by brute force. They then pressed formal disciplinary charges against the prisoner, which resulted in his work wages being reduced as punishment for refusing to get his hair cut. In the resulting lawsuit, the district court granted summary judgment in favor of the prison officials. On appeal, the Eighth Circuit Court of Appeals affirmed the district court's decision. In his concurring opinion, senior Circuit Judge Heaney wrote:

> I concur only because our opinion in *Iron Eyes* . . . leaves me no other alternative. I continue to believe that our opinion in *Iron Eyes* was not required by *Turner v. Safely.* . . .
>
> This case smacks of harassment and religious persecution to me. . . . The sooner our court *en banc* considers this question and resolves to do away with the penological myth that the director of this institution perpetuates, the better.
>
> . . . This case is even stronger than *Iron Eyes.* . . . No rational reason has been advanced as to why it was permissible to wear long hair in the Missouri State Penitentiary but not at the Farmington Correctional Center, even though the former is a more secure prison than the latter.[120]

Nevertheless, the [appeals] court affirmed the district court's decision, stating that, with respect to the hair length issue, the cases of *Turner v. Safely* and *Iron Eyes v. Henry* "require the result ordered by the district court. . . . We, accordingly, affirm on the basis of the well-reasoned opinion of the district court." What is particularly striking about this is that the district court did not even set forth any reasons for its finding that the hair length regulation satisfied the four *Turner* factors. The prison officials claimed that the regulation was necessary for security and identification purposes, but no evidence was presented to substantiate their claims, and the district court did not address any of the factual evidence presented in the case, beyond the apparently self-serving, unsubstantiated fears of the prison officials. In *Iron Eyes*, which the *Kemp* court relied on in arriving at its decision, prison officials' asserted justification for maintaining the short-hair rule at the Farmington Correctional Center was that long hair enables prisoners to conceal contraband, and that long hair makes it difficult to maintain the identities of prisoners. The plaintiff asserted that although Indian prisoners had been allowed to wear long hair in some Missouri prisons, contraband had never been found in long hair. The prison officials made no attempt to refute this or to present evidence to support their claims. And as the court of appeals noted:

> Iron Eyes argues that . . . he was never photographed with short hair, despite the fact that his hair was forcibly cut twice while incarcerated. We cannot deny the strength of Iron Eyes' argument here. If identification concerns are so important for security, it is *incredulous* that the prison officials, after forcibly cutting Iron Eyes' hair, failed to photograph him.[121]

What is even more incredible is that the [appeals] court ruled in favor of the prison officials anyway.

As for the sweat lodge issue raised in *Kemp*, there is no indication in the record that the ban on sweat lodges was related to any penological objectives. Rather, the [appeals] court held that since the plaintiff had access to *some* religious practices (e.g., the pipe ceremony), any remaining prohibition on American Indian free exercise was constitutionally permissible under *Turner*.[122]

PART III

INDIAN COURTS AND JURISDICTIONS

CHAPTER FIVE

UNEQUAL JUSTICE AND PUNISHMENT UNDER THE LAW

Aboriginal justice was at the clan or band level and did not require a separate judicial apparatus, although certain tribes assigned warriors with policing duties, and clan leaders, medicine men, and tribal leaders served as arbitrators or judges. With the early Cherokee, this included women serving in the judicial role. The nature of aboriginal restorative justice ran along a continuum from blood vengeance, like that exercised by the Cherokee, to the more gentle process of the Navajo and their Beauty Way, the harmonious method of the Peacemaker.

The introduction of Western judicial and martial justice came with the Europeans and their struggle over control of North America. Indian-European alliances changed the circumstances of dealing with traditional enemies. No longer was the enemy body count related to accommodating a balance for Native dead; now the tribes were indoctrinated with the European concept of annihilation. This introduction to the European concept of martial justice set the stage for the long and brutal history of Indian-white wars that began during the colonial era and extended to the early 1970s. During the early days of the United States, nonhostile administrative rules were developed that also outlined the nature of trade with Indian groups. The Trade and Intercourse Acts (1790, 1793, 1796, 1799, 1802, 1822, 1834) began shortly after the establishment of the War Department in 1789. From then on, the military played a critical role in policing Indian country.

Rules governing criminal justice emerged over the years as well. Initially, federal and state criminal jurisdiction pertained only to Indian-white inter-actions, either in or out of Indian country. Intratribal offenses were pretty much left to traditional Indian justice. Again, there was a wide variance between types of justice: the Five Civilized Tribes (Cherokee, Choctaw, Chickasaw, Creek, and Seminole) adopted the Euro-American style of justice in the early nineteenth century and carried this form of government with them to Indian Territory (Oklahoma) following removal, while other tribes continued to maintain their aboriginal forms of justice. Cohen noted that the historical precedent for criminal justice within Indian country rested with the Trade and Intercourse Acts:

> The exercise of federal jurisdiction over non-Indian offenders against Indi-ans in Indian country was first put on a statutory basis by the original Trade and Intercourse Act, the Act of July 22, 1790. . . . These provisions were reenacted with minor modifications in the later temporary Trade and Intercourse Acts of 1793, 1796, and 1799, and were embodied in the first permanent Trade and Intercourse Act of 1802 as sections 2 to 10, inclu-sive. The general rule established by these statutes was confirmed in the Act of March 3, 1817 (Federal Enclaves or General Crimes Act). . . . The Trade and Intercourse Act of June 30, 1834, reenacted the rule developed in the earlier statutes. This rule was subsequently incorporated in the Revised Statutes as section 2145 and in title 25 of the United States Code as sec-tion 217. The exceptions contained in title 25 of the United States Code, section 218, relating to offenses by Indians against Indians and to offend-ers punished by tribal law have no application to offenses committed by non-Indians against Indians.[1]

This basis of Indian jurisprudence emerged out of the U.S. Supreme Court decisions forged under Chief Justice John Marshall. Three cases, known as the "Marshall trilogy," determined early on what the relationship between American Indians and the United States would be as well as what authority each branch of government would have in these matters. In 1823, in *Johnson v. McIntosh*, the Court determined that, with the establishment of the United States, Indian tribes could no longer transfer their land to other parties without the consent and approval of the federal government.[2] This establishment of federal supervision over tribes was based on the Court's determination that the tribes' sovereignty was diminished with the establish-ment of the United States. Then, in 1831, in *Cherokee Nation v. Georgia*, the

U.S. Supreme Court determined that tribes, specifically the Cherokee Nation, were not foreign states but merely domestic dependent nations existing within the confines of the greater United States. This ruling established the federal trust relationship with tribes. Consequently, the Court ruled that tribes could not sue states in federal court.[3] A year later, in 1832, in *Worcester v. Georgia*, the U.S. Supreme Court ruled that states could not interfere with tribal jurisdictions, given that tribes (Indian country) constituted distinct communities, occupying their own territory with clearly defined boundaries.[4] The results of Marshall's trilogy gave the U.S. Congress total and exclusive authority over Indian country, even if this meant abrogating previous treaties. Essentially, the U.S. Supreme Court empowered Congress to regulate the tribes. We will soon see that this power included interfering with the sovereign powers of a tribe when dealing with criminal offenses within Indian country.

In these early years of the republic, the War Department provided the enforcement arm in Indian country, while the Indian agent (later upgraded to the position of commissioner of Indian affairs in 1832) determined which issues required adjudication. The regulation of non-Indians within Indian country was first articulated by Congress in 1817 with the Federal Enclaves Act, also known as the General Crimes Act. The purpose of the Federal Enclaves Act was to extend the entire body of federal law into Indian country. The justification for this action was that the federal government held exclusive jurisdiction in Indian country, especially for crimes committed against Indians by non-Indians.[5] The Federal Enclaves Act was subsequently modified by the Assimilative Crimes Act of 1825, the Major Crimes Act of 1885, and Public Law 280 in 1953.

The Assimilative Crimes Act stipulated that offenses in Indian country, while still under federal jurisdiction, would use state or territorial statutes and sentences as a guide for federal adjudication. Hence, the local state or territorial laws where the reservation was located would be used by the federal government for those crimes not specifically defined under the federal criminal code.[6] And while the intent was for tribal justice to operate within Indian country for crimes by Indians against Indians, the white Indian superintendent held virtually absolute authority in dealing with issues in Indian country. Most significantly, he had the U.S. Army at his disposal as an enforcement agent for his dictates. Initially, the Indian superintendent was responsible for: (1) providing the provisions to the tribe that were guaranteed by treaty; (2) keeping the Indians within the confines of Indian country as it was defined by treaty; and (3) enforcing methods for civilizing (Christianizing) the Indian.

The Trade and Intercourse Act of 1834 spelled out the Indian superintendent's judicial duties within Indian country.

Section 19. *And be it further enacted,* That it shall be the duty of the super-intendents, agents, and sub-agents, to endeavour to procure the arrest and trial of all Indians accused of committing any crime, offense, or misdemeanor, and all other persons who may have committed crimes or offenses within any state or territory, and have fled into the Indian country, either by demanding the same of the chiefs of the proper tribe, or by such other means as the President may authorize; and the President may direct the military force of the United States to be employed in the apprehension of such Indians, and also, in preventing or terminating hostilities between any of the Indian tribes.[7]

This method of justice in Indian country deteriorated during the Civil War when U.S. society was torn apart. Unfortunately, American Indians often became a target for exploitation and white hostilities. Clearly, the act of criminal justice that best represents this era of turmoil was the trial and execution of the Santee Sioux warriors who rebelled against starvation and injustices at the hands of the Indian superintendent. The injustices precipitating the Great Sioux Uprising in 1862 were reported to President Lincoln in October 1862 by Government Agent George A.S. Crooker:

> The outbreak of the Sioux was caused by the wretched conditions of the tribes, some of them were almost at the point of starvation, the neglect of the Government agents to make the annuity payments at the proper time and the insulting taunts of the Agents to their cries for bread of whom told them "they must eat their own shit" and also in a very great degree to the rapacious robberies of the Agent Traders and Government officials who always connive together to steal every dollar of their money that can be stolen. Where else can it be true as is the adage here that "if an agent can hold his office through one yearly payment of annuities he can retire rich for life" when his salary is never more than $1,500.00 a year and often less. A kind and considerate Agent who had the interests of his government and the well being of the Indians at heart would have avoided and prevented the whole of the bloodshed that followed. The Indians were told to be a set of demons in the shape of white men that now was their time to get their just revenge for all the past because all of our fighting men were gone to the War at the south. These demons all live in Minnesota.[8]

No whites were charged with this clearly provoked outbreak, and once the Santee surrendered, government retaliation was swift, severe, and disproportionate to the events. While only a small segment of the tribe was involved in the outbreak, the tribe as a whole was punished with all annuities from earlier treaties (1805, 1837, 1851) terminated and the entire tribe forcefully removed across the Missouri River onto what once was the Ponca Reservation in northern Nebraska. Moreover, 302 Indians and a mulatto were sentenced to be executed, while another 18 were given prison sentences. All were tried without counsel, and many of the Indians could not even understand English. As many as forty cases a day were heard by the special military court assigned to carry out this judicial task. Only a presidential pardon by Lincoln saved all but 38 of the convicted defendants. A mixed French-Canadian and African-American mulatto married to a Santee woman had his sentence commuted in exchange for turning state's evidence.

The presidential review found only 39 of the defendants guilty of a federal capital crime. This included the 38 Santee and the mulatto, who was granted immunity. Those whose sentences were overturned were subjected to extreme hardships and attacks by white mobs—actions encouraged by the U.S. Army. At the public execution of the 38 Santee Sioux warriors, a civilian was selected to cut the rope that sprung the trapdoors. Among those executed were two Sioux pardoned by President Lincoln for "heroic acts in saving white settlers." The pardon was ignored by the angry white civilian and army personnel adjudicating the Sioux, as was the order to not execute the mulatto. What resulted was the single largest mass execution in U.S. history. On the day after Christmas in 1862, 38 Santee Sioux warriors were hanged together on a single gallow, tied and hooded, chanting their traditional death song. And to add insult to injury, the bodies, buried in a shallow grave, were soon exhumed by local physicians for use as cadavers. This example of criminal justice in Indian country served notice to the entire Sioux Nation and was the deciding act that caused the Sioux to resist white advancement into their territory up until 1890.[9]

Crow Dog and the Major Crimes Act

It was another Sioux case that extended the Federal Enclaves (General Crimes) Act in 1885 to include the "Major Crimes." An element of Congress was attempting to further apply state jurisdictions within Indian country at the time of the killing of Spotted Tail in 1881 on the Brulé Reservation at Rosebud. Although considered to be a puppet of the U.S. government, Spotted Tail was a warrior and war chief who was seriously injured fighting the U.S. Army at Bluewater, Nebraska, in the Sioux War of 1855. This resulted in his incarceration at Fort Leavenworth, Kansas. But by 1865, he emerged as the head chief of the Brulé, and along with Red Cloud and the Oglala Sioux, participated in the treaties, held at Fort Laramie in the late 1860s, that determined the Great Sioux Reservation. His status with the United States was elevated considerably when he kept the Brulé out of the 1876 Sioux war, which resulted in the defeat of Lieutenant Colonel George A. Custer and the Seventh Calvary at the Little Big Horn River. By the early 1880s, extralegal retribution by both the U.S. Army and the Indian superintendents in the Dakotas was fierce and severe, resulting in the questionable execution of Crazy Horse in 1877 and the exile of Sitting Bull—two of the leaders of the Little Big Horn River group that defeated Custer.

Crow Dog, on the other hand, was a more traditional Sioux leader, given that traditionally the Sioux never had a strong head chief until this position was made necessary when dealing with the U.S. government relevant to treaties and the emergence of leaders such as Red Cloud and Spotted Tail. Crow Dog was once the chief of the Orphan band of the Brulé Sioux and remained a leader of the survivors of Big Raven's band following the massacre of Big Raven and all his warriors in the 1844 conflict with the Shoshone. Crow Dog was closely associated with Crazy Horse and even accompanied him when he surrendered in 1877. Crow Dog is credited with preventing bloodshed when soldiers attempted to kill Crazy Horse at the time he surrendered. Crow Dog also went to Canada and met with Sitting Bull while he and his band were in exile. Thus, in the early 1800s, while Spotted Tail was seen as an ally of the United States, Crow Dog was seen as the leader of Sioux traditionalism and antagonistic to the U.S. government. Just prior to the altercation that took Spotted Tail's life, Crow Dog served as the chief of the Indian police at the Rosebud BIA Indian agency from 1879 until 1880.

Clearly, both Spotted Tail and Crow Dog were vying for positions of power within the new Rosebud agency, established in 1878. These leaders reflected the two camps existing at that time—the progressives (accommodation with the United States) led by Spotted Tail and the traditionalists led by Crow Dog. The hostility between Spotted Tail and Crow Dog has been attributed to ideological differences, bitterness, and jealousy. Some believed that Crow Dog was angry at Spotted Tail for dismissing him as chief of police, while others saw this as a personal problem involving a woman, Light-in-the-Lodge. Here, Spotted Tail is accused of taking Light-in-the-Lodge away from her disabled, elderly husband and making her his second wife. Crow Dog then took it upon himself to represent the wronged husband. At any rate, on August 5, 1881, the forty-seven-year-old Crow Dog shot the fifty-eight-year-old Spotted Tail as they approached each other on a road near the agency. Crow Dog killed Spotted Tail during this altercation.

Given that this was an Indian versus Indian crime and was exempt at that time from federal jurisdiction under the Federal Enclave/General Crimes Act, the matter was resolved between the clans involved utilizing the traditional Peacemakers. The resolution, according to Brulé traditions, was for Crow Dog's clan to compensate Spotted Tail's clan with a payment of $600, eight horses, and one blanket. This determination was quickly met, and harmony was then restored to the tribe according to their customary law.

The U.S. Supreme Court decision regarding Crow Dog was unpopular with a number of factions, including the U.S. Army, the Indian agency and Spotted Tail's supporters (except family and clan, which agreed to the dictates of tribal justice). Agent Lelar sent Chief Hollow Horn Bear to arrest Crow Dog and his alleged co-conspirator, Black Crow, after Eagle Hawk, the chief of the agency police failed to do so. Once he was arrested, Crow Dog was brought to Fort Niobrara, Nebraska. (This is the site of the removed Santee Sioux following the Great Sioux Uprising in the early 1860s.) Within twenty days of the killing, the U.S. attorney general and the secretary of the Department of Interior jointly concluded that the Federal Enclaves Act, as modified by the Assimilative Crimes Act and incorporated into the various Sioux treaties, allowed the territorial death qualified statute to apply to Crow Dog.

Interestingly, Crow Dog was only one of a number of parallel murder cases that the BIA was attempting to get the courts to qualify as falling under state or territorial law, a clear forerunner to Public Law 280. At this time, BIA Commissioner Henry Price stated that the BIA wanted to impose any available criminal jurisdiction, federal, state, or territorial, over the tribes. The U.S. attorneys joined the BIA in this early Public Law 280 effort, but the Nevada Supreme Court rejected this argument, stating that states had no jurisdiction over Indians because of the exclusive federal authority in Indian affairs set by the Marshall Court.

Crow Dog's trial itself reflected the political emotions surrounding it and the assertion that he represented the "bad Indians" such as Crazy Horse and Sitting Bull and needed to be punished in order to send a message to other renegades. It was clear from the outset that the trial and all-white jury would find Crow Dog guilty despite his claim of self-defense. In the jury selection, the defense attorney, A. J. Plowman, questioned the jurors about their prejudices against Indian witnesses. The general consensus was that the testimony of a white would greatly outweigh that of an Indian. One juror stated that the testimony of one white man would outweigh that of a hundred Indians. Nonetheless, the jury was quickly approved and seated.

The lead prosecution eyewitness was the Brulé Indian agent, John Cook, who was in Chicago on private business when the killing occurred. However,

Indian eyewitnesses testified that Spotted Tail not only had a pistol but drew it on Crow Dog while he was repairing his wagon. He fired one shot with his rifle in self-defense of himself, his wife, Pretty Camp, and their young child, who were with him at the time. Others, including the agency police chief, Eagle Hawk, testified that not only did Spotted Tail have a pistol but he had a bad temper as well. The Indian witnesses did not paint a favorable picture of Spotted Tail, even noting that he shot and killed another competitor, Big Mouth, in 1869. Contrary to this depiction, the white officials, who were selected as character witnesses for Spotted Tail, spoke highly of him, especially his cooperation with the U.S. government and the agency. Besides, Plowman's efforts to introduce the local laws and customs of the Brulé tribe and their stipulation in U.S.-approved treaties were all suppressed by the prosecution. In the end, the jury convicted Crow Dog of capital murder.

Sentenced to hang, Crow Dog set about attempting to get funds for his appeal. This was no easy task, given that the secretary of the interior was not sympathetic to Crow Dog. However, Commissioner of Indian Affairs Henry Price felt that it was the responsibility of the federal government to protect all Indian rights, however distasteful to the government. Toward this end, he attempted to take the money from the Sioux holdings. Plowman knew that this was not a likely course and instead pursued monies from Congress. Ten months later Plowman was awarded $1,000 for Crow Dog's appeal. This money came from the Sundry Civil Act of March 3, 1883. Judge G. C. Moody presided over the original trial, held at the First Judicial District Court of Dakota; he excluded crucial information relevant to treaty designated Indian justice, sentenced Crow Dog to be hanged, and heard the appeal in territorial court, which he dismissed. The U.S. Supreme Court, on December 17, 1883, in turn, upheld Crow Dog's petition and released him in *Ex parte Crow Dog*.[10] In its decision, the Court upheld the Marshall Court's contention of tribal sovereignty in *Worcester v. Georgia*. It posed a serious challenge to the BIA policy of cultural genocide and instead upheld the equality of tribal traditions and sovereignty.[11]

The Major Crimes Act emerged as a conservative reaction to the U.S. Supreme Court decision in *Ex parte Crow Dog* but also had the support of an unlikely source, the Indian Rights Association (IRA), a group of eastern liberal reformers, who also shared the tenet of civilizing and Christianizing American Indians. The Major Crimes Act extended original and exclusive federal jurisdiction in Indian country to include murder, manslaughter, rape, assault with intent to kill, arson, burglary, and larceny.[12] Crow Dog's prosecution violated the Enclaves Act, which precluded federal prosecution of Indian defendants who had been punished by their tribe. Now tribal justice was exempt from adjudicating these crimes. (The Index Crimes listed under the Major Crimes Act has been expanded to now include thirteen crimes.) This also set the stage for state (or territorial) statutes to become the standard for the adjudication of all other crimes committed by anyone, including Indians off the reservation as well as non-Indian offenders in Indian country.[13] The Major Crimes Act initially gave federal exclusive jurisdiction only in Indian country, but was later extended to any federal lands not covered by the Uniform Code of Military Justice (UCMJ). J. Edgar Hoover is credited with this expansion in order to curtail lawlessness in the United States during the turbulent years following World War I and during the Great Depression. Hoover then used federal major crime statistics to gather data for what he called the "Index Crimes"; these data are published yearly in the FBI *Uniform Crime Reports*. These Index Crimes are also the reason that the FBI has such a presence in Indian country. In 1886, the U.S. Supreme Court upheld the constitutionality of the Major Crimes Act in *United States v. Kagama*, a case involving murder among Indians on the reservation. The Court now argued that due to the federal trust relationship with Indian tribes, Congress has the duty and authority to regulate tribal matters.[14] Later, in *Lone Wolf v. Hitchcock*, the U.S. Supreme Court went a step further, stating that Congress could, by statute, abrogate the provisions of an Indian treaty. These congressional powers were deemed so powerful that complaints against these actions had to be brought to the same body that dictated them—the U.S. Congress. This ruling specifically had significance for not only allotment but Public Law 280 as well.[15]

The Court of No Appeal in Indian Territory

At the time of the Crow Dog incident, the Interior Department and its enforcement and administrative arm, the Bureau of Indian Affairs (BIA), were attempting to consolidate their power and authority in Indian country clearly at the expense of traditional rites and customs. This led to the establishment of the Courts of Indian Offenses in 1883, also known as BIA courts. Secretary of the Interior Henry M. Teller initiated the congressional action that provided the Courts of Indian Offenses. These courts were the first attempt to legislate morality in Indian country, given that Teller's intent was to use these BIA courts to eliminate the heathenish practices that he felt plagued American Indians and impeded their Christianization and civilization. These were, in fact, courts of cultural genocide.[16] Previous to the establishment of the BIA Courts of Indian Offenses, the BIA agent held martial law status, serving as prosecutor and judge with the authority to summarily charge, prosecute, and sentence Indians under his control. Revisions in 1892 established district courts within Indian country and provided for the appointment of Indian judges in the BIA Courts of Indian Offenses. The commissioner of Indian affairs or the BIA agent appointed both the tribal police and judges using the patronage system. While the district judges were now Indians, they kept their job as long as they held allegiance to the white BIA agents. Not only did the BIA determine the judges and police, who served as prosecutors, but any judgment had to be approved by the white BIA official.[17]

These courts were effective in carrying out their mandate of cultural genocide, punishing the practice of Indian customs and religious rituals such as the sun dance, use of medicine men, and joint clan ownership of property. On the other hand, certain tribal customs were sanctioned by the BIA courts, including banishment and restitution. The BIA Courts of Indian Offenses set the stage for allotment and the attempt to dissolve Indian country.

Following the Civil War, the displaced (removed) tribes residing in Indian Territory (Oklahoma), especially the Five Civilized Tribes, were subjected to harsh treatment from the federal government, which held trust and guardian authority over all Indians in Indian country. At the same time, Indian Territory was designated as the model for tribal extinction under the General Allotment Act. During this time, Indian country fell under the jurisdiction of the U.S. Court for the Western District of Arkansas, which had Fort Smith as its judicial seat. After the Civil War, Indian country became a sanctuary for white, black, and Indian misfits and outlaws, making it one of the most, if not *the* most, lawless sections of the United States.

In 1875, Isaac Charles Parker, a former U.S. congressman from Missouri, was appointed by President Grant to be the federal judge of the Western District of Arkansas. Parker, at age thirty-six, was the youngest judge on the federal bench at that time. This was the only federal court with jurisdiction in Indian Territory, a vast land mass of nearly seventy-four thousand square miles, which included Texas, Kansas, and Colorado in addition to Indian Territory. His court along with two hundred U.S. marshals were responsible for law and order in this sparsely populated region of about sixty thousand people. What is unique about Judge Parker's court is that for fourteen years, from 1875 until 1889, his was the only federal court without the right to appeal. This fact becomes more significant when it is realized that this was the largest federal district jurisdiction and the one where the death penalty was doled out more often. During his tenure, 65 of his marshals were killed in the line of duty, and 160 men were sentenced to die with

Parker hanging 79 of them, sometimes in multiple executions involving up to 6 men at a time.

Judge Parker's court had greater authority than the U.S. Supreme Court at this time, since it held both original and final jurisdiction, including the death sentence. Parker's decisions were absolute and irrevocable. Only a presidential pardon could overturn a Parker judgment, and this did not happen given his influence in Washington and the White House. Judge Parker also had considerable latitude in his decisions given that little federal case law existed either from the federal enclaves laws or the newly created Major Crimes Act enacted later in his administration in 1885.

Judge Parker became known as the "hanging judge" throughout the country. This image eventually led to changes in both his jurisdiction and his authority. In January 1883, Congress split up his district, assigning the western half of Indian Territory to the U.S. Judicial District of Kansas and its courts in Wichita and Fort Scott and the southern region to the Northern District of Texas and the federal court at Graham. This still gave Judge Parker authority over the Five Civilized Tribes. And the Major Crimes Act took away considerable discretion from federal judges by articulating the felony crimes that could be prosecuted in Indian country. An 1883 Missouri newspaper editorial raised the cry over the lack of common justice in Judge Parker's court: "The Judge of the Fort Smith district alone has passed the sentence of death upon more convicted criminals than we care to guess at, not one of whom, red, white, or black, ever had the poor privilege of having his case reviewed in any manner."[18]

This led U.S. Representative John H. Rogers and U.S. Senator James K. Jones, both representing Arkansas, to advocate appellate courts in these districts. In 1889, Congress acted, abolishing the circuit court powers of the district courts of the Western District of Arkansas, the Northern District of Mississippi, and the Western District of South Carolina. After May 1, 1889, all capital cases tried before a U.S. court had to be reviewed by an appellate court before judgment could be exercised. This action stripped Judge Parker of his unique status of having a court of last resort. Unlike Parker's court, the other courts mentioned in this action had multiple judges who could act at the district level as an appellate review board. This law, however, abolished these circuit court powers at the district court level, regardless of the number of judges available for this review process.

Despite these changes, Judge Parker continued to adjudicate over his federal district, serving twenty-one years in this capacity until the district and circuit courts of the Western District of Arkansas were dismantled on September 1, 1896, in lieu of territorial courts. This resulted when Indian Territory

was carved up for non-Indians according to the dictates of the General Allotment (Dawes) Act of 1887. State law replaced territorial law when Oklahoma
became a state in 1907. Judge Isaac Charles Parker died on November 17,
1896, ending one of the most unusual chapters in American jurisprudence.
During his tenure as federal judge of the Western District of Arkansas, Judge
Parker adjudicated 13,490 cases with 344 for capital offenses. Of these, 165
were convicted and 160 sentenced to die. Seventy-nine were hanged, 2 were
killed attempting to escape, 2 died in jail, 2 were pardoned, while 46 had their
death sentence commuted by the U.S. president to terms of ten years to life
imprisonment. Two of these death-qualified offenders sentenced to death by
Judge Parker had new trials resulting in acquittal. Another 27 death-sentenced
inmates were assigned new trials on appeal to the U.S. Supreme Court, resulting in 9 acquittals and 15 convicted on lesser, nondeath-qualified offenses. Of
the other 5 sentenced to death, 2 died awaiting the execution of their sentence, 1 was declared insane and sent to an asylum, 1 was returned to Indian
court for lack of jurisdiction, and 1 fled while on bail. Those cases modified
on appeal all occurred after 1889, when a separate and independent appeals
process was mandated by the U.S. Congress.[19]

CHAPTER SIX

TRIBAL COURTS: SELF-DETERMINATION AND LIMITED JUSTICE

The Synder Act and Meriam Report Influence

BIA Courts of Indian Offenses set the stage for subsequent courts within Indian country, even when more autonomy and authority was awarded to tribes for the adjudication of crimes involving Indians. A sociolegal dilemma occurred as a result of the BIA's efforts to Christianize and civilize American Indians in Indian country. The effects of cultural genocide, that is, the outlawing of traditional rituals and customs, left a significant psychocultural gap among those tribes that could not integrate Christian and aboriginal ways into a meaningful ethnomethodological worldview. The unsuccessful attempt to walk in two worlds led to cultural ambiguity and personal alienation, a form of cultural death, which resulted in a marked increase in alcoholism and related social, economic, legal, and mental and physical health problems in Indian country. The effects of this sociocultural plague were recognized by the authors of the Synder Act of 1921.

The Synder Act specified the expenditure of appropriations made to the Bureau of Indian Affairs in Indian country. It provided: "for the employment of inspectors, supervisors, superintendents, clerks, field matrons, farmers, physicians, Indian police, Indian judges, and other employees."[1]

It was the Meriam Report of 1928 that set the stage for the pendulum to swing back to recognition of Indian choice in social and cultural lifestyle, thus planting the seeds of self-determination:

> The position taken, therefore, is that the work with and for the Indians must give consideration to the desires of the individual Indians. He who wishes to merge into the social and economic life of the prevailing civilization of this country should be given all practicable aid and advice in making the necessary adjustments. He who wants to remain an Indian and live according to his old culture should be aided in doing so. . . . The fact is, however, as has been pointed out, that the old economic basis of his culture has been to a considerable extent destroyed and new problems have been forced upon him by contacts with the whites. Adjustments have to be made, economic, social and legal. Under social is included health. . . . In every activity of the Indian Service the primary question should be, how is the Indian to be trained so that he will do this for himself. Unless this question can be clearly and definitely answered by an affirmative showing of distinct educational purpose and method the chances are that the activity is impeding rather than helping the advancement of the Indian. . . .[2]

Congressional power and authority of federal paternalism was specified in 1913 in *United States v. Sandoval,* in which the U.S. Supreme Court upheld the application of a federal liquor law to the New Mexico Pueblos, even though, due to their Spanish pueblo land grant status, they were not designated as reservation land. Here, the U.S. Supreme Court defined "Indian country" in broad strokes, attributing to the United States a superior status vis-à-vis Indian tribes, which it assigned dependent status, with the U.S. Congress playing the guardian role.[3] The Meriam Report merely refined the guardian's options within Indian country. Essentially, it took the Meriam and other reports on the plight in Indian country to get Congress to act. Despite the authorization in the Synder Act for Indian police and courts, Congress was still inhospitable toward Indians and Indian country and felt that the BIA with its stern and strict law-and-order methods in Indian country was adequate for this group.

The Indian Reorganization Act and the Establishment of Tribal Courts

It took the Roosevelt administration and the Indian Reorganization Act of 1934 (Wheeler-Howard Act) to change things in Indian country. Section 18 applied the recommendation of the Meriam Report by allowing each tribe to either accept or reject the IRA (Indian Reorganization Act) through a majority vote by adult enrolled members within two years of the act's approval. This action, in itself, set a significant precedent for Indian self-determination. During this two-year IRA acceptance period, elections were held; 181 tribes accepted it and 77, including the largest tribe, the Navajo, rejected it. Within the next twelve years, 161 tribal constitutions and 131 corporate chapters were adopted and approved according to the dictates of the IRA.[4]

Those tribes that accepted the changes proposed under the IRA also had the option of establishing tribal courts. However, given the strong influence of the BIA/CFR (Courts of Federal Regulations) Courts of Indian Offenses in Indian country, most of the tribal courts fashioned themselves after them. Slowly, however, tribes have adapted their tribal codes to include some traditional rules that were not allowed under the BIA/CFR system. Indeed, very few tribes went back to traditional customs, with the exception of the Pueblos of New Mexico and Arizona, where traditional religious leaders still play a significant role in tribal social and criminal justice.

The dilemma created by the IRA was that it created two types of Indian courts: the BIA/CFR Courts of Indian Offenses and the tribal courts. Felix Cohen provided an early assessment of the newly enacted tribal courts (circa late 1930s, early 1940s), noting the differences between tribal versus state criminal codes:

> II. The number of offenses specified in a tribal code generally runs between 40 and 50, whereas a state code (exclusive of local municipal ordinances) generally specified between 800 and 2,000 offenses.
>
> III. The maximum punishment specified in the Indian penal code is generally more humane, seldom exceeding imprisonment for 6 months, even for offenses like kidnapping, for which state penal codes impose imprisonment for 20 years or more, or death.
>
> IV. Except for fixing a maximum penalty, the Indian penal codes leave a large discretion to the court in adjusting the penalty to the circumstances of the offense and the offender.
>
> V. The form of punishment is typically forced labor for the benefit of the tribe or of the victim of the offense, rather than imprisonment.

VI. The tribal penal codes, for the most part, do not contain the usual catch-all provisions to be found in state penal codes (vagrancy, conspiracy, criminal syndicalism, etc.), under which almost any unpopular individual may be convicted of crime.

VII. The tribal penal code is generally put into the hands of every member of the tribe, and widely read and discussed, which is not the case with state penal codes.[5]

The Influence of Public Law 280 on Indian Courts

William Canby, on the other hand, provides a contemporary pre-Dura comparison of criminal jurisdiction in Indian country excluded from the dictates of Public Law 280. With crimes by Indians against Indians there is concurrent federal and tribal jurisdiction for the "major" crimes, while the tribe has exclusive jurisdiction for other crimes. For crimes by Indians against non-Indians there again exists concurrent federal and tribal jurisdiction for "major" crimes, and this jurisdiction is extended to other crimes as well. Regarding crimes without victims perpetrated by Indians, the tribe holds exclusive jurisdiction, while the federal authorities hold exclusive jurisdiction over crimes by non-Indians against Indians. And the state where the reservation is located holds exclusive jurisdiction over all crimes by non-Indians committed in Indian country.[6]

The policies of termination and relocation, and Public Law 280 in the early 1950s, served to strip a number of tribes of their criminal justice authority and set the stage for another era of a lack of congressional support for Indian justice, especially tribal-centric self-determination. (The Public Law 280 debate is presented in Part One.) As far as criminal justice and self-determination were concerned, Public Law 280 was designed as a supportive instrument for termination and relocation—the last-ditch effort in the twentieth century for Congress to enforce a policy of cultural genocide. Initially designed for California only, it soon was expanded to include five other mandatory states and, later, a number of optional states. The pretense for extending state criminal jurisdiction into Indian country, for what the federal policymakers at the time hoped would include all tribes, was lawlessness of the reservations and the accompanying threat this posed to the Anglos living nearby.[7] Many felt that the absence of an Indian consent provision clearly reflected the punitive nature of Congress and the administration at this time. This element of Public Law 280, along with the extension of civil jurisdiction to states without any corresponding rationale, was seen as an attempt to abrogate treaty-funding responsibilities to the tribes. The states were not happy with their unfunded extended criminal and civil mandate. Public Law 280 states still have jurisdiction within Indian country located in their states, not including those tribes exempted. This experiment lasted from 1953 until 1968.

The Influence of the Indian Civil Rights Act on Tribal Justice

In 1968, Congress provided the tribal consent provision for additional Public Law 280 states but did not make this retroactive. This was one of the few positive aspects of the Indian Civil Rights Act of 1968 for tribal authority and self-determination. Essentially, the Indian Civil Rights Act was seen as yet another attempt to undermine tribal authority in the area of criminal justice in that it extended constitutional rights to individual Indians at the expense of tribal authority. Two provisions of the 1968 Indian Civil Rights Act (ICRA) place limits on tribal courts: (1) it states that no tribe shall imprison a convicted offender in excess of six months or exact a fine over $500; and (2) it avails habeas corpus reviews to all Indian offenders convicted in tribal courts relevant to any sentence involving incarceration. Before the ICRA, tribes were not subject to the federal Constitution since the IRA was designed to allow the incorporation of traditional ways and customs into the tribal code. Now tribal courts have jurisdiction over all criminal and civil matters, excluding "major crimes," as long as "due process" is observed in criminal cases. Omitted in this refinement of the authority of tribal courts are the areas of probate, juvenile problems, domestic relations, and housing matters. Clearly, the 1968 Indian Civil Rights Act served notice in Indian country that the U.S.-style of civil and criminal justice will be allowed and that tribal authority will be greatly restricted to only minor criminal and civil judicial issues.[8]

A number of subsequent cases have refined the strengths and limitations of tribal authority in the realm of criminal justice, ending with *Duro v. Reina* in 1990. In 1959, the U.S. Supreme Court, in *Williams v. Lee*, ruled that the state of Arizona did not have civil jurisdiction in a case involving a non-Indian who owned a store on the Navajo reservation and attempted to sue an enrolled Navajo for an alleged breach of contract that occurred in the Navajo Nation. The Court ruled that state adjudication of this civil matter would erode the authority of tribal courts, a clear infringement of the right of Indian self-determination.[9]

However, other cases set limits on tribal authority over nonmembers. In 1978, the U.S. Supreme Court, in *United States v. Wheeler*, ruled that tribes and tribal courts held inherent criminal jurisdiction over only their enrolled members, even though this was not a salient issue in the case.[10] The same year, the U.S. Supreme Court ruled, in *Oliphant v. Suquamish Indian Tribe*, that tribal jurisdiction did not extend to non-Indians. The reason given is that this authority would not be in concert with the tribes' status as dependent sovereignties as stipulated by the Enclaves Act and its subsequent revisions.[11] The *Oliphant* decision, however, did uphold the tribal court's authority to enforce decorum (issue and act on contempt orders) against disruptive non-Indian criminal defendants.

Later, in *Merrion v. Jicarilla Apache Tribe*, the federal courts recognized the tribes' power of exclusion for unwanted persons, including member Indians, nonmember Indians, and non-Indians, as long as these individuals do not hold federally conferred rights to be in Indian country.[12] This last issue was determined by *Harding v. White Mountain Apache Tribe*.[13] It was *Dura v. Reina*, however, that led to statutory changes relevant to tribal judicial authority over nontribal Indians. In 1990, the U.S. Supreme Court, in *Dura*, stated that tribes do not hold criminal jurisdiction over nonmember Indians who commit crimes on the reservation. Here, the Court limited the tribe's judicial authority to only its own members even if the crime occurs on the reservation and would otherwise be covered by the tribal code.[14]

In 1991, the U.S. Congress exercised its authority as ultimate guardian in all matters within Indian country, passing Public Law 102–137, an act entitled Criminal Jurisdiction over Indians. This was another example of Congress exercising its authority over the U.S. Supreme Court in matters regarding Indian country. Unlike their action in *Crow Dog*, over one hundred years before, the Congress this time sided with the tribes, reinstating their judicial authority over all Indians on the reservation, including nonmember Indians.[15]

The Indian Tribal Act of 1993 and Tribal Codes

Two years later, Congress passed the Indian Tribal Act of 1993 in an attempt to consolidate the Anglo-based judicial codes within Indian country, whether the tribes used the old BIA Courts of Indian Offenses or their own tribal courts. There is a disclaimer in the act that its purpose is not to impose justice standards on Indian tribes but only to provide technical assistance and training. The areas addressed by the new Office of Tribal Justice Support include the following:

1. Tribal codes and rules of procedure.
2. Tribal court administrative procedures and court records management systems.
3. Methods of reducing case delays.
4. Methods of alternative dispute resolution.
5. Tribal standards for judicial administration and conduct.
6. Long-range plans for the enhancement of the tribal justice system.

These initiatives are supported by fiscal rewards. Moreover, the secretary of the interior is authorized by this act to provide funds to tribal judicial conferences under Section 3611, pursuant to contracts authorized under the Indian Self-Determination and Education Act of 1975, if these conferences address the following training initiatives:

1. The employment of judges, magistrates, court counselors, court clerks, court administrators, bailiffs, probation officers, officers of the court, or dispute resolution facilitators;
2. The development, revision, and publication of tribal codes, rules of practice, rules of procedure, and standards of judicial performance and conduct;
3. The acquisition, development, and maintenance of a law library and computer-assisted legal research capacities;
4. Training programs and continuing education for tribal judicial personnel;
5. The development and operation of records management systems;
6. Planning for the development, enhancement, and operation of tribal justice systems; and
7. The development and operation of other innovative and culturally relevant programs and projects, including (but not limited to) programs and projects for:
   (a) Alternative dispute resolution;
   (b) Tribal victims assistance or victims services;
   (c) Tribal probation services or diversion programs;
   (d) Juvenile services and multidisciplinary investigations of child abuse; and
   (e) Traditional tribal judicial practices, traditional justice systems, and traditional methods of dispute resolution.[16]

Clearly, given the majority U.S.-style judicial mandates being funded through this act, it obviates the traditional initiatives, which appear as awkward supplements.

THE NAVAJO COURT SYSTEM

The Navajo Nation is the largest Indian tribe in the United States, comprising some 25,000 square miles in a section of the Southwest that includes sections of three states: Arizona, New Mexico, and Utah. It is estimated to be the size of West Virginia and has close to half the enrolled members of American Indians in the country. The Navajo Nation estimates its total population to be over 160,000 enrolled members with 80 percent residing on the reservation. Another ten thousand non-Navajo also reside on the Navajo reservation. The tribe's complex social system revolves around the clan system and the Beauty Way. The four original clans are Towering House Clan (*Kinyaaáani*), One Walks-Around Clan (*Honaghaahnii*), Bitter Water Clan (*Todichiinii*), and Mud Clan (*Hashilishnii*).

The Beauty Way is the Navajo's concept of the Harmony Ethos. Here, the purpose of justice is the restoration of harmony (*Hozho*). And, like most aboriginal belief systems, the Navajo view their world as being divided into four quadrants, with Mount Blanco protecting the east; Mount Taylor, the south; Mount Humphrey, the west; and Mount Hespurus, the north. The four Navajo colors are white, yellow, blue, and black; blue and black represent the night and white and yellow, the day.

An undated tribal document by Nelson J. McCabe, written while he was chief justice of the Navajo Nation, claims that the Navajo do not receive their governmental powers from the United States since the Navajo Nation is an

Indian state that has independent powers of self-government and is recognized under international law:

> The Navajo do not receive their governmental powers from the United States—they come from the fact of Indian statehood. Indian nations are legally states under international law, having independent powers of self-government. When the Navajo Nation entered into treaties with the United States, it made some concessions to the United States but reserved all the powers of statehood which were not specifically surrendered. Therefore the source of Navajo governmental power and sovereignty is the Navajo People and not a United States government which dispenses governmental authority. The Navajo Nation is like an open-charter municipal government—under the laws of the United States the Navajo Nation may do everything which has not been *specifically* given up by it. [Emphasis added][1]

The designation of the Navajo Nation cited in chapter 5, sections 301 and 302, of the Navajo Tribal Code:

**Section 301. Use of term "Navajo Nation";
certification of resolutions: address**

(a) The Advisory Committee of the Navajo Tribal Council hereby directs the Chairman of the Navajo Tribal Council and all departments, divisions, agencies, enterprises, and entities of the Navajo Tribe to use the phrase "Navajo Nation" in describing the lands and people of the Navajo Tribe.

(b) The Advisory Committee further directs that all resolutions of the Tribal Government be certified as being duly enacted at "Window Rock, Navajo Nation (Arizona)."

(c) The Advisory Committee further directs that all correspondence, stationery and letterheads, of all the above-referred-to divisions, agencies, etc., of the Navajo Tribe, use the designation "Navajo Nation" to locate the Tribe. . . .

Section 302: Spelling of "Navajo"

The Treaty of 1868 recognized the Navajo People as a sovereign nation and spelled "Navajo" with a "j," therefore, the Advisory Committee directs and urges that all use of the name "Navajo" use the spelling "j," not "h."[2]

Navajo Adult Court System

The Navajo court system is best described by Chief Justice Robert Yazzie, who states that it came into existence on April 1, 1959, and was revised under the 1985 Judicial Reform Act to provide more flexibility and to promote Navajo common law, setting the stage for the Navajo Peacemakers model of justice. Here, the essence of "law" and "justice" comes from the Navajo word *beehazáannii*, which signifies the essence of life within the Beauty Way. Yazzie points out that the purpose of the Navajo Nation courts is not to punish or alienate the people, but to bring harmony back into the Beauty Way. Within this system, the Navajo Nation Council (Legislative Branch) makes the laws; the president and Executive Branch execute these laws; and the Navajo Nation courts apply and enforce the laws.

The Navajo Nation has a two-level court system: district trial courts and the Navajo Nation Supreme Court. The Navajo Nation Supreme Court serves as the appellate court for the district trial courts. There are seven judicial districts in the Navajo Nation; each district has a court, and five of the seven districts have a separate family court. The district courts are located in Tuba City, Kayenta, Chinle, and Window Rock, Arizona, and in Shiprock, Crownpoint, and Ramah, New Mexico. New Mexico also has two satellite courts. Together, the district courts serve all 110 chapters of the Navajo Nation. The Navajo judiciary consists of seventeen judges, with fourteen trial judges presiding at the district and family courts and three appellate judges from the Supreme Court. The Navajo courts are funded by both the federal government and the Navajo Nation general funds, and hear over ninety thousand cases a year.

Since 1958, Navajo judges are appointed and no longer elected. Applicants must be enrolled members of the tribe and at least thirty years of age. The initial screening, interviewing, and scoring of potential judges is done by the Judiciary Committee of the Navajo Nation Council. Names of qualified applicants are sent to the president of the Navajo Nation, who makes the appointment that then needs to be confirmed by the Navajo Nation Council. Upon confirmation, new judges serve a two-year probationary term. Only the Navajo Nation Bar Association (NNBA) can practice in the Navajo courts. The three hundred members of the NNBA include law school graduates as well as legally trained lay advocates. All NNBA applicants must pass both an examination and suitability screening. The Judicial Branch of the Navajo Nation employs 137 personnel, including the court solicitor, bailiffs, court clerks, secretaries, and probation and parole officers. Chief Justice Yazzie explains the courts' jurisdiction as follows:

Jurisdiction is the power of a court to decide a case. The Navajo trial courts have general civil jurisdiction and limited criminal jurisdiction. Navajo civil jurisdiction extends to all persons (Indian and non-Indian) who reside in Navajo Indian Country or have caused an action to occur in Navajo Indian Country. The Navajo courts' criminal jurisdiction extends to all crimes codified in the Navajo Nation Code along with its terms of punishment. The Navajo courts have criminal jurisdiction over Indians only and not over non-Indians. The Navajo courts have the power to sentence a person to a maximum of six months in jail or a $500 fine or both.

Juries are used in criminal and civil cases, but not in domestic relations, decedent's estate or miscellaneous cases. Juries are not used in the Court of Appeals. Navajo Court juries consist of six residents 21 years old or greater and are selected from a list of eligible jurors by the judge. Jury verdicts, in both criminal and civil cases, require only a majority vote (preponderance of probability).

The Navajo Nation Supreme Court has jurisdiction over appeals from final decisions of the trial courts and certain administrative agencies. The Supreme Court decides only on issues of law raised on the record of appeal. The district courts have jurisdiction over all other matters that the family courts do not hear. The Navajo family courts have jurisdiction over matters involving children, probate, name changes, quiet title, and domestic relations. Parties to a case can present their case without an attorney to a district court using small claims proceedings. People can use the Navajo Peacemaker Division to solve their disputes. The division is attached to the trial courts. It uses Navajo traditional laws and procedures in a Navajo mediation setting to arrive at consensual solutions to disputes.

Navajo common law and statutory laws are the laws of preference in the Navajo courts. Otherwise, federal law, if applicable, is used. Lastly, state law may be applied. Navajo common law includes the traditional ways of the Navajo people. Navajo common law is found in books and articles on Navajo culture and in Navajo court opinions. Navajo elders and teachers of Navajo culture are also sources of Navajo common law. The statutory law of the Navajo Nation is found in the Navajo Tribal Code. Legal opinions of the Navajo Nation Supreme Court and of the trial courts are found in the *Navajo Reporter* and the *Indian Law Reporter*. The Indian Civil Rights Act (a federal law) and the Navajo Nation Bill of Rights require the Navajo courts to safeguard the rights of individuals.[3]

Despite claims of state or national autonomy, the Navajo Nation courts are BIA Courts of Indian Offenses regulated by the United States Code

Annotated, Title 25, "Indians." This regulation states that: "No court of Indian Offenses will be established on reservations where justice is effectively administered under state laws and by state law enforcement agencies."[4] This indicates that the Navajo Nation does not fall under Public Law 280 jurisdictions per se even though their own code indicates that state laws (Arizona, New Mexico, Utah) can be utilized when tribal or federal codes do not address a criminal or civil issue. Offenses in the Navajo Tribal Code fall under the following categories: general; abduction; animals and livestock; bribery; children; disorderly conduct; drunkenness; embezzlement, theft and shoplifting; extortion; fish and game violations; forgery; fraud; gambling; health and safety; intoxicating liquors; malicious mischief; perjury; prostitution; public property; stolen property; trespass; weapons; false pretenses and false impersonation; solicitation by charitable organizations or association with the Navajo Nation; conspiracy; and preservation of antiquities.

Under the general subchapter a number of offenses are listed including: violation of tribal ordinances; disobedience of court orders; unauthorized fences on tribal lands without a permit; nonsupport of dependent persons, including children born out of wedlock; sale, concealment, or removal of chattel subject to mortgage or other lien; and failure of parents to send children ages six to sixteen to school. Abduction, which corresponds to the federal offense of kidnapping, has the maximum sentence that the tribal court can impose—six months of labor. Adultery and illicit cohabitation, on the other hand, have a thirty-day maximum sentence, while a conviction of bigamy has a ninety-day sentence of hard labor or a fine not to exceed $100, or both conditions. Four offenses relate to resisting arrest or escape. Refusing to aid an officer during an arrest can lead to a ten-day labor conviction, while resisting lawful arrest can bring a sentence up to thirty days of labor. Escape and resisting or obstructing a public officer using threat or violence can result in the maximum six-month sentence, with the latter also having the option of a $500 fine in addition to imprisonment.

The subchapter on assaults includes assault and battery as well as sexual assault on a child and indecent assault on an adult. Certain forms of assault are federal offenses under the Major Crimes Act. And, since 1990, the federal Indian child protection statute (Title IV of Public Law 101-630—Indian Child Protection and Family Violence Prevention Act) requires that abuse of Indian children be made known to the appropriate authorities (tribal, state, federal) and that the failure to do so actually is a crime itself.[5] Contributing to the delinquency of a minor also falls in this category of offenses.

A number of codes address riots and unlawful assembly, including the obstruction of teachers or students, which can carry the most severe fine and imprisonment allowed by law. Riots, inciting riots, and unlawful assembly also can result in the maximum sentences. Embezzlement, theft, forgery, carrying a concealed weapon, and perjury offenses adjudicated in tribal courts also hold the possibility of the maximum of six months of labor, while perhaps the most common offense, drunkenness, specifically public drunkenness, has a maximum five days of incarceration and a $50 fine. It needs to be noted that federal authority now allows Indian courts to administer a maximum criminal penalty of one year of imprisonment and a $5,000 fine, or both and that these new maximum punishments may be reflected in more current volumes of the Navajo Tribal Code. This authorization is noted in the United States Code Annotated—Title 25 (2000 Supplementary Pamphlet Covering Years 1984 to 1999).

Gambling, a heated controversy both in and out of Indian country, failed to win a majority vote of the Navajo Tribal Council recently, even though many of the Navajos' neighbors, the New Mexico Pueblos, have successful gaming operations. Hence, poker, blackjack, monte, and similar games of chance are violations of the Navajo Tribal Code. Another interesting code is 1506: "Impersonation by a Non-Indian." Individuals posing as Navajo Indians or Indians of other tribes may be excluded from tribal lands according to this code. Indeed, according to code 1902 nonmembers of the Navajo tribes, including American Indians enrolled elsewhere, can be excluded on the following grounds:

1. Unauthorized prospecting.
2. Unauthorized mining, timber-cutting, or other activity causing physical loss or damage of any nature to Tribal property.
3. Commission of a crime, as defined by state or Federal law.
4. Immorality.
5. Forcing entry into any Navajo home without consent of the occupant or occupants.
6. Interfering with or photographing Navajo ceremonies without permission of the Navajos involved.
7. Unauthorized trading.
8. Committing frauds, confidence games, or usury against Navajo people, or inducing them to enter into grossly unfavorable contracts of any nature.
9. Recruiting Navajo labor for off-Reservation employment without prior permission of the Tribal Council and the General Superintendent.
10. Defrauding any Navajo of just compensation for his labor or service of any nature done at the request of the nonmember.
11. Breach of the peace, or repeated public drunkenness.
12. Contagious disease.

13. Violation of traffic regulations.
14. Entering an area of the Navajo Reservation in violation of an order of the Tribal Council and General Superintendent designating such area as closed because of fire hazard or for any other reason.
15. Removing or attempting to remove any Navajo minor from the Navajo Reservation without prior approval of the Advisory Committee of the Tribal Council, except for the purpose of attending school under a non-sectarian program approved by the Bureau of Indian Affairs. However, this ground for exclusion shall not apply in cases where a Navajo minor is removed from the Navajo Reservation by his/her adopted parents, or by persons who have received custody of such child pursuant to an order of the Trial Court of the Navajo Tribe.
16. Conducting missionary activities without a mission site permit or a mission site on fee-patent land within the Reservation boundaries.

Section 1904. Hearing; Order of Exclusion:

a) Upon request of the Tribal Council, the Advisory Committee shall hold a hearing to decide whether or not the nonmember shall be excluded from Navajo Tribal land. Such nonmember shall be given an opportunity to present his defense at such hearing and may be represented by counsel.

b) After such hearing, or after the time set for such hearing, if after notice the person proposed for exclusion does not appear, the Advisory Committee may order such person excluded from all or any part of the Navajo Tribal lands, or may permit the person to remain upon Navajo Tribal land on such conditions as the Committee see fit to impose. All orders of exclusion shall remain in force until revoked by the Advisory Committee, unless the order specifically provides otherwise.[6]

By the same token, the Navajo Tribal Code prohibited asylum from prosecution within the Navajo Nation for Indians who committed crimes outside Indian country. Here, the Tribal Council could order the Navajo police to apprehend such individuals and to deliver them to proper state authorities at the reservation boundary.[7]

Navajo Juvenile Court System

Juvenile court judges are appointed in the same manner and with the same qualifications as are judges of the trial courts and serve in the seven districts.

Juvenile courts have original jurisdiction over all persons within the Navajo Nation:

- Concerning any child who is alleged to have violated any Federal, Tribal, state, or local law or municipal ordinance, regardless of where the violation occurred.
- Concerning any child:
  who is a neglected or dependent child; or
  who is beyond the control of his parent, custodian, or school authorities.
- To determine the custody of any child or appoint a guardian of the person of any child who comes within the purview of the court's jurisdiction under other provisions of this chapter.
- To determine the legal parent-child relationship, including termination of residual parental rights and duties, as to a child who comes within the purview of the court's jurisdiction under other provisions of this chapter.
- For judicial consent to the marriage, employment or enlistment of a child in the armed forces, and to emergency medical or surgical treatment of a child who comes within the purview of the court's jurisdiction under other provisions of this chapter.
- For the treatment or commitment of a mentally defective or mentally ill child who comes within the purview of the court's jurisdiction under other provisions of this chapter.

Section 1055. Jurisdiction over Adults:

The Juvenile Court shall have exclusive original jurisdiction to try all adults subject to the jurisdiction of the Navajo Tribe for offenses committed against children, as follows:

- Any adult who induces, aids, or encourages a child to violate any Federal, state, or local law or municipal or Tribal ordinance, or who aids or contributes to the dependency or neglect of any child;
- Any adult having a child in his legal or physical custody, or in his employment, who willfully ill-treats, neglects or abandons such child in any manner likely to cause the child unnecessary suffering or serious injury to his health or morals;
- Any adult who forcibly takes away a child from, or induces him to leave, the legal or physical custody of any person, agency or institution in which the child has been legally placed for the purpose of care, support, education or adoption, and any person who detains or harbors such child after

demand is made for the return of the child by an officer of the court or by the person, agency, or institution concerned;

• Any adult who commits the crime of child beating.

Section 1061. Duties and Powers of Probation Officers:

The probation officers shall make preliminary inquiries and social studies, and such other investigations as the judge may direct, and shall keep written records of such investigations or studies, and shall make reports to the judge as provided in this chapter or as directed by the judge. Upon the placing of any person on probation or under protective supervision, the probation officer shall explain to the child, if old enough, and to the parents and other persons concerned, what the meaning and conditions of probation or protective supervision are and shall give them the necessary instructions. The probation officer shall keep informed concerning the conduct and condition of each person on probation or under protective supervision and shall report thereon to the judge as he may direct. Probation officers shall use all suitable methods to aid persons on probation or under protective supervision to bring about improvements in their conduct or condition, and shall perform such other duties in connection with the care, custody, or transportation of children as the judge may require. Probation officers shall have the powers of peace officers for purposes of this chapter, but shall, whenever possible, refrain from exercising such powers except in urgent situations in which a regular peace officer is not immediately available.

Section 1156. Examinations:

The court may order that a child concerning whom a petition has been filed shall be examined by a physician, surgeon, psychiatrist or psychologist, and may place the child in a hospital or other facility for such examination. However, the child shall not be held in such hospital or facility longer than 24 hours unless necessary for treatment of physical injuries, without a hearing before the court. After due notice and a hearing set for the specific purpose, the court may order a similar examination of a parent or guardian whose ability to care for a child is at issue, if the court finds from the evidence presented at the hearing that the parent's or guardian's physical, mental or emotional condition may be a factor in causing the neglect, dependency or delinquency of the child.

Section 1174. Conduct of Hearings:

Hearings in children's cases shall be before the court without a jury and may be conducted in an informal manner; provided that any child if accused of an offense punishable by detention shall upon request be entitled to a trial by jury. The general public shall be excluded and only such persons admitted as the judge finds have a direct and legitimate interest in the case or in the work of the court. At the discretion of the court, the child may be separately interviewed at any time if represented by his/her counselor. The hearing may be continued from time to time to a date specified in the order.

Section 1184. Taking a Child into Custody:

A child may be taken into custody by any peace officer or probation officer pursuant to an order of the court.

A child may be taken into custody by any peace officer or probation officer without order of the court for the following reasons:

- when in the presence of the officer the child has violated a state, Federal, or local law or a municipal or Tribal ordinance;
- when there are reasonable grounds to believe that he/she has committed an act which if committed by an adult would be a felony;
- when he/she is seriously endangered in his/her surroundings, and immediate removal appears to be necessary for his/her protection;
- when there are reasonable grounds to believe that he/she has run away or escaped from his/her parents, guardian, or custodian;
- when there are reasonable grounds to believe that he/she has committed an act, which if committed by an adult, would be a breach of peace; and
- when he/she has reason to believe that the child requires immediate care or medical attention.

Section 1187. Detention of Child:

A child shall not be detained by the Tribal police or in a police station any longer than is reasonably necessary to obtain his/her name, age, residence and other identifying information and to contact and avoid [sic] the appearance of his parent, guardian or custodian. Notwithstanding the above, if the child is not thereupon released, he/she must be taken without unnecessary delay to the court probation officer or to the place of detention or shelter designated by the court, but no child shall be held in detention longer than 48 hours unless upon order of the court or until positive identification is made.

Section 1188. Notification and Report to Court:

The officer or other person who takes a child to a detention or shelter facility must notify the court at the earliest opportunity that the child has been taken into custody and where he/she was taken; he/she shall also promptly file with the court a brief written report stating the occurrences or facts which bring the child within the jurisdiction of the Tribal Juvenile Court and giving the reason why the child was not released.

Section 1351. Procedure:

An appeal to the Navajo Court of Appeals may be taken from any order, decree, or judgment of the Tribal Juvenile Court. Such appeal shall be taken in the same manner in which appeals are taken from judgments or decrees of the Trial Court, provided that the appeal must be made within 30 days from the entry of the order, decree, or judgment appealed from.

Section 1402. Records Accessibility:

The court shall keep such records as may be required by the judge and by this chapter. Records in children's cases shall not be deemed criminal records and shall not be open to public inspection; but the court may, at its discretion, by order, authorize inspection by persons having a legitimate interest in the proceedings, and by persons conducting pertinent research studies.[8]

Navajo Peacemaker Court

Reintroduced in 1982, the Navajo Peacemaker Court has gained international attention, especially in these days of restorative justice and community policing. Chief Justice Yazzie explains the differences between this concept of restoring harmony and the adversarial U.S. justice model, which also is instituted on the Navajo Nation:

> Currently, there are two distinct systems of justice at work in the Navajo Nation. One is an adversarial adjudication system, based on the practices of the Anglo-American courts. The other is based on the traditional Navajo

conception of justice, which emphasizes consensual problem-solving to achieve dispute resolution.

In the former system, resolutions to people's problems are forced on them from on high. In the latter, people solve their own problems with the help of a "naatáanii," or Peacemaker. Peacemakers are part of the Peacemaker Project, an attempt by the Navajo Court System to return to the traditional Navajo conception of justice.

The adversarial system of the Anglo-American courts is a "vertical" system of justice. In this vertical system, judges sit at the top over lawyers, jury members, parties, and all the other participants in court proceedings. Judges possess a tremendous amount of power to affect human lives, either to harm them or bring goodness to them. The parties involved in the dispute do not have as much power. Someone from on high dictates how the dispute must be handled, and everyone must obey the judge's order. This vertical system relies on coercion to control and force people to do or not do something, according to the judge's decision. There is a high degree of control and force over those who come to court.

Navajo Supreme Court Justice Homer Bluehorse always said that when someone prevails in the adversarial system, he or she walks out of the courtroom with "tails up," and the loser walks out with "tails down." It is a win-lose situation, a zero-sum game. It is not a win-win situation. The adversarial system is a system of absolutes. One part is the "bad guy," and another is the "good guy." One party is wrong or at fault while the other is right.

In the adversarial system the goal is to punish wrongdoers and teach them a lesson. In a criminal case, the defendant is usually punished by serving a jail term or paying a fine. It is punishment for the sake of punishment, but nothing is done to solve the underlying problems that caused the dispute in the first place. In a criminal case, the victim is essentially without power, having little or nothing to say about what relief the court should grant. Thus, the real rights and the real needs of the victim may be ignored, and the end result is that little or no real justice is done. In this system, there is not just one victim, there are victims: family members, relatives, and the community are all affected by the dispute and the decision. They are in the courtroom without a voice, and they leave the courtroom empty-handed.

The adversarial system has a relatively short history in the Navajo courts. It was created by the federal government in 1892 with the CFR courts. Later, the Navajo Nation Council established the current judicial system—the Navajo Nation Courts. We have lived with the Anglo-American adjudication system for only 100 years. The Navajo Peacemaker system, on the other hand, has existed for many, many years. It existed long before the adversarial system was ever introduced to Navajos.

What is the Navajo Peacemaker system? Traditionally, Navajos used a Peacemaker, called a "naatáanii," to mediate disputes. Peacemakers helped preserve ongoing relationships, both within immediate and extended families. The parties settled their disputes in a forum where they could talk and settle their problems by consent. In this way harmony was restored. Today, the Peacemaker Courts of the Navajo judicial system seek to implement these methods of dispute resolution. The core idea behind the Navajo Peacemaker Courts is to allow people to solve their own problems without the interference of judges or attorneys.

Is the Peacemaker system better than the adversarial system of justice? Let us make some comparisons. As we have said before, the Anglo-American system is a vertical system of justice. In the vertical system, human beings are placed in ranks from top to bottom. In the Navajo Peacemaker system all human beings are treated as equals. This is the "horizontal" system.

The vertical system uses judges, lawyers, parties, bailiffs, and police officers. The Peacemaker process does not divide people into divisions. There is no need. Anglo-American courts rely on control, coercion, and force. How cases are resolved is determined by rules and regulations, instead of according to the needs of the individuals involved in the dispute. In the process of peacemaking, there are no rules to dictate how proceedings should be controlled. Force, coercion, and control are completely left out.

In the Anglo-American courts, parties are always labeled as being on one side or the other. In the Peacemaker process, parties are not labeled as plaintiffs or defendants. No one is treated as the "good guy" or the "bad guy." Rich or poor, educated or not, everyone is treated as equal. Social and economic status has no place in the Peacemaker process.

In the Anglo-American courts justice can sometimes be bought with money. Money buys lawyers, and the best lawyers cost the most money. The party with the most money can "buy" justice because he can afford the best lawyer and legal procedures money can buy. In the Peacemaker process, legal fees are not needed because lawyers are not hired to represent parties. Rather, a Peacemaker works so that justice can be done for everyone involved in the dispute. Another difference is that in Anglo-American courts, parties may not freely communicate with judges. To do so might prejudice the rights of the other party. In the Peacemaker process you can speak with the mediator. The mediator is there to help you work out the dispute and come to a solution, not to act as a policeman.

In the Anglo-American courts, when justice is rendered it is "blind" justice. It is not true justice that repairs damaged relationships and restores harmony to the family, community, and society. Adversarial court systems promote greater adversarial relationships and disharmony, rather than true justice.

For example, husband and wife divorce. They fight more after their divorce, and in the process, their children are forever wounded from the experience.

In the Peacemaker process, the mediator aims at one goal, and one goal only—restoring true justice among individuals, families and the larger community and society. This is done by allowing the wrongdoer and the victim to "talk things out." Navajos have always believed that the more individuals are restored to harmony, the more the family, community, and society will live and function in a harmonious fashion. In the adversarial system there is little or no chance of restoring what Navajos call "ké bil nil," or harmony. The ultimate goal of the Peacemaker process is to restore the minds, physical being, spirits, and emotional well-being of all people involved.

The selection of Peacemakers is based upon the respect, integrity, and good character of an individual who lives in the community. When a chapter does not elect a Peacemaker, the Navajo court may appoint one. The Peacemaker does not have to possess any special knowledge, position in society, or education degree to be a maker of peace. He or she need only possess the skill of being able to get people to talk out their problems with one another. In the Peacemaker Courts, Peacemakers help resolve all types of cases, both civil and criminal.

Why have a Peacemaker system? It is obvious that alien ways do not solve people's problems. Imposed methods which are not in harmony with people's notions of right and wrong do not enforce right or deter wrong. Navajos deal with the same problems as the general American society—domestic violence, gang activity, fighting, disorderly conduct, public intoxication, and driving while intoxicated. The general society attempts to deal with these problems by using force (in the form of jails). That does not work, and it will not work for Navajos. Rather, if the Navajo courts institutionalize Navajo justice concepts—equality, talking things out, and consent—that will respond to expectations that Navajos already have.

Adversarial methods of adjudication ignore concepts of harmony and the restoration of ongoing relationships. They do not always bring justice; they often feed a sense of injustice; they represent conflict which is suppressed by force. As it was with the Rodney King situation in Los Angles, injustice fuels underlying problems and sparks a discontent which comes from ignoring real problems. Instead, we must work to solve problems among individuals so that they can resolve the ones which affect the community.

Can serious cases, such as a homicide, be handled by a Peacemaker? Perhaps they can. If a Peacemaker can get the commitment of people to seriously address their conduct, their intentions, and how they can repair the division between them, almost any situation can be addressed through peacemaking. Many Indian tribes have the tradition of a temporary banishment or cool-off period following a homicide. An offender could later open negotiations for a peaceful return to the community with the victim's family. Other tribes had traditions of mediation and compensation to the clan where there was a homicide. Rather than dismiss certain categories of cases, we must recognize that most Indian tribes had their own ways of dealing with even the most serious offense.[9]

The *Peacemaker Court Manual* specifies the rules and procedures for this form of adjudication, which, in its contemporary format, is a blend of aboriginal ways and Anglo-American adjudication. First, these rules are written in English. The manual states that the Peacemaker Court is meant mainly for everyday problems, including the following:

- Problems among husbands and wives and their families;
- Disputes among parents and children;
- Minor problems between neighbors, such as nuisances, animal trespass or annoyance, conduct which bothers others and so on;
- Problems due to the use or abuse of alcohol by members of the family or neighbors;
- Problems caused by sexual misconduct;
- Conduct that harms people or property, or causes annoyance or disunity in the family or chapter;
- Business matters of $1,500 or less; and
- Any other matter the district court judge feels should or can be taken care of in the Peacemaker Court.

While there is no formal legal representation (e.g., lawyers) in the Peacemaker Court, once a district court judge appoints a Peacemaker, all parties involved are compelled to cooperate in the process. The Peacemaker is usually selected on a case-by-case basis and needs to be a respected member of the community—one who has a thorough knowledge of Navajo religious traditions. This could prove problematic for those Navajos who subscribe solely to traditional Christian faiths, the Mormon faith, or the Native American Church. What follows are the formal Peacemaker Court rules:

General Rules

1.1 *Purpose.*
These rules fix the practice and procedure for the handling of disputes among members of the Navajo Tribe by the intervention of members of the

community where the dispute arises. These rules are intended to give formal support, structure and enforcement to traditional Navajo methods of resolving disputes through mediation and the use of traditional ways without the imposition of judges or lawyers.

1.2 *Authority*:

These rules are authorized by 7 NTC Sec. 204(a), which permits the use of customs of the Navajo People in civil matters before the Courts of the Navajo Nation. The judges of the Navajo Nation find there is a long-standing custom and usage with the Navajo Tribe and the Navajo Courts for judges to appoint members of a community who are respected as being elders, wise in traditional ways, holy or otherwise respected, for the purpose of resolving disputes. These rules are for the purpose of formalizing that custom and usage.

1.3 *Establishment of Peacemaker Court*:

The Peacemaker Court of the Navajo Nation is hereby established as a department of the district court of each judicial district of the Navajo Nation. The trial judge of each judicial district shall supervise the activities of the Peacemaker Court of the district and shall exercise supervisory control over any Peacemaker appointed pursuant to these rules.

1.4 *Scope*:

A judge of the Navajo Nation may appoint a Peacemaker in a community where the parties to the dispute are members of the Navajo Tribe and where the matter in dispute involves certain personal and community relationships including but not limited to, the following:

- Marital disputes and disputes involving family strife;
- Disputes among parents and children;
- Minor disputes between neighbors as to community problems such as nuisance, animal trespass or annoyance, disorderly conduct, breaches of the peace and like matters;
- Alcohol use or abuse by family members or neighbors;
- Sexual misconduct;
- Conduct causing harm, annoyance or disunity in the immediate community or chapter;
- Minor community business transactions of a sum of $1,500 or less.
- Any other matter which the District Court finds should or can be resolved through the use of the Peacemaker Court.

1.5 *Compulsory Nature of Peacemaker Court*:

An order compelling individuals to submit to Peacemaker Court proceedings as parties, witnesses or participants is binding upon any member of the Navajo Tribe and any Indian living among the members of the Navajo Tribe. Non-Indians may be compelled to participate in Peacemaker Court proceedings as a witness or participant but not as a party. A non-Indian may voluntarily submit to the proceedings of the Peacemaker Court and be bound by its conclusion or any agreed judgment under these rules.

1.6 *Council Forbidden*:

Members of the Navajo Nation Bar and all attorneys are barred from participating in any proceeding of the Peacemaker Court with the exception of assisting persons with respect to protective orders, complaints and judgments, under Sections 4.1, 4.2, 4.3, 4.4, 4.5, 4.6 and 5.2.

1.7 *Interpretation and Implementation of Rules*:

These rules will be interpreted liberally and informally with the goal of providing a fair, informal, inexpensive and traditional means of resolving local disputes within the communities of the Navajo Nation. The rules will be used and applied in as close an accordance with Navajo tradition and custom as is possible.

2.1 *Appointment and Qualifications*:

- *General Qualifications*: Any person who has the respect of the community of his or her residence, an ability to work with Chapter members, and a reputation for integrity, honesty, humanity and an ability to resolve local problems shall be eligible to be appointed as a Peacemaker. Members of the Navajo Tribal Council, Chapter governments, Native American Church chapters, medicine men or members of any other organization or group which has the respect of the individuals who will come before the Peacemaker Court may be appointed as Peacemakers.
- *Appointment by Chapter*: Each Chapter may select and certify the names of individuals as proposed Peacemakers to the District Court district in which the Chapter lies. The individuals selected by the Chapters must agree to serve under the direction of the Court. The clerk of the District Court shall maintain a roll of Peacemakers by Chapter, and Peacemakers shall be appointed from that roll. Any Chapter may add or delete names to or from the list from time to time.

- *Action Where No Chapter Appointment*: Where a Chapter fails to certify Peacemakers for the Chapter, the District Court may appoint a Peacemaker from qualified persons known to it or any person recommended as being qualified as a Peacemaker.
- *Agreement as to Peacemaker*: The parties to any dispute may agree to a given individual as a Peacemaker for the resolution of their dispute. In such cases the Peacemaker need not be a member of the Navajo Tribe or be Indian, but such an individual must be agreed to by all the parties to the dispute.

2.2 Powers of the Peacemaker:

Peacemakers are officers of the Navajo Tribal Courts when acting as a Peacemaker and performing the functions of the Peacemaker Court under these rules, and they shall have the privileges and immunities of court officers. Peacemakers shall have the power to:

- Mediate disputes among persons involved in the peacemaking process by attempting to get them to agree as to the nature and effect of the problems affecting them and to agree on what should be done to resolve those problems;
- Use traditional Navajo religious and other ways of mediation and community problem-solving;
- Instruct or lecture individuals on the traditional Navajo teachings relevant to their problem or conduct;
- Compel persons involved in a dispute, affected by it or in any way connected with it to meet to discuss the problem being worked on and to participate in all necessary peacemaking efforts;
- Use any reasonable means to obtain the peaceful, cooperative and voluntary resolution of a dispute subject to peacemaking. No force, violence or the violation of rights secured to individuals by the Navajo Bill of Rights will be permitted.

2.3 Limitations; Peacemakers Not Judges; Agreed Arbitration:

Peacemakers shall only have the authority to use traditional and customary Navajo methods and other accepted nonjudgmental methods to mediate disputes and obtain the resolution of problems through agreement. Peacemakers shall not have the authority to decide a disputed matter unless all parties to the dispute agree to such authority. Parties to a dispute may agree in writing or before the District Court to permit a Peacemaker to arbitrate a dispute by hearing all sides of it and making a decision. Any such decision will have the effect of a court judgment when submitted to the District Court for entry of a written judgment.

2.4 *Duties of Peacemakers*:

Upon notice to an individual of his or her appointment as a Peacemaker for an individual matter, the Peacemaker shall notify the court of any disqualification or inability to serve in the matter or acceptance of the appointment. . . . The Peacemaker will informally contact the parties to the dispute and any other persons involved, advise all interested persons of his authority to compel them to participate in the peacemaking, and make other necessary arrangements to conduct peacemaking sessions. The Peacemaker may conduct a reasonable number of sessions in an attempt to achieve peacemaking, and may conduct peacemaking efforts using procedures and techniques which are accepted in the community. Where the parties involved accept or practice a given religious belief, discipline or following, the accepted methods and teaching of that religious way may be used.

2.5 *Reports to District Court*:

Either at the conclusion of the peacemaking or at such time as the Peacemaker finds there can be no resolution of the matter, the Peacemaker must report the results of his or her efforts to the Court. The report may be informal, and if the Trial judge permits, they may be given orally rather than in writing. The District Judge or (at the direction of the judge) the clerk of Court may make an informal (including handwritten) notation of an oral report in the file of the matter.

3.1 *Request for Peacemaking*:

Any individual may ask the assistance of the Peacemaker Court by filing a written request with the District Court in the district in which the individual resides. The request may be informal and hand-written, and it may be made either on a form provided by the Court or in any way which gives the Court the following information:

- The name and address of the person who requests the use of the Peacemaker Court;
- The names of the persons involved in the dispute and their addresses and Chapters;
- The reason the individual wants to use the Peacemaker Court and a short statement of the problem involved;

- The names and addresses of each person who should be contacted by the Peacemaker and involved in the peacemaking;
- A statement that all individuals involved directly in the dispute are members of the Navajo Tribe or are Indians residing among members of the Navajo Tribe or that non-Indians are involved as parties to the dispute.

3.2 *Who Can Request Peacemaking*:
Only the following persons can request the services of the Peacemaker Court:

- Persons who are injured, hurt or aggrieved by the action of another;
- Chapter officers, either by their own action as officers or upon a resolution of the Chapter, where there is a problem or dispute which affects the people of the Chapter as a whole, which constitutes what would otherwise be a crime which is against public peace or which affects Chapter government;
- Tribal Council Delegates, where the problem or dispute is one as in the above subsection;
- Non-Indian individuals who are injured, hurt or aggrieved by the actions of another if such non-Indians agree to fully participate in and be bound by the Peacemaker process as would any member of the Navajo Tribe. . . .

4.4 *Method of Presenting Proposed Judgment*:
The parties need not be represented by counsel, and the Court may make its written judgment following an informal oral conference with the parties. Where necessary the Court may require a member of its staff to assist the Peacemaker in preparing a proper form of judgment.

4.5 *Form of Judgment*:
All judgments must contain the following information:

- The names and jurisdictional information with regard to each party (i.e., tribal affiliation, residence, consent to jurisdiction);
- A statement of the fact that all necessary parties to the dispute have actual knowledge of it and that they have all agreed to the proposed judgment;
- If the dispute was resolved by the agreement of all the parties that it would be submitted for the Peacemaker's decision, a statement of that fact;

- A statement the judgment is based upon Peacemaker Court proceedings, and the name of the Chapter affiliation of the Peacemaker:
- A general description of the dispute;
- The actual judgment of the District Court.

4.6 Enforcement of Judgment:

A judgment of the District Court upon Peacemaker Court proceedings may be enforced as any other judgment of the District Court may be enforced. . . .

Transfer of cases from District Court to Peacemaker Court:

6.1 General Policy:

Certain civil and criminal actions in District Court may be transferred to the Peacemaker Court where they fall within one of the kinds of matters within the jurisdiction of the Peacemaker Court described in Section 1.4, or where it is in the interests of justice to make such a referral for good cause shown.

(f) *Civil Matters*:

Civil actions falling within the provisions of Section 1.4 may be referred to the Peacemaker Court with the written stipulation of all the parties to the action or for good cause shown to the District Court.

(g) *Criminal Matters*:

Any criminal matter may be transferred to the Peacemaker Court where:

- The case does not involve injury to person or property; or
- Where the victim to the alleged offense consents; or
- Where the offense is a victimless crime; or
- Where there is a finding of guilty and peacemaking would be an appropriate condition of probation for achieving harmony and reconciliation with the victim.

(h) *Criminal Probation*:

The District Court may, as a condition of criminal probation, require the defendant to submit to the Peacemaker Court for traditional and customary counseling, instruction and lectures appropriate to his or her offense. The District Court may require the defendant to pay the fee required of other parties before the Peacemaker Court.[10]

Clearly, the Navajo Peacemaker Court is not as cut-and-dried as one would expect. Its symbiotic entanglement with the Anglo-American–driven district courts obviates a truly stigma-free adjudication process. Interviews with traditional elders, those selected to serve as Peacemakers, indicated to me that the current process is a far cry from the aboriginal process that occurred in a legal vacuum involving only the relevant clans. In the Navajo Nation, a matriarchal society, one's mother's clan is the significant clan (the clan "born to"), and the community is secondary. In aboriginal times, the Navajo (Diné) were a homogeneous society with a single belief system. This is a far cry from the numerous Christian-based religions and the Native American Church, which compete with the traditional Beauty Way spirituality. Obviously, trying to be everything for everyone has greatly compromised the original Peacemaker process. Moreover, during aboriginal times, harmony restoration was a process without a record. It dealt with the here-and-now and was forgotten once harmony was restored. In its current application a record exists, even if it does not lend itself to case law.

Profile of Criminal, Civil, and Juvenile Cases in Navajo Courts

A profile of adjudication within the Navajo Nation is reflected in the following statistical reports from district and family courts.

Criminal cases shown in table 7.1 include those discussed earlier as well as prostitution, fish and wildlife violations, and forests and woodlands violations. Out of the seven districts and three satellite (circuit) courts, Window Rock had the greatest number of criminal cases (4,541), followed by Crownpoint (4,475) and Chinle (4,074). Chinle had the highest number of DWI (driving while intoxicated) cases (1,641), followed by Window Rock (1,400) and Shiprock (954).[11]

TABLE 7.1

**Navajo District Court Criminal Cases
(October 1, 1998, to September 30, 1999)**

	Criminal	DWI
Case load	22,665	6,358
Closed cases	14,629	4,629
Pending	8,026	1,729

TABLE 7.2

Navajo District Court Civil Cases
(October 1, 1998, to September 30, 1999)

	Civil	Civil Traffic
Case load	4,669	32,746
Closed cases	3,630	24,244
Pending	1,039	8,502

TABLE 7.3

Navajo Family Court Children's Cases
(October 1, 1998 to September 30, 1999)

	Delinquency	CHINS	Dependency	Total
Case Load	2,197	768	626	3,591
Closed cases	1,672	642	441	2,755
Pending	525	126	185	836

Civil cases (table 7.2) include: contracts, torts/injuries, land disputes, specific relief, civil rights, prisoners' relief, and other small-claims and miscellaneous categories, while civil traffic cases include the following: general operations offenses, equipment violations, and size/weight/load violations. Window Rock had the most civil cases, with 1,018 (22 percent of total), and 11,722 civil traffic cases (36 percent of total). None of the other six districts courts or three satellite circuit courts came close to these numbers.[12]

In table 7.3, Crownpoint had the greatest number of delinquency cases (478), followed by Chinle (474) and Shiprock (348); Crownpoint also had the highest number of CHINS (children in need of supervision) with 205 cases, followed by Chinle. Shiprock had the most dependency cases (190), followed by Window Rock (153). None of the other district or satellite courts matched these numbers.[13]

Domestic relations cases (table 7.4) include: divorce, order to show cause, probate matters, paternity suits, child support, validation of marriages, change

TABLE 7.4

Navajo Family Court Domestic Relations
(October 1, 1998, to September 30, 1999)

Case load	5,609
Closed cases	4,625
Pending	984

of name, protective orders, quiet title, and a number of other related situations. Window Rock had the greatest number of cases, with 1,204, followed by Chinle with 1,014 cases and Shiprock with 993 cases.[14]

The federal profile on Indian crime, as presented in the U.S. Department of Justice bulletin *American Indians and Crime*, February 1999, provides the following comparisons of crime in Indian country (American Indians in this report include Alaska Natives and Aleuts):

Violent victimizations: American Indians experience per capita rates of violence that are more than twice those of the U.S. resident population.

Murder: The murder rate among American Indians is 7 per 100,000, a rate similar to that found among the general population. The rate of murder among blacks is more than five times that among American Indians.

Age: Rates of violence in every age group are higher among American Indians than those of all races. Nearly a third of all American Indian victims of violence are between ages eighteen and twenty-four. This group of American Indians experienced the highest per capita rate of violence of any racial group considered by age—about one violent crime for every four persons of this age.

Sex: Rates of violent victimization for both males and females are higher among American Indians than for all races. The rate of violent crime experienced by American Indian women is nearly 50 percent higher than that reported by black males.

Offender race: At least 70 percent of the violent victimizations experienced by American Indians are committed by persons not of the same race—a substantially higher rate of interracial violence than that experienced by white or black victims.

Alcohol use by offender: American Indian victims of violence were the most likely of all races of victims to indicate that the offender committed the offense while drinking.

Weapon use by offender: More than 10 percent of American Indian nonlethal violent victimizations involved a firearm. American Indian murder victims were less likely to have been murdered by a handgun than victims of all other races.

Crimes reported to police: American Indian victims of violence reported the crime to the police at about the average rate for all races.

Arrest of adults and youths: American Indian arrest rates for violence among youths were about the same as the rates among white youths in 1996. Violent crime arrest rates for American Indian adults were similar to those for youths. Among other racial groups, arrest rates for adults are lower than for youths.

Arrests for drug and alcohol offenses: The 1997 arrest rate among American Indians for alcohol-related offenses (driving under the influence, liquor law violations, and public drunkenness) was more than double that found among all other races. Drug arrest rates for American Indians were lower than average.

Under correctional supervision or control: An estimated 63,000 American Indians are under the care, custody, or control of the criminal justice system on an average day—about 4 percent of the American Indian population age eighteen or older. On average in 1997, about 2,000 American Indians per 100,000 adults (persons age eighteen or older) were serving a sentence or were on probation, about half the rate found among blacks.

In state or federal prisons: In 1997 about 16,000 American Indians were held in local jails—a rate of 1,083 per 100,000 adults, the highest of any racial group. The rate of American Indians on parole is similar to that of the general population, about 300 per 100,000 adults. On a per capita basis, American Indians had a rate of prison incarceration about 38 percent higher than the national rate.

Federal convictions: American Indians accounted for 1.5 percent of federal case filings in U.S. district courts in 1997, and half of these were for violent offenses. Eight hundred fifty-four American Indians were convicted in federal court—9 percent for murder and 20 percent for rape.[15]

CHAPTER EIGHT

LAW ENFORCEMENT AND CORRECTIONS IN INDIAN COUNTRY

Justice during aboriginal times was often a clan function and was doled out only as needed. Warrior societies were the most likely to be assigned the duties of enforcement. This informal format changed with European contact and the reintroduction of the horse (prehistoric horses were small and unlikely to be used as domesticated animals). The horse and forced migration upset traditional alliances among American Indian groups, causing changes in traditional lifestyles as well. Tribes were more mobile, forcing the warrior societies to adapt their policing techniques. Not only was competition for limited resources intensified, intergroup blood vengeance increased accordingly. The introduction of firearms and European-style mutilation also contributed to changes in the traditional rules of engagement, making it more violent. The constant threat from both Europeans and other tribes increased the need for intragroup controls and a greater need for more policing.

Formal Policing in Indian Country

The Five Civilized Tribes were among the first tribes to modify their police standards by creating a more permanent tribal police force, which superseded the clan/warrior model. The Cherokee adaptation is discussed in chapter 3, including the creation of a mounted tribal police force in 1797 known as "regulating companies." This was the beginning of Euro-American adaptations made in Indian country. The relationship between law enforcement, the courts, and corrections also had a Cherokee link with the establishment of the position of a "national marshal" in the early 1800s prior to removal. The national marshal served as the officer of the court and was responsible for those convicted and sentenced to incarceration. The adapted Euro-American justice system was reintroduced in Indian Territory (Oklahoma) following removal. The seeds for destruction of the Five Civilized Tribes' cultural-centric adaptations to the U.S. justice system were sown during the Indian war–Reconstruction era, which saw a shift to military justice and eventually white-led Indian police forces.

Thomas Lightfoot, the Indian agent for the Iowa, Sac, and Fox tribes in southeastern Nebraska, is credited with the movement to recruit Indians as police in Indian country outside the Five Civilized Tribes in Indian Territory (Oklahoma), doing so in 1869. Three years later, in 1872, as part of the conditions of the Treaty of 1868, the military special Indian commissioner for the Navajos organized a horse cavalry of 130 Navajos to guard the newly drawn up reservation from theft, especially that of livestock. Meanwhile, the Cherokee Nation authorized its National Prison in 1873. It was built in the Cherokee Nation capital square in Tahlequah (Oklahoma) and completed in 1874. The National Prison also served as the national jail and was the only such facility in Indian Territory (Oklahoma) until 1901. Consequently, it was used to hold prisoners throughout Indian Territory. The money used with the sale of the Cherokee outlet was used to build the Indian prison. It had its own scaffold in the backyard used to execute condemned prisoners. The position of high sheriff of the Cherokee Nation was created in 1875; this individual was responsible to the Cherokee National Council. The high sheriff served as warden and treasurer of the National Prison as well as custodian of the other capital buildings in capital square. Principal Chief Charles Thompson appointed Samuel Sixkiller as the high sheriff. He served for four years until he was charged with the murder of Peter Thompson in 1879. Though he was eventually acquitted of the murder, Sixkiller was not able to regain his position as high sheriff.[1]

At about the same time, Indian Agent John Clum was experimenting with his own Indian police force on the San Carlos (Arizona) Apache Reservation. Clum did this in an attempt to wrest civilian control from the military in Indian country. Although not entirely successful, agents Clum and Lightfoot were successful in establishing a parallel Indian police in Indian country. The Apache police also served as scouts when operating with the U.S. Army. Tom Horn, a noted civilian white scout leader, and chief of the Apache scouts, described his Apache police-scouts in their pursuit of Geronimo and his Chiricahua band:

> Captain Crawford was now stationed at San Carlos with his troop of cavalry. I also put in a big portion of my time there. All the Cibicus were as good and quiet as mean Indians could be. The hanging of Dead Shot, Dandy Jim, and Loco has a good effect on them. . . .
>
> Crawford said we looked a good deal more like a band of border outlaws than we did like the military commander of San Carlos and the Chief of Scouts. The only thing military in the whole outfit was our rifles. We all had Springfield rifles, but our clothes and horses and equipments [sic] were of every kind of buckskin to calico shirts, and from corduroy pants to no pants at all. There was not a soldier's uniform in the whole outfit. Crawford and I both had Mexican saddles, as did Micky, but the rest of our escort had no saddles at all.
>
> Usually the Apache just puts a raw-hide or hair rope in a horse's mouth and that is a complete outfit for him. The Apaches said that the Americans were always leaving something in camp; but an Apache never. With an Indian rig [a horse-hair rope], you had all that was needed. When you went into camp, the rope was used to stake out the horse, and when you wanted to move, all you had to do was to tie it around his under jaw and you had a bridle and no traps or parts of your equipment were left in camp.[2]

Two years after the Cherokee initiative, and Clum and Lightfoot's influence, Indian Commissioner Ezra A. Hayt officially petitioned the U.S. Congress for authorization for Indian police on reservations:

> As a means of preserving order upon an Indian reservation, an Indian police has been found to be of prime importance. I have recommended an additional outlay of money to enable the government to extend the usefulness of a police system now in its infancy with us. In Canada, the entire body of Indians are kept in order by such force. In this country, as far as it has been tried, it works admirably. I would recommend that the force be composed of Indians, properly officered and drilled by white men, and where capable Indians can be found, that they be promoted to command, as reward for faithful service. The Army has used Indians for scouts with great success, and wherever employed the Indian has been found faithful to the trust confided to him. I would also recommend that the police force be supplied with

a uniform similar to the style of clothing which I shall hereafter suggest to be furnished for all Indians, with the addition of a few brass buttons by way of distinction. The employment of such a force, properly officered and handled, would, in great measure, relieve the Army from doing police duty on Indian reservations. I am thoroughly satisfied that the saving in life and property by the employment of such a force would be very large, and that it would materially aid in placing the entire Indian population of the country on the road to civilization. . . .[3]

Based on Commissioner Hayt's recommendations, Congress authorized pay for 430 Indian privates and 50 white officers in 1878 and raised this to 800 privates and 100 officers for fiscal 1879. Forty-three men served on the Indian police force in Indian Territory, a division which gave each police officer a 712-square-mile jurisdiction. The Indian police had to work with U.S. deputy marshals and local non-Indian police forces in bringing law to this vast haven for outlaws. The duties of the Indian police included arresting intruders; removing squatters; pursuing cattle, horse, and timber thieves; serving as guards at ration and annuity distributions; protecting buildings and property; serving as truant officers; and looking for bootleggers, disorderly conduct, drunkenness, and other crimes; as well as documenting births and deaths and strangers in Indian country.

Ironically, some of the Indian police were also outlaws or accused of crimes, as was Sixkiller. Bob Dalton, of the infamous Dalton gang, once served as chief of the Osage police in Indian Territory. The lives of Indian police were as colorful as the outlaws they sought. Sixkiller was bushwacked in 1886 by two men as he walked out of a drugstore in Muskogee. Known as a gunfighter, Sixkiller was unarmed at the time, and while his assailants were caught, they were never convicted. Chief Dalton died along with his brothers in the act of bank robbery. And Crowdog served as a captain in the Brulé Indian police under Chief Spotted Tail. Outside of Indian Territory, Indian police were regulated by the Indian agent. Clearly, Indian police were agents of the federal government, and often this was met with resentment, especially among the Plains Indians.

One of the most noted conflicts involved the killing of Sitting Bull on December 15, 1890, on his reservation in North Dakota. On the orders of Indian Agent James McLaughlin the Indian police attempted to arrest Sitting Bull because of their fears about his influence in the Ghost Dance movement. Thirty-nine Indian police and four volunteers went to Sitting Bull's home before dawn and awoke him and placed him under arrest. Soon, over one hundred of his supporters confronted the police, and in the ensuing melee,

Sitting Bull, eight of his supporters, and eight Indian police were killed. And Clum's Chiricahua Indian police were forcefully imprisoned along with the decorated scouts following Geronimo's capture by Tom Horn in 1886. A Presidential Order mandated General Miles to arrest all the remaining Chiricahua Indians on the reservation and to have them all removed to a military prison in Florida. The Chiricahua Apache remained interned in military prisons in Florida, Alabama, and eventually Oklahoma until 1914. They remained imprisoned for a twenty-eight-year period, and children born in captivity were automatically given prisoner status. The conditions of their imprisonment were deplorable, resulting in a death rate twice the national average.[4]

In Indian Territory (Oklahoma) tribal and federal jurisdiction often conflicted, resulting in the disbanding of the Five Civilized Tribes' dual criminal justice system. This included the dual jurisdiction over capital punishment. In June 1897, the U.S. Congress prevented the Cherokee Nation from implementing its equal-but-separate form of justice, stating that effective January 1, 1898, all crimes within Indian Territory (Oklahoma) were to be tried in U.S. federal courts. Since 1875, ten years before enactment of the Major Crimes Act, the Cherokee National Council codified their national laws, which included treason and conspiracy, murder and manslaughter, excusable and justifiable homicide, assault with intent to kill, burglary, robbery and larceny, mayhem, arson, perjury, abortion, poisoning, bribery, embezzlement, forgery and counterfeiting, escape of prisoners, liquor laws, prostitution, gambling, public disturbances, malicious trespassing, false pretense, burning prairie or woods, weights and measures, slander, and libel. The Curtis Act of June 28, 1898, effectively destroyed tribal governments in Indian Territory.[5] Not only was the Cherokee National Council emasculated, the National Prison was forced to close, absolute and unconditional pardons were granted to those incarcerated in the National Prison at this time, and full rights were awarded to all those convicted by the courts of the Cherokee Nation. This pre–Public Law 280 initiative was replayed during the termination era, from 1953 until passage of the Indian Civil Rights Act in 1968.

Elsewhere in Indian country, it was clear that the appointment of Indian police and Indian judges by the Indian agent was a clear attempt to abrogate traditional tribal authority and traditions and to replace these with Euro-American ways. Once Indian Territory was dissolved and the state of Oklahoma created, a renewed focus was placed on enforcing prohibition in Indian country. These special agents were white and had considerable authority within Indian country, thus setting the stage for their replacement in Indian country—the Federal Bureau of Investigation (FBI).

After the turn of the Century, while the Courts of Indian Offenses continued to function under the control of the Indian agents, the primary thrust of law enforcement became liquor suppression. More money was provided for police, but by 1925 appropriations for Indians courts had decreased to $6,500, almost one-half the 1892 level of $12,540. The number of Indian judges declined similarly. Indian courts waned in importance and were little more than tools of the Indian agents who had to approve of all court decisions.[6]

Toward Greater Federal Control over Indian Law Enforcement

The Indian Reorganization Act of 1934 merely reinforced the concept of U.S.-type laws and law enforcement in Indian country while the termination-relocation era of the early 1950s forced state laws and law enforcement upon certain tribes. Often, this was a bad mix, since there appears to have been considerable prejudice among those non-Indians who resided closest to Indian country. These prejudices have extended to courts and law enforcement as well. Both the BIA and FBI resorted to military interventions from the 1970s through the 1990s in Indian country. Wounded Knee II and the Mohawk gambling war quickly reminded tribal leaders that a strong sense of federal paternalism, especially when looking at law enforcement, is still a presence during this current era of self-determination.

More than any other law enforcement force, the FBI is the most contentious element in Indian country today. The animosity between the FBI and traditional Native Americans is best illustrated with the Leonard Peltier conviction in 1977 for the execution-style death of two FBI agents on the Pine Ridge Reservation during the post–Wounded Knee II turmoil played out between the American Indian Movement (AIM) and what many Sioux believed to be an oppressive white-influenced tribal government. AIM came to Pine Ridge in the early 1970s because of concerns over the corrupt government of the tribal chairman, Dick Wilson. Wilson, apparently with the blessings of the BIA and FBI, controlled the Oglala police. They were known as "Wilson's Guardians of the Oglala Nation," also known as Wilson's GOONs. Following a number of murders by the GOONs and no recourse provided by the BIA or FBI, AIM came to Pine Ridge on February 27, 1973, and occupied the town of Wounded Knee—the site of the massacre of Chief Big Foot and his followers by the U.S. Army in December 1890. The following battle of Wounded Knee II is history.

Here, as in the Mohawk war, the BIA and FBI brought in outside forces, including the U.S. Army. In May 1990, bloodshed occurred at the Akwesasne (St. Regis) Mohawk Nation. Located in both Quebec, Canada, and New York State, this incident had an international flavor. Of the twenty-five thousand Mohawk Indians, over eight thousand reside in the United States on six reservations, while the rest reside on reserves in Quebec, Canada, across the St. Lawrence River. While the BIA and FBI have a strong influence on the U.S. Mohawks, New York State also has considerable influence by virtue of its pseudo Public Law 280 status, which extends back to the 1880s. Tribal gaming divided the historically international Mohawk Nation. In July 1989, the FBI and New York state troopers raided the gaming houses in Akwesasne at the request of the antigambling segment of the tribe. A nine-month standoff erupted in violence in May 1990, resulting in the deaths of two Indians. Following the deaths, the New York state troopers and the Royal Canadian Mounted Police entered the Akwesasne on the U.S. and Canadian sides of the reservation. The FBI was interested in this conflict because of the apparent influence of the New York City Gotti Mafia family in the gambling controversy among the Mohawk factions.[7]

Another incident occurred on the eastern band of Cherokee Indians' Qualla boundary in the early 1970s. Like New York, North Carolina served as a quasi–Public Law 280 state, assuming this authority back in 1838 when approximately one thousand Appalachian Cherokees were allowed to stay in the mountains instead of being forcefully removed to Indian Territory. Part of this federal-state-tribal agreement was that they subscribe to North Carolina laws. Following 1885 and passage of the Major Crimes Act, a federal presence was included in this plan. In 1925 they received federal recognition as an Indian reservation, thus bringing the BIA onto the Qualla boundary. Today, the twelve thousand eastern Cherokees continue to have both federal and state jurisdictional influences on the reservation in addition to the tribal government.

This complex jurisdictional issue was challenged in 1975 following the death of three young adult Cherokee males arrested by tribal police on the reservation and then transported to the white-run Jackson County jail twenty-five miles away in Sylva, North Carolina. All three young Cherokee men were found hanged in their cells during a twenty-one-month period, from early 1974 through 1975. No non-Indians suffered a similar fate. Tensions between whites and Indians were high throughout the country at this time, with the wide media coverage of Wounded Knee II and the actions of the American Indian Movement, which had its influence and followers among the eastern Cherokees. Moreover, North Carolina was seen as one of the most conservative and punitive states at this time. It had the distinction of having the largest number of death-qualified prisoners on death row at the time of the 1972 U.S. Supreme Court decision *Furman v. Georgia*, which found the death penalty to be discriminatory as it was then administered. At this time, I was a sociology professor at Western Carolina University (WCU). I also served as the faculty advisor to the Native American Club. The parents of the deceased requested an outside investigation since they did not believe that their sons would commit suicide. All were future oriented, and one had just left the military. The probability of three Cherokee males, arrested and jailed overnight for minor misdemeanors, committing suicide within this short period defied logic. I and members of the WCU Native American Club contacted the American Indian Historical Society, and they, in turn, had the U.S. Civil Rights Commission investigate the deaths of Donald E. Lambert, Johnson L. Littlejohn, and Francis P. Jackson. The case was written up in the American Indian Historical Society's nationwide newspaper, *Wassaja*.

The story that emerged from these inquiries was that the local white jailer killed the Cherokees in retaliation for his teenage son being beaten by a Cherokee girl whom he was harassing at the local bowling alley in Sylva. And while the jailer was not indicted, the system of cross-deputization of Cherokee police and the transportation of Indians arrested on the reservation to the white county jail was seriously faulted. The U.S. Civil Rights Commission notified the local white jailers and sheriffs (the Qualla boundary falls in two North Carolina counties, Jackson and Swain) that this was not to happen again. Moreover, they were to install monitors in each cell. The Cherokee police now became a more autonomous force, with the chief holding the status of a federal deputy marshal. The Cherokee police are now deputy special officers. However, despite a new courthouse and police station, the eastern band still does not have its own jail. In the past, the cross-deputized Cherokee police were compelled to transport their clients to the county jails. Now they are reluctant to do so. The FBI transports Major Crimes Act violators seventy miles to Asheville where the federal court and magistrate reside.[8]

The BIA police training intensified following the 1968 Indian Civil Rights Act. The first BIA Indian Police Academy (IPA) was established in Roswell, New Mexico, in 1969. Jim Hornbuckle, co-author of *The Cherokee Perspective* and once a Cherokee law enforcement officer, was one of its first graduates. The academy moved to Brigham City, Utah, and was located there from 1973 until 1984. It then moved to Marana, Arizona, and operated there from 1985 until 1992, when it moved to its present location at the Federal Law Enforcement Training Center in Artesia, New Mexico.

The current BIA police training is based on the 1990 Indian Law Enforcement Reform Act (Public Law 101-379). The makeup of the BIA police is stipulated under Indian law enforcement responsibilities:

Division of Law Enforcement Services: Establishment and Responsibilities:

There is hereby established within the Bureau of Law Enforcement Services which under the supervision of the Secretary, or an individual designated by the Secretary, shall be responsible for:

- carrying out the law enforcement functions of the Secretary in Indian country; and
- implementing the provisions of this section.

Additional Responsibilities of Division:

Subject to the provisions of this chapter and other applicable Federal or tribal laws, the responsibilities of the Division of Law Enforcement Services in Indian country shall include:

- the enforcement of Federal law and the consent of the Indian tribe- tribal law;
- in cooperation with appropriate Federal and tribal law enforcement agencies, the investigation of offenses against criminal laws of the United States;
- the protection of life and property;
- the development of methods and expertise to resolve conflicts and solve crimes;
- the provision of criminal justice remedial actions, correctional and detention services, and rehabilitation;
- the reduction of recidivism and adverse social effects;
- the development of preventive and outreach programs which will enhance the public conception of law enforcement responsibilities through training and development of needed public services skills;
- the assessment and evaluation of program accomplishments in reducing crime; and
- the development and provisions of law enforcement training and technical assistance.

Branch of Criminal Investigations: Establishment, Responsibilities, Regulations, Personnel, etc.:

- The Secretary shall establish within the Division of Law Enforcement Services a separate Branch of Criminal Investigations which, under such inter-agency agreement as may be reached between the Secretary and appropriate agencies or officials of the Department of Justice and subject to such guidelines as may be adopted by relevant United States attorneys, shall be responsible for the investigation, and presentation for prosecution, of cases involving violations of sections 1152 and 1153 of Title 18, within Indian country.

- The Branch of Criminal Investigations shall not be primarily responsible for the routine law enforcement and police operations of the Bureau in Indian country.

- The Secretary shall prescribe regulations which shall establish a procedure for active cooperation and consultation of the criminal investigative employees of the Bureau assigned to an Indian reservation with the governmental and law enforcement officials of the Indian tribe located on such reservation.

- Criminal investigative personnel of the Branch shall be subject only to the supervision and direction of law enforcement personnel of the Branch or of the Division. Such personnel shall not be subject to the supervision of the Bureau of Indian Affairs Agency Superintendent or Bureau of Indian Affairs Area Office Director. Nothing in this paragraph is intended to prohibit cooperation, coordination, or consultation, as appropriate, with nonlaw enforcement Bureau of Indian Affairs personnel at the agency or area levels, or prohibit or restrict the right of a tribe to contract the investigative program under the authority of Public Law 93-638 or to maintain its own criminal investigative operations.

- At the end of one year following the date of establishment of the separate Branch of Criminal Investigation, any tribe may, by resolution of the governing body of the tribe, request the Secretary to reestablish line authority through the Agency Superintendent or Bureau of Indian Affairs Area Office Director. In the absence of good cause to the contrary, the Secretary, upon receipt of such resolution, shall reestablish the line authority as requested by the tribe.

Division of Law Enforcement Services Personnel; Education, Experience, etc.; Classification of Positions:

- The Secretary shall establish appropriate standards of education, experience, training, and other relevant qualifications for law enforcement personnel of the Division of Law Enforcement Services who are charged with law enforcement responsibilities pursuant to section 2803 of this title.

- The Secretary shall also provide for the classification of such positions within the Division of Law Enforcement Services at GS grades, as provided in section 5104 of Title 5, consistent with the responsibilities and duties assigned to such positions and with the qualifications established for such positions.
- In classifying positions in the Division of Law Enforcement Services under paragraph (2), the Secretary shall ensure that such positions are classified at GS grades comparable to those for other Federal law enforcement personnel in other Federal Agencies in light of the responsibilities, duties, and qualifications required of such positions.

Law Enforcement Authority:

The Secretary may charge employees of the Bureau with law enforcement responsibilities and may authorize those employees to:

- carry firearms;
- execute or serve warrants, summonses, or other orders relating to a crime committed in Indian country and issued under the laws of (A) the United States (including those issued by a Court of Indian Offenses under regulations prescribed by the Secretary), or (B) an Indian tribe if authorized by the Indian tribe.
- make an arrest without a warrant for an offense committed in Indian country if (A) the offense is committed in the presence of the employee, or (B) the offense is a felony and the employee has reasonable grounds to believe that the person to be arrested has committed, or is committing, the felony;
- offer and pay a reward for services or information, or purchase evidence, assisting in the detection or investigation of the commission of an offense committed in Indian country or in the arrest of an offender against the United States;
- make inquiries of any person, and administer to, or take from, any person an oath, affirmation, or affidavit, concerning any matter relevant to the enforcement or carrying out in Indian country of a law of either the United States or an Indian tribe that has authorized the employee to enforce or carry out tribal laws;
- wear a prescribed uniform and badge or carry prescribed credentials;
- perform any other law enforcement related duties; and
- when requested, assist (with or without reimbursement) any Federal, tribal, State, or local law enforcement agency in the enforcement or carrying out of the laws or regulations the agency enforces or administers.

Assistance by Other Agencies:

The Secretary may enter into an agreement for the use (with or without reimbursement) of the personnel or facilities of a Federal, tribal, State or other government agency to aid in the enforcement or carrying out in Indian country of a law of either the United States or an Indian tribe that has authorized the Secretary to enforce tribal laws. The Secretary may authorize a law enforcement officer of such an agency to perform any activity the Secretary may authorize under section 2803 of this title.

- Any agreement entered into under this section relating to the enforcement of the criminal laws of the United States shall be in accord with any agreement between the Secretary and the Attorney General of the United States.
- The Secretary may not use the personnel of a non-Federal agency under this section in an area of Indian country if the Indian tribe having jurisdiction over such area of Indian country has adopted a resolution objecting to the use of the personnel of such agency. The Secretary shall consult with Indian tribes before entering into any agreement under subsection (a) of this section with a non-Federal agency that will provide personnel for use in any area under the jurisdiction of such Indian tribes.

Reports to Tribes:

- In any case in which law enforcement officials of the Bureau or the Federal Bureau of Investigation decline to initiate an investigation of a reported violation of Federal law in Indian country, or terminate such an investigation without referral for prosecution, such officials are authorized to submit a report to the appropriate governmental and law enforcement officials of the Indian tribe involved that states, with particularity, the reason or reasons why the investigation was declined or terminated.
- In any case in which a United States attorney declines to prosecute an alleged violation of Federal criminal law in Indian country referred for prosecution by the Federal Bureau of Investigation or the Bureau, or moves to terminate a prosecution of such an alleged violation, the United States attorney is authorized to submit a report to the appropriate governmental and law enforcement officials of the Indian tribe involved that states, with particularity, the reason or reasons why the prosecution was declined or terminated.[9]

The BIA Office of Law Enforcement Services (OLES) is located within the Office of the Commissioner of Indian Affairs and is under the authority of the deputy commissioner of Indian affairs within the U.S. Department of the Interior. The director operates under the authority of Public Law 101-379 and has the Criminal Investigation Division, the Drug Enforcement Division, the Internal Affairs Division, the Police and Detention Division, the Special Investigations Divisions, and the Training Division (Indian Police Academy). (The Criminal Investigations Division was articulated under the provisions of Public Law 101-379.) The Internal Affairs Division is the quality assurance arm of the BIA police investigating allegations of misfeasance, malfeasance, and nonfeasance by BIA law enforcement personnel. The Drug Enforcement Division promotes project DARE (Drug Awareness Resistance Education) and similar programs in Indian schools. It also is responsible for the eradication of marijuana cultivation and the interdiction and control of illegal drug trafficking within Indian country. The division now also complies with the dictates of the Violent Crime Control and Law Enforcement Act of 1994. The Police and Detention Division is responsible for all BIA law enforcement and detention program evaluations and reviews and provides technical assistance in Indian country. It is also responsible for developing liaisons with other federal, state, and local law enforcement agencies. This division operates within the authority of Public Law 101–379 and the subsequent rules specifying both adult and juvenile detention in Indian country. This mandate extends to the sixty-nine Indian country detention programs and facilities. The Special Investigations Division provides services to BIA and other police relevant to special investigations, like child abuse articulated by Public Law 101-630, the Indian Child Protection and Family Violence Prevention Act.[10] Lastly, the Training Division refers to the Indian Police Academy.

Today, the Indian Police Academy (IPA) falls under the authority of the director of the Federal Law Enforcement Training Center (FLETC). W. Ralph Basham is the current director, having been appointed on February 15, 1998. The FLETC serves seventy Federal agencies, providing training to state, local, and international police much like the FBI Academy. The FLETC serves the majority of federal officers and agents (FBI excluded). It graduates some twenty-three thousand students annually and is the largest law enforcement training facility in the United States. FLETC has its central training headquarters near Brunswick, Georgia, and has an annual budget of over $100 million. The Indian Police Academy (IPA) in Artesia, New Mexico, is a satellite training center of FLETC. The FLETC most current statistics, those for fiscal 1999, indicate that 3,758 individuals graduated from the Indian Police Academy in Artesia, New Mexico, or about 7 percent of the 25,168 officers trained by FLETC for that year.

The Bureau of Indian Affairs, Office of Law Enforcement Services, operates in five districts: District I, Aberdeen, South Dakota; District II, Muskogee, Oklahoma; District III, Phoenix, Arizona; District IV, Albuquerque, New Mexico; and District V, Billings, Montana. The minimum qualifications for BIA law enforcement officers are:

be a U.S. citizen between ages twenty-one and thirty-seven;
have a high school diploma or equivalent;
pass a written examination;
pass a medical examination;
pass a background investigation;
successfully complete a rigorous basic police training course;
possess a valid state driver's license;
be in excellent physical condition.

Indian preference is another consideration for employment as a BIA law enforcement officer.

The Indian Police Academy offers a fourteen-week Basic Police Training Program as well as four weeks of Basic Detention Training; one week of Basic Radio Dispatcher Training; ten weeks of Basic Criminal Investigator Training; one week of Criminal Investigation and Police Officer In-service Training; one week of Chiefs of Police In-service Training as well as Outreach Training (Indian country criminal jurisdiction; community policing, gangs, and domestic violence; use of force; patrol tactics and procedures; investigative techniques; and range officer safety and survival); and multiple advanced training programs. A twelve-week training program at the FBI National Academy is also available, as is one week of training at the Law Enforcement Executive Command College. The U.S. Attorney's Office and the Office of Victims of Crime (OVC) also provide five one-week Regional Training Conferences yearly. Graduation data indicate that 33 percent of the officers trained at the IPA come from the Great Plains; 31 percent from the Southwest; 20 percent from the Northeast; 7 percent from Oklahoma tribes; and 6 percent from the southeastern tribes.

The fourteen-week Basic Police Officer Training Program curriculum consists of: report writing; communications; interpersonal skills; interviewing; ethics; stress management; gangs, and so on.

The latest (1995) BIA Annual Law Enforcement Program Report indicates the incident of Major Crimes in Indian country[11]:

Major Crime Offense	Total Number of Actual Offenses
Homicide	
Murder and non-negligent manslaughter:	146
Manslaughter by negligence:	48
Forcible Rape	
Rape by force:	346
Attempts to commit forcible rape:	292
Robbery	
Firearm:	43
Knife or cutting instrument:	16
Strong arm:	38
Other dangerous weapons:	11
Aggravated Assault	
Firearm:	507
Knife or cutting instrument:	308
Other dangerous weapons	503
Hands, fists, feet, etc.:	2,036
Burglary	
Forcible entry:	3,518
Unlawful entry, no force:	447
Attempted forcible entry:	204
Larceny-Theft	
(except motor vehicle)	5,193
Motor Vehicle Theft	
Autos:	721
Trucks and buses:	303
Other vehicles:	293
Arson	
Structural:	129
Mobile:	69
Other:	156
Total	**15,327**

Offenses Other Than Part One—Major Crimes:

Offense	Total Number of Actual Offenses
Assaults (no weapons used):	13,063
Forgery/counterfeiting:	310
Fraud:	588
Embezzlement:	95
Stolen property (buying, receiving, possessing):	2,275
Vandalism:	10,241
Weapons:	1,904
Prostitution/commercial vice:	9
Sex offenses:	1,334
Drug abuse violations (sell/manufacture):	957
Possession:	1,524
Gambling:	1,697
DWI:	12,064
Liquor laws:	6,430
Drunkeness	42,151
Disorderly conduct:	13,813
ARPA violations:	112
All other offenses:	33,637
Suspicion:	9,637
Curfews & loitering (under age 18)	3,206
Runaways (under age 18):	1,901
Part II Totals	**156,948**

In 1993, the National Native American Law Enforcement Association (NNALEA) was formed. It includes federal, state, county, local, and tribal police agencies. The objectives of NNALEA are: (1) to provide for the exchange of ideas and new techniques used by criminal investigators; (2) to conduct training seminars, conferences, and research into educational methods for the benefit of American Indians in the law enforcement profession; (3) to keep the membership and public informed of current statute changes and judicial decisions as they relate to the law enforcement community; (4) to establish a network and directory consisting of Native American enforcement officers, agents, and employees; (5) to provide technical and/or investigative assistance to association members within the various aspects of law enforcement investigations; (6) to promote a positive attitude toward law enforcement in the American Indian community and other communities; and (7) to provide a support group for Native American officers, agents, and employees through a national organization.

A profile of the Navajo police indicates that a police force was established in 1872, once the Navajos returned from their forceful removal by the U.S. Army (Long Walk) to New Mexico. Apparently this effort was short lived, and policing was conducted by the U.S. Army and later the BIA. The current police system emerged in 1958. The police fall under the Division of Public Safety and operate in the seven judicial districts. A captain heads each district. The head of the Navajo Nation police holds the rank of chief and is in charge of the three law enforcement components—Criminal Investigation, Patrol, and Corrections. The head of each of these components also holds the title of chief. Within the districts there are lieutenants, sergeants, and patrol officers. The Navajo police are responsible for a vast region the size of New Jersey and need to know the laws of the three states, Arizona, New Mexico, and Utah, in which the 25,000 square mile reservation lies. They also need to know the laws of the nine counties where the Navajo Nation intersects these states.

Perhaps more than anyone, Tony Hillerman, the author of the popular Sergeant Jim Chee and Lieutenant Joe Leaphorn series, has drawn attention not only to the Navajo culture but to Indian police as well. In *Hunting Badger*, Hillerman focused on the 1998 manhunt for three survivalists who killed a police officer in Cortez, Colorado, and then vanished into the vast wilderness along the Utah-Arizona border. This joint police effort illustrated the lack of coordination often observed among federal, state, local, and tribal police. Hillerman quoted the then Chief of Navajo Tribal Police Leonard Butler as saying that the search became a circus, with search parties tracking each other. They were unable to communicate due to mismatched radio frequencies. And local and tribal police, those who knew the area best, were relegated to man roadblocks, while the FBI flaunted its ultimate authority in coordinating the search.[12]

Politics has been a factor in Indian police since the days of Spotted Tail and continues today. When writing his book in July 1999, Hillerman spoke highly of Chief Butler, and to his credit the first female chief was assigned to head the Navajo Department of Criminal Investigations—Dorothy Lameman Fulton. Recently, Butler fell out of favor with tribal leaders and was fired. His replacement at the time of this writing (December 2000) is Chief Fulton, now the first female chief of the Navajo Tribal Police.

Nonetheless, tribal policing is a dangerous job. Kevin Gover, head of the BIA under the Clinton administration, told Congress that people living on Indian reservations fear for their safety and that of their families. While violent crime has been on the decline nationally in the United States, it has been on the increase in Indian country. Claiborne noted, in his 1998 article in the *Washington Post*, that the homicide rate in Indian country rose 87 percent from 1992 to 1996, while dropping 22 percent nationwide during this same time frame. At the same time, Indian police services have also declined due to relentless budget cuts by Congress. Using the FBI's *Uniform Crime Reports*, he noted that there are 2.9 police officers per 1,000 citizens in non-Indian communities with populations of less than 10,000 but only 1.3 officers per 1,000 citizens in Indian country.[13] In an article in the *Albuquerque Journal*, December 1999, Matt Kelley reported on the tribal police shortages by focusing on the death of a White Mountain Apache Indian police officer, Tenny Gatewood. Gatewood was the only officer on duty on the Fort Apache Indian reservation, a 1.6 million acre mountainous region larger than Delaware. Quoting Ted Quasula, head of law enforcement for the BIA, he noted that one-person shifts and lonely patrols, hours from any backup, are the norm in policing Indian country. This has led to seventeen Indian police being killed in the line of duty during the 1990s alone.[14]

Miriam Jorgensen and Stewart Wakeling, writing on Indian police for the John F. Kennedy School of Government at Harvard University, noted that the BIA police have an image problem, given that not so long ago their mandate was to keep tribal members confined to the reservation, to forcibly remove children from their homes and place them in boarding schools, to ration food, and to support the policies of resident agents of the U.S. government. Essentially, Indian police, to many residents of Indian country, convey the image of an occupying army. Jorgensen and Wakeling call for more financial support and greater cultural autonomy for Indian police, something not likely while they are under the strict control of the BIA.[15]

The issue of Indian-run jails and prisons is another area of neglect. It is estimated that there are seventy-three jails serving 57 of the 224 reservations under BIA influence. Ten of these are for juveniles only while the remaining thirty-six facilities' beds are dedicated to juveniles. Like the situation among the eastern band of Cherokee Indians, this is a critical justice issue in Indian country. Following Wounded Knee II, the Native American Rights Fund (NARF) was instrumental in attempting to get a regional Indian prison for the Plains Indians. This followed the model of the Cherokee National Prison, which closed at the turn of the twentieth century. This prison was to occupy an abandoned Jobs Corp facility on the Cheyenne River Reservation in the lower-middle portion of South Dakota. It was designed to serve American Indians from five northern Plains states: South Dakota, North Dakota, Nebraska, Minnesota, and Montana as well as Indian inmates from the Federal Bureau of Prisons. The rehabilitative concept of the Swift Bird Correctional Facility was to provide individualized cultural reprogramming for short-term Indian clients convicted and sentenced in either federal court and/or in the courts of the participating states. The facility was to open late in 1979, but the states involved were reluctant to surrender their control over their Indian prisoners so the plan was never fully realized.[16] Clearly, law enforcement and corrections remain critical issues within Indian country.

THE ISSUE OF SOCIAL JUSTICE IN INDIAN COUNTRY

Over five hundred years of Indian-white contact has resulted only in a continued battle over cultural differences. The dominant U.S. society continues to impose its ethnocentrism in Indian country. And while the theme of the twentieth century was one of token recognition of elements of Native American cultures, strong economic ties, those guaranteed in treaties, are linked with compliance to dominant societal standards, especially in the area of criminal justice.

The twentieth century saw some efforts on the part of the U.S. government to acknowledge the blatant exploitation of Native Americans and American Indian culture. Part one ended with Kevin Gover's apology for the Bureau of Indian Affairs' legacy of racism and inhumanity toward the group of people it was to protect. But Gover's tenure as head of the BIA ended when the George W. Bush administration came to power. And if history is an accurate predictor of future actions, then problems in Indian country are likely to continue, given that this has been the most consistent theme emerging from Republican administrations. Indeed, one of the first acts during these new elections was for the Washington State Republican Party to call for the elimination of American Indian tribal governments.[1] John Fleming, the main sponsor of the GOP resolution, related to the *Spokane Spokesman-Review* that if the tribes resisted, then the U.S. military would enforce it. Leaders in Indian country know all too well that the U.S. military, especially the U.S. Army, would be a willing accomplice in these endeavors, given their sordid past regarding eliminating, removing, and controlling American Indian groups. Forced removal to Indian Territory and unprovoked massacres by the U.S. Army in 1864, Sand Creek, and in 1890, Wounded Knee, as well as their ready intervention in the 1973 Wounded Knee II uprising are but a few of the examples of the U.S. Army's other My Lai's.

Colonel John M. Chivington, the "Fighting Parson" of Civil War fame, wanted to get elected to the U.S. Congress and knew that Americans rewarded its war heroes and Indian fighters. With this in mind, on November 29, 1864, with a force of a thousand soldiers, he attacked the peaceful Cheyenne and Arapaho camped along Sand Creek. The soldiers killed more than one hundred fifty Indians, mostly women, children, and elderly men. Chivington's response was: "I have come to kill Indians, and I believe it is right and honorable to use any means under God's heaven to kill Indians."[2] This began twelve years of continued war against these Plains Indians and greatly influenced the treaty violations and attacks on Indians that led to Lieutenant Colonel Custer's demise at the Little Big Horn in 1776 and the last retaliatory U.S. Army massacre, which took place at Wounded Knee on December 29, 1890.

Again, religious and cultural intolerance played a role in the Wounded Knee massacre. During those desperate times, a Paiute medicine man, Wovoka (also known as Jack Wilson), had a vision that portended a return of the buffalo, dead Indian ancestors, and the old ways. His vision prompted a new religious fervor among the Plains Indians and what became known as the Ghost Dance. They believed that by wearing a special ribbon-shirt they would be protected from harm by the U.S. Army. This anti-Christian movement led to a renewed, unwarranted fear of the Plains Indians. These fears led to plans to neutralize Sitting Bull, a strong proponent of the Ghost Dance movement and to his eventual assassination on December 15, 1890. Fearing for their lives, a number of his followers went to Big Foot's camp and were among those executed by Colonel James Forsyth's troops on December 29, 1890. Here, the U.S. Cavalry and Light Battery E of the First Artillery, a combined force of 487 men, attacked the unarmed and weary Sioux at Wounded Knee, South Dakota, with rifles, carbines, and four rapid-fire Hotchkiss mountain cannons, killing over two hundred fifty Indian women, children, and men. Despite tactical errors, including placing the army in such a fashion that they were wounding each other with friendly fire, Colonel Forsyth not only survived charges of incompetence filed against him by General Miles, but twenty Congressional Medals of Honor were awarded to army personnel for their involvement in this massacre. This despite Miles's assessment of the massacre:

> Wholesale massacre occurred and I have never heard of a more brutal, cold-blooded massacre than that at Wounded Knee. About two hundred women and children were killed and wounded; women with little children on their backs, and small children powder burned by the men who killed them being so near as to burn the flesh and clothing with the powder of their guns, and nursing babes with five bullet holes through them. . . . Colonel Forsyth is responsible for allowing the command to remain where it was stationed after he assumed command, and in allowing his troops to be in such a position that the line of fire of every troop was in direct line of their own comrades or their camp.[3]

Neither the U.S. government nor the U.S. Army has ever apologized for these actions. They have never said that they were wrong or that they are sorry. Indeed, the sentiment in the West, the home of these massacres, was clearly stated in 1977 by the Western Conference of The Council of State Governments:

Resolution of the American Indian Policy Review Commission

> Whereas, the American Indian Policy Review Commission has recently completed its report to Congress; and
> Whereas, the Commission report has assumed as first principles that all policy and legal issues in favor of the Indians; and
> Whereas, the Western Conference of The Council of State Governments believes that the Commission report fails to recognize the following facts:
>
> 1. That the Constitution of the United States provides for only two sovereign powers—the United States and the several states within their spheres of influence.
> 2. Indian tribes are political subdivisions of the United States and are not sovereign in their own sphere.
> 3. Powers not specifically denied by treaty are not reserved to the tribes.
> 4. The intent of the Federal Congress in establishing Indian self-government was purposive in nature, to maintain tribal integrity and identity. Therefore, Congress did not intend Indian government to be general or territorial in nature.

5. There is no legal doctrine whereby one entering the land of another consents to [the] general lawmaking and enforcing authority of the landowner.

6. The Commission Report fails to recognize that Indian tribes are no longer isolated communities; and

Whereas, the granting of sovereignty to Indian tribes and the necessary inclusion of non-Indians under their jurisdiction will destroy the ability of Indian peoples to make their own laws and be governed by them.

Therefore, be it resolved, by the Western Conference of The Council of State Governments, that it agrees with the Minority Report of Congressman Lloyd Meeds, Vice Chairman of the American Indian Policy Review Commission, that Americans are justified in believing that 400 years have been sufficient to quiet title to the continent; and

Be it further resolved that the Western Conference also agrees with the following recommendations and opinions of the Minority Report:

1. That Congress should enact comprehensive legislation defining the scope and nature of tribal self-government, making clear that tribal governmental powers are limited.

2. Legislation should be enacted directly prohibiting Indian courts from exercising criminal jurisdiction or civil jurisdiction over any non-Indian or Indian who is not a member of the tribe which operated the court.

3. Congress should enact legislation allowing civil jurisdiction in state courts against Indian defendants in all cases where states would have jurisdiction were it not for the Indian status of the defendant, and tribal government does not provide a judicial forum. Tribal interests could be protected by providing that rules of decision must be given appropriate weight in state court.

4. Congress should bar actions by Indians against non-Indians for claims arising on reservations where tribes have not provided forums for similar actions by non-Indians against Indians.

5. Congress should enact legislation confirming that states have the same power to levy taxes, the legal incidence of which falls upon non-Indian activities or property, on Indian reservations as they have off Indian reservations. The exemptions to this blanket state authority should come in instances where federal regulation of special subject matter would preempt state regulation.

6. Congress should expressly proscribe the authorization for tribal taxation of nonmembers or property of nonmembers.

7. With regard to the Indian Civil Rights Act of 1968, if Indian governments are to exercise governmental powers as licensees of the United States, it is imperative that they be fully answerable for the improper exercise of those powers.

8. To the extent that chosen national Indian policy entails financial burdens on persons other than Indians, it is neither fair nor rational for those burdens to be cast disproportionately on the taxpayers of the states in which Indian reservations are situated.

9. Congress should undertake to define "Indian Country" for the various purposes for which the term is used.

10. In regard to the operation of Public Law 280, if withdrawal from state jurisdiction is to be done on grounds of federal policy, the policy choices should be made by Congress, which can weight fairly the cost of balkanizing state jurisdictions as well as the advantages to Indians.

11. In the absence of ultimate authority over Indian land use planning lying with federal officials, the fairest system would be to place final authority in state planning agencies in which Indians would participate equally with other affected citizens;

and

Be it further resolved, that copies of this resolution be delivered to the President of the United States, the President Pro Tempore of the United States Senate, the Speaker of the United States House of Representatives, the Secretaries of Agriculture and the Interior and the Congressional Delegation of each of the member states of the Western Conference of the Council of State Governments and each of the six easterly adjoining states.

As Approved by the Western Conference of The Council of State Governments, September 28, 1977.[4]

This reaction to the comprehensive works of the American Indian Policy Review Commission and its many noted Indian leaders, including Reuben Snake, clearly indicates the ongoing stand of the western governors; that any action against the Indians is justified under the superior rights afforded white Christians under the God-given mandate of Manifest Destiny.

These western sentiments were made prior to the acceptance of Indian gaming and the battle over oil, gas, and water rights in Indian country. The long-term leasing of tribal lands by the BIA and U.S. Department of the Interior to ranchers and farmers, many of whom are anti-Indian and bigoted, is but one example of the cooperation between whites and the government at the expense of the Indians, whom the U.S. government is charged with protecting. These twenty-five-year leases often are contracted without the knowledge or consent of the tribes. The Sioux in the Dakotas and Nebraska have been threatened by armed white ranchers and farmers for trespassing on their leases within Indian country. These battles continue to be fought today, with fierce battle lines being drawn over the West's biggest problems—water rights and the need for increased electrical power. Both of these issues deeply involve Indian country and the continued exploitation of natural resources found on the reservations and supposedly protected by the U.S. government in the interest of the tribes.

The concept of Manifest Destiny, as it is presented in the Anglo-dominated American culture, is a perverted version of the Protestant ethic and the spirit of capitalism. Here, any form of deceit or misjustice is justified under the moral imperative of Manifest Destiny—or the right of whites over American Indians. This theme has been played out throughout U.S.-Indian contact. One aspect of this theme is to divide the tribe(s) and then find an Indian leader who can be swayed to do the government's bidding in Indian country relevant to the exploitation of natural resources held in government trust or otherwise protected by treaty. Spotted Tail was one such leader. Peter Mac-Donald was another.

Following the devastating Long March, when the Navajo were forcefully removed from their traditional lands, and the eventual return of the Navajo to a much smaller reservation in the mid-1860s, efforts were made to keep the Navajo from forming a unifying tribal organization. Toward this end, the reservation was divided into separate Indian agencies in 1910, which eventually resulted in six distinct jurisdictions, including the Hopi Pueblo tribe, which also had its lands greatly reduced by the U.S. government. A few years later, oil was discovered on the Navajo Reservation, and thus began the eighty-year exploitation of both the Navajo and Hopi relevant to valuable resources, including oil, gas, coal, uranium, and water. Another resource exploited was the health of these Native Americans as well. This exploitation became easier once the Navajo were allowed to form a unified government under the Indian Reorganization Act of the early 1930s.

Peter MacDonald, a college-educated Navajo, was appointed to head the Office of Navajo Economic Opportunity in 1963 and was quickly groomed by the BIA to aid in the exploitation of mineral riches on the Navajo Reservation. Elected chairman of the Navajo Tribal Council in 1970, MacDonald was instrumental in allowing the U.S. government to approve Peabody Coal's exploitation of coal in Indian country on both the greater Navajo Nation and on the smaller Hopi Pueblo enclosed by the Navajo Reservation. This latter point led to the still contentious issue of the 1974 Navajo-Hopi land partitioning law and the eventual removal of Navajos from Hopi-partitioned lands onto newly acquired lands per the Navajo-Hopi Land Settlement Act of 1996. This Navajo-Hopi land dispute and its eventual settlement also spelled the fall of Chairman MacDonald.

A brief chronology of these events since MacDonald's rise to tribal chairman in 1970 is as follows. In 1970, Peabody Coal started supplying fuel to the Mohave Generating Station in Nevada by the first slurry pipeline. This secret deal, made with the approval of the BIA and the U.S. Department of Interior, involved using over a billion gallons of Indian-righted water per year in order to transport the slurry through its 275-mile pipeline. The electricity produced was for big urban areas such as Los Angeles, Las Vegas, Phoenix, and Tucson. (Less than half of the Navajo and Hopi used electricity at this time.) Then, in 1974, the U.S. Congress passed the Hopi Land Settlement Act (Navajo Relocation Act), which was designed to forcibly remove some twelve thousand Navajos from lands Peabody Coal wished to strip mine in order to continue to supply the big cities of the western United States. The head of the BIA at the time of this action, Assistant Secretary of the Interior Harrison Loesch, the person most responsible for this removal act, soon left the U.S. government to become vice president of Peabody Coal.

In 1975, energy-resource tribes formed a coalition, the Council of Energy Resource Tribes (CERT), in an effort to gain better control over their resources. By 1993, CERT more than doubled its membership to fifty-three tribes. Bad deals made by the U.S. government, which tended to benefit big business at the expense of the tribes, was one of the organization's major concerns. On July 16, 1979, although not widely publicized, the largest nuclear accident in the United States occurred at the United Nuclear Company plant located on the Navajo Nation in Church Rock, New Mexico. Over eleven hundred tons of uranium waste contaminated some 100 million gallons of water that ran into the Rio Puerco alluvium, killing livestock and sickening those who used this water. When tested, the water showed six thousand times the allowable level of radioactivity. This was in addition to the poor working conditions the United States allowed when employing the Navajo to mine uranium found on the reservation, uranium that was commandeered by the government.

Seen as a reasonable solution to the Hopi-Navajo land dispute created by U.S. treaties, the U.S. government purchased off-reservation ranches that were contaminated from the Rio Puerco to house the thousands of Navajos being forcibly removed from the Black Mesa area so that Peabody Coal could continue its strip-mining project. Not to be outdone, MacDonald got the Navajo Nation to buy the 491,000-acre Big Boquillas Ranch near Seligman, Arizona, for $33.6 million. In this deal, designed to fleece the tribe and the

U.S. government, two real estate agents bought the ranch first for $26.2 million and then sold it the same day to the tribe for the $33.6 million. Apparently, Peter MacDonald, his son, and a few friends also benefited from this deal. Ostensibly, the U.S. government had tired of MacDonald by this time and granted the white real estate agents immunity from prosecution if they turned state's evidence against MacDonald. Not only were the white real estates agents not prosecuted, but they were allowed to retain their ill-gained $4 million profit from this corrupt deal. Under indictment, MacDonald was removed as tribal chairman with pay.

The situation intensified on July 20, 1989, when a group of two hundred of MacDonald's followers, known as "Peter's Patrol," stormed tribal headquarters in Window Rock in an attempt to overthrow the tribal government. The tribal police fired on the group, killing two of MacDonald's patrol members. Thirty-two of Peter's Patrol were indicted, and this incident was added to the list of charges against MacDonald. MacDonald and six of his patrol received prison sentences. One of the patrol members was Donald Benally, a former tribal councilman from Shiprock and New Mexico county commissioner from San Juan County.

The next year, following years of effort by Stewart Udall, former secretary of the interior, the U.S. Congress passed a compensation bill for Navajo uranium miners. But under the unrealistic conditions of proof demanded by Congress, less than a third of the families affected received any benefits. In 1993, MacDonald was sentenced to fourteen years in federal prison in Pennsylvania. On April 25, 1995, the Navajo Nation Council (the old Navajo Trial Council) granted Peter MacDonald a tribal pardon. It was signed by Navajo President Albert Hale, who also had to resign due to his own personal scandal. In 1999, the U.S. government was still trying to evict the Navajos living on Hopi-partitioned land. On June 21, 1999, the Navajo Nation filed a lawsuit against Peabody Western Coal Company and its utility customers, Southern California Edison Company and the Salt River Project, for over $1.5 billion.[5] On January 20, 2001, on his last day in office, President Clinton granted 140 pardons, one of which was for Peter MacDonald. This news was well received within the Navajo Nation in that it now allowed the tribe to again reach harmony—a critical component of the Diné's harmony ethos. Not pardoned, however, was Leonard Peltier, who was serving two life sentences in federal prison for allegedly killing two FBI agents.

New Mexico, a state still playing out its neo-colonial war between Anglos (whites) and Hispanics (Mexican Americans), has been extremely harsh on its original residents—the Pueblo and Athapaskan (Navajo and Apache) Indians. In this state with a high proportion of Hispanics (38%), both major political parties support the state's long-held position of Indian exploitation.

Here, Hispanics are more likely to be Democrats, while Anglo-Americans are most likely to be Republicans. Nonetheless, both Republican Governor Gary Johnson and Democratic Attorney General Patricia Madrid back a state effort to exploit a high proportion of profits from Indian gaming endeavors despite objections from the tribes. And to make matters worse, U.S. District Judge Bruce D. Black upheld the state's right to sue the tribes for their 16 percent off-the-top taxes from Indian gaming enterprises. This comes from a state that has done little to help Indians and was the last state to enfranchise them.

At the federal level, President Bill Clinton made attempts at improving U.S.-Indian relations by visiting the Pine Ridge Reservation and attempting to better articulate U.S.-Indian government-to-government relations. In a speech on March 10, 2000, on the status of his efforts to bring the nation closer to racial healing, President Clinton noted that the United States' goal ought to be the fundamental empowerment of the Native American tribes in this country as envisioned by the Constitution and required by the Supreme Court. He cited Census Bureau and BIA data that indicated that of the 1.43 million Indians living in or near Indian country, only 63 percent are high school graduates, while 29 percent are homeless and 59 percent live in sub-standard housing.[6]

Principles of Indian Sovereignty and the Trust Responsibility

The Clinton administration reinforced the Indian self-determination policy, spelled out in Attorney General Janet Reno's June 1, 1995, memorandum:

> Though generalizations are difficult, a few basic principles provide important guidance in the field of Indian affairs: 1) the Constitution vests Congress with plenary power over Indian affairs; 2) Indian tribes retain important sovereign powers over "their members and their territory," subject to the plenary power of Congress; and 3) the United States has a trust responsibility to Indian tribes, which guides and limits the Federal Government in dealing with Indian tribes. Thus, federal and tribal law generally have primacy over Indian affairs in Indian country, except where Congress has provided otherwise.

Department of Justice Recognition of Indian Sovereignty and the Federal Trust Responsibility:

The Department resolves that the following principles will guide its interactions with the Indian tribes.

The Sovereignty of Indian Tribes:

The Department recognizes that Indian tribes as domestic dependent nations retain sovereign powers, except as divested by the United States, and further recognizes that the United States has the authority to restore federal recognition of Indian sovereignty in order to strengthen tribal self-governance.

The Department shall be guided by principles of respect for Indian tribes and their sovereign authority and the United States' trust responsibility in the many ways in which the Department takes action on matters affecting Indian tribes. For example, the Department reviews proposed legislation, and administers funds that are available to tribes to build their capacity to address crime and crime-related problems in Indian country. The Department represents the United States, in coordination with other federal agencies, in litigation brought for the benefit of Indian tribes and individuals, as well as in litigation by Indian tribes or individuals against the United States or its agencies. In litigation, as in other matters, the Department may take actions and positions affecting Indian tribes with which one or more tribes may disagree. In all situations, the Department will carry out its responsibilities consistent with the law and this policy statement.

Government-to-Government Relationships with Indian Tribes:

In accord with the status of Indian tribes as domestic dependent nations, the Department is committed to operating on the basis of government-to-government relations with Indian tribes.

Consistent with federal law and other Department duties, the Department will consult with tribal leaders in its decisions that relate to or affect the sovereignty, rights, resources or lands of Indian tribes. Each component will conduct such consultation in light of its mission. In addition, the Department has initiated national and regional listening conferences and has created the Office of Tribal Justice to improve communications with Indian tribes. In the Office of the United States Attorneys with substantial areas of Indian country within their purview, the Department encourages designation of Assistant U.S. Attorneys to serve as tribal liaisons.

In order to fulfill its mission, the Department of Justice endeavors to forge strong partnerships between the Indian tribal governments and the Department. These partnerships will enable the Department to better serve the needs of Indian tribes, Indian people, and the public at large.

Self-Determination and Self-Governance:

The Department is committed to strengthening and assisting Indian tribal governments in their development and to promoting Indian self-governance. Consistent with federal law and Departmental responsibilities, the Department will consult with tribal governments concerning law enforcement priorities in Indian country, support duly recognized tribal governments, defend the lawful exercise of tribal governmental powers in coordination with the Department of the Interior and other federal agencies, investigate government corruption when necessary, and support and assist Indian tribes in the development of their law enforcement systems, tribal courts, and traditional justice systems.

Trust Responsibility:

The Department acknowledges the federal trust responsibility arising from Indian treaties, statutes, executive orders, and the historical relationship between the United States and Indian tribes. In a broad sense, the trust responsibility relates to the United States' unique legal and political relationship with Indian tribes. Congress, with plenary power over Indian affairs, plays a primary role in defining the trust responsibility, and Congress recently declared that the trust responsibility "includes the protection of the sovereignty of each tribal government." 25 U.S.C. Section 3601.

The term "trust responsibility" is also used in a narrower sense to define the precise legal duties of the United States in managing property and resources of Indian tribes and, at times, of individual Indians.

The trust responsibility, in both senses, will guide the Department in litigation, enforcement, policymaking and proposals for legislation affecting Indian country, when appropriate to the circumstances. As used in its narrower sense, the federal trust responsibility may be justifiable in some circumstances, while in its broader sense the definition and implementation of the trust responsibility is committed to Congress and the Executive Branch.

Protection of Civil Rights:

Federal law prohibits discrimination based on race or national origin by the federal, state and local governments, or individuals against American Indians in such areas as voting, education, housing, credit, public accommodations and facilities, employment, and in certain federally funded programs and facilities. Various federal criminal civil rights statutes also preserve personal liberties and safety. The existence of the federal trust responsibility toward Indian tribes does not diminish the obligation of state and local governments to respect the civil rights of Indian people.

Through the Indian Civil Rights Act, Congress selectively has derived essential civil rights protections from the Bill of Rights and applied them to Indian tribes. 25 U.S.C. Section 1301.

The Indian Civil Rights Act is to be interpreted with respect for Indian sovereignty. The primary responsibility for the enforcement of the Act is invested in the tribal courts and other tribal fora. In the criminal law context, federal courts have authority to decide habeas corpus petitions after tribal remedies are exhausted.

The Department of Justice is fully committed to safeguarding the constitutional and statutory rights of American Indians, as well as all other Americans.

Protection of Tribal Religion and Culture:

The mandate to protect religious liberty is deeply rooted in this Nation's constitutional heritage. The Department seeks to ensure that American Indians are protected in the observance of their faiths. Decisions regarding the activities of the Department that have the potential to substantially interfere with the exercise of Indian religions will be guided by the First Amendment of the United States Constitution, as well as by statutes which protect the exercise of religion such as the Religious Freedom Restoration Act, the American Indian Religious Freedom Act, the Native American Graves Protection and Repatriation Act, and the National Historic Preservation Act.

The Department also recognizes the significant federal interest in aiding tribes in the preservation of their tribal customs and traditions. In performing its duties in Indian country, the Department will respect and seek to preserve tribal cultures.

Directive to All Components of the Department of Justice:

The principles set out here must be interpreted by each component of the Department of Justice in light of its respective mission. Therefore, each component head shall make all reasonable efforts to ensure that the component's activities are consistent with the above sovereignty and trust principles. The component heads shall circulate this policy to all attorneys in the Department to inform them of their responsibilities. Where the activities and internal procedures of the components can be reformed to ensure greater consistency with this Policy, the component head shall undertake to do so. If tensions arise between these principles and other principles which guide the component in carrying out its mission, components will develop, as necessary, a mechanism for resolving such tensions to ensure that tribal interests are given due considerations. Finally, component heads will appoint a contact person to work with the Office of Tribal Justice in addressing Indian issues within the component.

Disclaimer:

This policy is intended only to improve the internal management of the Department and is not intended to create any right enforceable in any cause of action by any party against the United States, its agencies, officers, or any person.

Signed by Janet Reno, U.S. Attorney General, June 1, 1995[7]

Despite this memorandum, the Department of Justice remains a highly political entity much like the Department of the Interior. Janet Reno, attorney general during the Clinton administration, showed a genuine concern over justice in Indian country and initiated a number of initiatives, some jointly with other departments, in an attempt to ascertain the true nature of criminal justice issues pertaining to American Indians. One initiative was crime and justice research in Indian country. Strategic planning meetings were conducted nationwide with the involvement of the National Institute of Justice, the American Indian and Alaska Native Affairs Office, and the Office of Juvenile Justice and Delinquency Prevention. Here, major research universities were paired with American Indian leaders and scholars in an attempt to initiate research on basic justice issues in Indian country. A monograph on the results is currently being compiled. It must be realized, however, that the attorney general often has little influence on its subunits, like U.S. attorneys and the FBI, which often better reflect the political rather than the professional realm. And it is the FBI and U.S. attorneys who most often enforce their own perceptions of justice in Indian country, regardless of what the attorney general dictates in a memorandum. And Indian country certainly needs to be concerned about President George W. Bush's attorney general, a religious-right, anti-affirmative-action conservative. John Ashcroft certainly fits the stereotype of a staunch supporter of Manifest Destiny.

The same can be said for Clinton's Interior appointees. Secretary Babbitt was Indian-friendly as was his assistant secretary and BIA head, Kevin Gover. Indeed, since the appointment of American Indians as BIA directors, Gover was one of the most sensitive to Indian needs. Nonetheless, both Babbitt and Gover, in addition to Lawrence Summers, secretary of the treasury, were named in a tribal suit filed against the United States for the blatant mismanagement of the Indian trust funds. Those holding these ex-official titles change with each new administration. But the suit will continue. This suit was filed with the aid of the Native American Rights Fund (NARF) on June 10, 1996, when Babbitt was in office. In the original suit, the assistant interior secretary (BIA director) was Ada Deer, and Robert Rubin was the secretary of the treasury. The suit was filed by Elouise Pepion Cobell, a Blackfoot Indian and Montana banker, who, along with the NARF lawyers, accuse the U.S. government of violating their trust responsibility for the collection of monies from the leasing of Indian lands to non-Indian businesses for grazing, logging, mining, and oil drilling. The plaintiffs note a $10 billion shortfall due to either theft, corrupt deals, or shoddy bookkeeping practices.

In describing the suit, John Echohawk, executive director of the Native American Rights Fund, noted that: "The Bureau of Indian Affairs has spent more than 100 years mismanaging, diverting and losing money that belongs to Indians. They have no idea how much has been collected from the companies that use our land and are unable to provide even a basic, regular statement to Indian account holders. Every day the system remains broken, hundreds of thousands of Indians are losing more and more money."[8] The catch-22 is that the Department of the Interior approves all leases of resources in Indian country. Moreover, the law requires Indians to use the federal government as their bank, so these transactions occur without Indian input or accountability.

Declarative Judgment of the Indian Suit against the U.S. Government

A comprehensive text describes *Elouise Pepion Cobell, et al., v. Bruce Babbitt, Secretary of the Interior, Lawrence Summers, Secretary of the Treasury, and Kevin Gover, Assistant Secretary of the Interior* (*Cobell v. Babbitt*, U.S. District Court, District of Columbia, 30 F. Supp. 2d 24). In the text the plaintiffs, representing federally recognized Indian tribes whose monies are administered by the BIA and the U.S. Department of the Interior, claim that the defendants, the BIA and the U.S. Department of the Interior, have mismanaged the federal program known as the Individual Indian Money (IIM) trust. In the introduction to the memorandum decision it was noted:

> It would be difficult to find a more historically mismanaged federal program than the Individual Indian Money (IIM) trust. The United States, the trustee

of the IIM trust, cannot say how much money is or should be in the trust. As the trustee admitted on the eve of the trial, it cannot render an accurate accounting to the beneficiaries, contrary to a specific statutory mandate and the century-old obligation to do so. More specifically, as Secretary Babbitt testified, an accounting cannot be rendered for most of the 300,000-plus beneficiaries, who are now plaintiffs in this lawsuit. Generations of IIM trust beneficiaries have been born and raised with the assurance that their trustee, the United States, was acting properly with their money. Just as many generations have been denied any such proof, however. "If courts were permitted to indulge their sympathies, a case better calculated to excite them could scarcely be imagined." *Cherokee Nation v. Georgia*, 30 U.S. (5 Pet.) 1, 15 (1831) (Marshall, C.J.).

The Court ordered the following action:

I. Dismissal of Certain Claims

1. Plaintiffs' common-law claims are HEREBY DISMISSED with prejudice.
2. Plaintiffs' claim for obstruction or interference with the Special Trustee are HEREBY DISMISSED with prejudice.

II. Declaratory Judgment

Pursuant to the Declaratory Judgment Act, 28 U.S.C. Section 2201, and the Administrative Procedure Act, 5 U.S.C. Sections 702 & 76, the court HEREBY DECLARES that:

1. The Indian Trust Fund Management Reform Act, 25 U.S.C. Sections 162a *et seq.* & 4011 *et seq.*, requires defendants to provide plaintiffs an accurate accounting of all money in the IIM trust held in trust for the benefit of plaintiffs, without regard to when the funds were deposited.
2. The Indian Trust Fund Management Reform Act, 25 U.S.C. Sections 162a *et seq.* & 4011 *et seq.*, requires defendants to retrieve and retain all information concerning the IIM trust that is necessary to render an accurate accounting of all money in the IIM trust held in trust for the benefit of plaintiffs.
3. To the extent that prospective relief is warranted in this case and to the extent that the issues are in controversy, it has been shown that defendant Bruce Babbitt, Secretary of the Interior, and defendant Kevin Gover, Assistant Secretary of the Interior, owe plaintiffs, pursuant to the

statutes and regulations governing the management of the IIM trust, the statutory trust duty to:

(a) establish written policies and procedures for collecting from outside sources missing information necessary to render an accurate accounting of the IIM trust;

(b) establish written policies and procedures for the retention of IIM—related trust documents necessary to render an accurate accounting of the IIM trust;

(c) establish written policies and procedures for computer and business systems architecture necessary to render an accurate accounting of the IIM trust; and

(d) establish written policies and procedures for the staffing of trust management functions necessary to render an accurate accounting of the IIM trust.

4. To the extent that prospective relief is warranted in this case and to the extent that the issues are in controversy, it has been shown that defendant Lawrence Summers, Secretary of the Treasury, owes plaintiffs, pursuant to the statutes and regulations governing the management of the IIM trust, the statutory trust duty to retain IIM trust documents that are necessary to render an accurate accounting of all money in the IIM trust held in trust for the benefit of plaintiffs.

5. Defendants are currently in breach of the statutory trust duties declared in subparagraphs II(2)-(4).

6. Defendants have no written plans to bring themselves into compliance with the duties declared in subparagraphs II(2)-(4).

7. Defendants must promptly come into compliance by establishing written policies and procedures not inconsistent with the court's Memorandum Opinion that rectify the breaches of trust declared in subparagraphs II(2)-(4).

8. To allow defendants the opportunity to promptly come into compliance through the establishment of the appropriate written policies and procedures, the court HEREBY REMAINS the required actions to defendants for further proceedings not inconsistent with the court's Memorandum Opinion issued this date.

III. Continuing Jurisdiction and Further Proceedings

To ensure that defendants are diligently taking steps to rectify the continuing breaches of trust declared today and to ensure that defendants take the other actions represented to the court upon which the court bases its decision today, the court will retain continuing jurisdiction over this matter for a period of five years, subject to any motion for an enlargement of time that may be made. Accordingly, the court ORDERS that:

1. Beginning March 1, 2000, defendants shall file with the court and serve upon plaintiffs quarterly status reports setting forth and explaining the steps that defendants have taken to rectify the breaches of trust declared today and to bring themselves into compliance with their statutory trust duties embodied in the Indian Trust Fund Management Reform Act of 1994 and other applicable statutes and regulations governing the IIM trust.

2. Each quarterly report shall be limited, to the extent practical, to actions taken since the issuance of the preceding quarterly report. Defendants' first quarterly report, due March 1, 2000, shall encompass actions taken since June 10, 1999.

3. Defendants Secretary of the Interior and Assistant Secretary of the Interior—Indian Affairs shall file with the court and serve upon plaintiffs the revised or amended High Level Implementation Plan. The revised or amended HLIP shall be filed and served upon completion but no later than March 1, 2000.

4. Defendants shall provide any additional information requested by the court to explain or supplement defendants' submissions. Plaintiffs may petition the court to order defendants to provide further information as needed if such information cannot be obtained through informal requests directly to defendants.

5. The court DENIES plaintiffs' request for prospective relief that have not already been granted by this order. The court based much of its decision today—especially the denial of more extensive prospective relief—on defendants' plans (in both substance and timing) to bring themselves into compliance with their trust duties declared today and provided for explicitly by statute. These plans have been represented to the court primarily through the High Level Implementation Plan, but also through the representations made by government witnesses and government counsel. Given the court's reliance on these representations, the court ORDERS defendants, as part of their quarterly status reports, to explain any changes made to the HLIP. Should plaintiffs believe that they are entitled to further prospective relief based upon information contained in these reports or otherwise learned, they may so move at the appropriate juncture. Such a motion will then trigger this court's power of judicial review.

IV. Certification of Order for Interlocutory Appeal

For the reasons stated in the court's accompanying Memorandum Opinion, and pursuant to 28 U.S.C. Section 1292(a)(4), the court HEREBY FINDS that it is of the opinion that this order involves controlling questions of law as to which there is substantial grounds for difference of opinion. An immediate appeal of the court's order may materially advance the ultimate termination of the litigation. Accordingly, the court HEREBY CERTIFIES this order for interlocutory appeal pursuant to 28 U.S.C. Section 1292(b). Further proceedings in this case shall not be stayed during the dependency of any interlocutory appeal that may be taken.

SO ORDERED. Royce C. Lamberth, United States District Judge[9]

Not only did the defendants not comply, but they were charged by the plaintiffs with engaging in a deliberate destruction of records. Judge Lamberth subsequently held the defendants in contempt of court in February 2000 for admitting to the improper destruction of thousands of records and for not filing the required quarterly reports.[10] The American Indian plaintiffs requested appointment of a "special master" to enforce Judge Lamberth's court order. And this action comes from one of the most Indian-friendly administrations in U.S. history! Clearly, contravening U.S. policy and procedures toward American Indians continues unabated into the twenty-first century.

NOTES

Chapter One

1. William C. Canby, Jr., "Federal Indian Law and Policy, "*American Indian Law*, 2nd ed. (St. Paul, MN: West 1988), 10.
2. G. Nash, *Red, White, and Black* (Englewood Cliffs, NJ: Prentice-Hall, 1974); T. Perdue, *Slavery and the Evolution of Cherokee Society, 1540–1866* (Knoxville: University of Tennessee Press, 1979); and L.A. French, *Psychocultural Change and the American Indian* (New York: Garland, 1987).
3. G. Simmel, *The Sociology of Georg Simmel* (New York: Free Press, 1969); L. Coser, *The Functions of Social Conflict* (Glencoe, IL: Free Press, 1955); and L. Coser, *Continuities in the Study of Social Conflict* (Glencoe, IL: Free Press, 1956).
4. G. Friederici, "Scalping in America," *Annual Report of the Smithsonian Institution* (Washington, DC: Smithsonian Institution, 1906), 423–38.
5. Laurence A. French, "Government Policy and Practices during the 'Indian War' Era," *The Winds of Injustice* (New York: Garland, 1994), 23–43.
6. Laurence A. French, "Aboriginal Uses of Psychoactive Agents," *Addictions and Native Americans* (Westport, CT: Praeger, 2000), 9.
7. William C. Canby, Jr., "Historical Overview of Federal Indian Law and Policy," *American Indian Law*, 2nd ed. (St. Paul, MN: West, 1988), 9–31.
8. R. Costo and J. Henry, *Indian Treaties: Two Centuries of Dishonor* (San Francisco, CA: Indian Historian Press, 1977), 208.
9. See "Report of the Committee on Indian Affairs," *Journals of the Continental Congress,* 25 (October 15, 1783), 681–83, 693; "Committee Report on the Southern Department," *Journals of the Continental Congress,* 33 (August 3, 1787), 456–59; and "Report of Henry Knox on the Northwestern Indians," *American State Papers: Indian Affairs,* 1 (June 15, 1789), 13–14.
10. See *An Act to Establish an Executive Department, to be Denominated the Department of War, U.S. Statutes at Large,* 1: 49–50 (August 7, 1789).
11. See *Trade and Intercourse Act, U.S. Statutes at Large,* 1: 137–38 (July 22, 1790).
12. See *Trade and Intercourse Act, U.S. Statutes at Large,* 2: 139–46 (March 30, 1802).
13. See *Indian Removal Act, U.S. Statutes at Large,* 4: 411–12 (May 28, 1830).

14. See *Trade and Intercourse Act, U.S. Statutes at Large,* 4: 729–35 (June 30, 1834); and L.A. French, "Psychocultural Factors," *Addictions and Native Americans* (Westport, CT: Praeger, 2000), 35–43.

15. See *Cherokee Nation v. Georgia,* 30 U.S. (5 Pet.) 1 (1831), 15–20; and W.C. Canby, Jr., "The Cherokee Cases and Indian Control: 1820 to 1850," *American Indian Law* (St. Paul, MN: West, 1988), 12–17.

16. See *Worcester v. Georgia,* 31 U.S. (6 Pet.) 515 (1832), 534–63.

17. Laurence A. French, "Forced Removal: The Trail of Tears," *The Qualla Cherokee: Surviving in Two Worlds* (Lewiston, NY: Edwin Mellin Press, 1998), 45–50.

18. See "Federally Recognized Tribes," *Federal Register,* 63 (250) (December 30, 1998), 71941–46.

19. S.L. Johnson, Item 42, "Report on the Poncas, 10 February 1879," *Guide to American Indian Documents, Congressional Serial Set: 1817–1899* (New York: Clearwater, 1977), 246.

20. J. Stoutenburg, Jr., "Standing Bear," *Dictionary of the American Indian* (New York: Philosophical Library, 1960), 395–96.

21. S.L. Johnson, Item 47, "On the Relief of the Winnebagoes," *Guide to American Indian Documents in the Congressional Serial Set: 1817–1899* (New York: Clearwater, 1977), 246–47.

22. C. Kluckhohn and D. Leighton, *The Navajo* (Cambridge, MA: Harvard University Press, 1946); G. Bailey and R.G. Bailey, *A History of the Navajos* (Santa Fe, NM: School of American Indian Research Press, 1986).

23. See "Report of the Board of Indian Commissioners," in *Annual Report of the Board of Indian Commissioners,* November 23 (Washington, DC: U.S. Government Printing Office, 1869).

24. Ibid., 8–11.

25. S.L. Johnson, Item 62, "Annual Message to Congress with Documents; President Grant, 6 December 1870," in *Guide to American Indian Documents, Congressional Serial Set: 1817–1899* (New York: Clearwater, 1977), 182–83.

26. R. Costo and J. Henry, "Indian Treaties: Supreme Law of the Land," in *Indian Treaties: Two Centuries of Dishonors* (San Francisco, CA: Indian Historian Press, 1977), 23.

27. Ibid., 216; and W. C. Canby, Jr., "Movement to the Reservations: 1850–1887," in *American Indian Law,* 2nd Ed. (St. Paul, MN: West, 1988), 17–19.

28. C. J. Kappler, "1851 Treaty of Fort Laramie," in *Treaties,* vol. 2 of *Indian Affairs: Laws and Treaties* (New York: AMS Press, 1904).

29. M.A. Sievers, "Westward by Indian Treaty: The Upper Missouri Example," *Nebraska History* 56 (1) (1975), 77–107; and R.L. Clow, "General Philip Sheridan's Legacy: The Sioux Pony Campaign of 1876," *Nebraska History* 57 (4) (1976), 461–71.

30. C. J. Kappler, "Treaty with the Sioux, 1868"; "Treaty with the Crows, 1868"; "Treaty with the Apache, 1852," *Indian Affairs: Laws and Treaties* (New York: AMS Press, 1904), 998–1015; 1008–11; 598–600.

31. M.E. Melody, "The Americans," *The Apache* (New York: Chelsea House, 1989), 73–91.

32. W.C. Canby, Jr., "Crimes Punishable under the Federal Enclaves Act, 18 U.S.C.A. 1152," *American Indian Law,* 2nd ed. (St. Paul, MN: West, 1988), 120–28.

33. N. Abrams and S.S. Beale, "The Assimilative Crimes Act and the Special Maritime and Territorial Jurisdiction," *Federal Criminal Law* (St. Paul, MN: West, 1993), 671–92.

34. H.M. Teller, *Annual Report of the Secretary of the Interior,* House Executive Document No. 1, 48th Congress, 1st Session, Serial 2190, 1883, x-xii.

35. *Ex parte Crow Dog*, 109 U.S. Reports, 557, 571–72 (1883).

36. *Major Crimes Act, U.S. Statutes at Large*, 23: 385 (18 U.S.C.: 1153, 1885).

37. William C. Canby, Jr., "Crimes Punishable under the Major Crimes Act, 18 U.S.C.: 1153," *American Indian Law* (St. Paul, MN: West, 1988), 128–33; and S. J. Brakel, "Tribal Courts: History, Jurisdiction, and Current Status," *American Indian Tribal Courts: The Costs of Separate Justice* (Chicago, IL: American Bar Foundation, 1978), 5–11.

38. T. J. Morgan, *Rule for Indian Courts*, House Executive Document No. 1, 52nd Congress, 2nd Session, Serial 3088, August 27, 1892, 28–31.

39. William C. Canby, Jr., "Allotments and Attempted Assimilation: 1887 to 1934," *American Indian Law*, 2nd ed. (St. Paul, MN: West, 1988), 19–22.

40. *General Allotment Act* (Dawes Act), *U.S. Statutes at Large*, 24: 388–91, February 8, 1887.

41. *Curtis Act, U.S. Statutes at Large*, 30: 497–98, 502, 504–5, June 28, 1898.

42. *Citizenship for Indians in the Indian Territory, U.S. Statutes at Large*, 31L 1447 (March 3, 1901).

43. See *Burke Act, U.S. Statutes at Large*, 34: 182–83, May 8, 1906; *Lacey Act, U.S. Statutes at Large*, 34: 1221–22, March 2, 1907; *Citizenship for World War I Veterans, U.S. Statutes at Large*, 41: 350, November 6, 1919; *Indian Citizenship Act, U.S. Statutes at Large*, 43: 253, June 2, 1924; and *New Mexico Constitution*, Article VII, Section I (1992 Replacement).

44. *Bursum Bill* (*Congressional Record*, 62: 12324–25, September 11, 1922); and *Pueblo Lands Board, U.S. Statutes at Large*, 43: 636–37, June 7, 1924.

45. Title 25, Indians, *United States Code* (St. Paul, MN: West, 1926).

46. William C. Canby, Jr., "Indian Reorganization and Preservation of the Tribes: 1934 to 1953," *American Indian Law*, 2nd ed. (St. Paul, MN: West, 1988), 23–25.

47. L. Meriam, *The Problem of Indian Administration* (Baltimore, MD: Johns Hopkins Press, 1928), 346.

48. K. Philip, *John Collier's Crusade for Indian Reform, 1920–1954* (Tucson: University of Arizona Press, 1977).

49. Laurence A. French, "The Accommodative Antithesis," *Psychocultural Change and the American Indian: An Ethnohistorical Analysis* (New York: Garland, 1987), 123–59.

50. J. Collier, "Annual Report of the Commissioner of Indian Affairs," *Annual Report of the Secretary of the Interior* (Washington, DC: U.S. Government Printing Office, 1934), 78–83.

51. *Indian Reorganization Act, U.S. Statutes at Large*, 48: 984–88, June 18, 1934.

52. *Indian Reorganization Act*, Section 19, 50.

53. *Oklahoma Indian Welfare Act, U.S. Statutes at Large*, 49: 1967–68, June 26, 1936.

54. Laurence A. French, "Reservations and Federal Paternalism," *The Winds of Injustice* (New York: Garland, 1994), 45–74.

55. H.C. James, "Indian Reorganization and the Hopi," *Pages from Hopi History* (Tucson: University of Arizona Press, 1974), 201–14.

56. R. C. Lamberth, "History Surrounding IIM Trust Establishment," *Memorandum Opinion: Findings of Fact and Conclusions of Law*, U.S. District Court for District of Columbia (*Cobell v. Babbit*, 30 F. Supp. 2d 24).

57. *House Concurrent Resolution 108*, 83rd Congress, 1st Session, 67 *U.S. Statutes at Large*, B132, August 1, 1953.

58. *Public Law 280, U.S. Statutes at Large*, 67: 588–90, August 15, 1953.

59. *Termination of Menominee Indians, U.S. Statutes at Large*, 68: 250–52, June 17, 1954.

60. *Transfer of Indian Health Services from BIA to Public Health Service (HIS), U.S. Statutes*

   at Large, 68: 674, August 5, 1954.

61. G.L. Emmons, "Relocation of Indians in Urban Areas," *Annual Report of the Secretary of the Interior* (Washington, DC: U.S. Government Printing Office, 1954), 243.

62. R. Costo and J. Henry, "The New War against the Indians," *Indian Treaties: Two Centuries of Dishonor* (San Francisco, CA: Indian Historian Press, 1977), 42.

63. *Menominee Restoration Act, U.S. Statutes at Large,* 87: 700ff, December 22, 1973.

64. S.L. Harring, "Early BIA Attempts to Prosecute Indians under State or Territorial Law," *Crow Dog's Case: American Indian Sovereignty, Tribal Law, and United States Law in the Nineteenth Century* (Cambridge, Eng.: Cambridge University Press, 1994), 115–18.

65. Laurence A. French, *Addictions and Native Americans* (Westport, CT: Praeger, 2000).

Chapter Two

1. Commission on the Rights, Liberties, and Responsibilities of the American Indian, *The Indian: America's Unfinished Business* (Norman: University of Oklahoma Press, 1966); and American Indian Chicago Conference, *Declaration of Indian Purpose* (Chicago: University of Chicago Press, 1961), 5.

2. P. Nash, Task Force on Indian Affairs, *Annual Report of the Commissioner of Indian Affairs* (Washington, DC: U.S. Government Printing Office, 1961).

3. V. Deloria, Jr., *Behind the Trail of Broken Treaties: An Indian Declaration of Independence* (New York: Delta Books, Dell, 1974); and E.S. Grobsmith, *Indians in Prison: Incarcerated Native Americans in Nebraska* (Lincoln: University of Nebraska Press, 1994).

4. L.A. French, "In the Spirit of Crazy Horse: Leonard Peltier and the AIM Uprising," *Wings of Injustice* (New York: Garland, 1994), 77–112.

5. *Civil Rights Act of 1968,* Titles II-VII (April 11), *U.S. Statutes at Large,* 82: 77–81.

6. Lyndon B. Johnson, President Johnson, Special Message to Congress, March 6, 1968, *Public Papers of the President of the United States: Lyndon B. Johnson 1968–69* (Washington, DC: U.S. Government Printing Office, 1968), vol. 1: 336–37; 343–44.

7. W. Wadlington, C.H. Whitebread, and S.M. Davis, *Children in the Legal System* (Mineola, NY: Foundation Press, 1983); W.C. Canby, Jr., "Tribal Self-Determination: 1968 to the Present, "*American Indian Law* (St. Paul, MN: West, 1988), 28–31; and Richard M. Nixon, President Nixon, Special Message to Congress, *Public Papers of the President of the United States: Richard Nixon* (Washington, DC: U.S. Government Printing Office, 1970), 564–76; *Indian Education Act* (June 23, 1972), *U.S. Statutes at Large,* 86: 335, 339–43; *Comprehensive Employment and Training Act* (December 28, 1973) *U.S. Statutes at Large,* 87: 839; 858–59; and *Supreme Court of the United States,* 1967 (387 U.S. 1, 87 S.Ct. 1428, 18 L. Ed. 2d 527).

8. *Indian Education: A National Tragedy—A National Challenge,* Senate Report, No. 501, 91st Congress, 1st Session, serial 12836–1, xi–xiv.

9. *Indian Self-Determination and Education Assistance Act* (January 4, 1975), *U.S. Statutes at Large,* 88: 2203–14.

10. *Indian Law Enforcement Improvement Act of 1975* (December 3, 1975), 94th Congress, 1st Session (Washington, DC: U.S. Government Printing Office) (63–950), 1–10. See "Opening Statement of Hon. James Abourezit," Hearing before the Sub-Committee on Indian Affairs of the Committee on Interior and Insular Affairs, United States Senate, 94th Congress, 1st Session, on S.20105, December 3 and 4, 1975.

11. Statement of Ed Cline, Chairman, Omaha Tribe, Macy, Nebraska, *Indian Law Enforcement Act of 1975*, 48–50.

12. M. Thompson, Commissioner of Indian Affairs' Letter to Hon. Peter W. Rodino, Chairman, Committee on the Judiciary, House of Representatives, dated May 20, 1975, *Criminal Jurisdiction in Indian Country*, Serial no. 33, 94th Congress, 2nd Session (1976), 25–26.

13. *Indian Crimes Act of 1976* (May 29, 1976), *U.S. Statutes at Large*, 90: 585–86.

14. *Oliphant v. Suquamish Indian Tribe* (March 6, 1978), 435 S. Ct., 206–12.

15. *Duro v. Reina* (1990), 110 S. Ct. 2953.

16. Public Law 102–137: *Criminal Jurisdiction over Indians* (1991), Souse Reports no. 102–61, 376–377; and Public Law 102–137, 105 *U.S. Statutes at Large*, 646 (October 28, 1991).

17. *Supreme Court of the Navajo Nation* (May 11, 1999), (1) No. SC-CV–61–98.

18. R. Snake, "The Indian People, Alcohol and Drugs," *Report on Alcohol and Drug Use Task Force Eleven: Alcohol and Drug Abuse* (Washington, DC: U.S. Government Printing Office, 1976), 12–15.

19. Public Law 99–570, *Anti-Drug Abuse Act of 1986* (October 27, 1986), 21 USC 801, 100 Stat. 3207–137–138.

20. Public Law 99–570 (1986), Part III—Indian Youth Programs, 100 Stat. 3207–143–146; and L.A. French, "The Unity Regional Youth Treatment Center at Cherokee," *Counseling American Indians* (New York: University Press of America, 1997), 98–110.

21. *American Indian Freedom Congressional Resolution* (August 11, 1978), *U.S. Statutes at Large*, 92: 469–70.

22. *Employment Division, Department of Human Resources of the State of Oregon, et al. v. Smith*, No. 86–946, U.S. Supreme Court (April 27, 1988), 660–79.

23. Public Law 103–344, *American Indian Religious Freedom Act Amendments of 1994* (October 6, 1994), H.R. 4230, 103rd Congress, 2nd Session, 1–3.

24. U.S. Senate, "Part One—The Executive Summary: A New Federalism for American Indians," *Final Report and Legislative Recommendations: A Report of the Special Committee on Investigations of the Select Committee on Indian Affairs* (November 1989), 101st Congress, 1st Session, S.Prt. 101–60, 9–10.

25. Public Law 101–630, *Indian Child Protection and Family Violence Prevention Act, Title IV* (November 28, 1990), 25 USC 3210.

26. *Seminole Tribe of Florida v. Butterworth*, 658, F.2d 310 (5th Cir. 1981); and Public Law 100–497, *Indian Gaming Regulatory Act* (October 17, 1988), 102 *U.S. Statutes at Large*, 2467–88; and *Constitution of New Mexico*, Article VII, Section 1 (1967 Amendment, p. 246; Indian suffrage, p. 247).

27. Public Law 101–379, *Indian Law Enforcement Reform Act* (August 18, 1990), 104 *U.S. Statutes at Large*, 473.

28. Public Law 103–176, *Indian Tribal Justice Act* (December 3, 1993), 107 *U.S. Statutes at Large*, 2004.

29. Public Law 103–322, *Special Provisions for Indian Country, Violent Crime Control and Law Enforcement Act of 1994* (September 13, 1994), 42 USC 1307, 108 *U.S. Statutes at Large*, 1796–1968 (quote at 1968).

30. Authorization of Appropriations and Expenditures for Indian Affairs, *Synder Act* (November 2, 1921), *U.S. Statutes at Large*, 42: 208–9.

31. U.S. Senate (November 1989) "I. The Principle Findings of the Special Committee on Investigations; and II. Principal Recommendations of the Special Committee on Investi-

gations," *Final Report and Legislative Recommendations: A Report of the Special Committee on Investigations of the Select Committee on Indian Affairs,* 101st Congress, 1st Session, S.Prt 101–60.

32. "300,000 Indians Sue Federal Government for Mismanaging Their Money," *NARF Legal Review,* 21(2) (Summer/Fall 1996): 6.

Chapter Three

1. E. Goode, "Marijuana and the Politics of Reality," *Journal of Health and Social Behavior,* 10 (June), 37–48.

2. Emile Durkheim, *The Rules of Sociological Methods,* ed. G. Catlin (New York: Free Press, 1950).

3. M. Weber, *The Protestant Ethic and the Spirit of Capitalism,* ed. T. Parsons (New York: Charles Scribner's Sons, 1958).

4. W. Mieder, "'The Only Good Indian Is a Dead Indian': History and Meaning of a Proverbial Stereotype," *Journal of American Folklore,* 6 (419) (Winter 1993), 38–60 (quote on p. 39).

5. J. Gulick, *Cherokees at the Crossroads* (Chapel Hill: University of North Carolina Press, 1960); L.A. French and J. Hornbuckle, *The Cherokee Perspective* (Boone, NC: Appalachian Consortium Press, 1981).

6. L.A. French, "The Cherokee," *Psychocultural Change and the American Indian: An Ethnohistorical Analysis* (New York: Garland, 1987), 43–68.

7. M. Opler, *An Apache Life-Way* (New York: Cooper Square, 1965); J.P. Reid, *A Law of Blood* (New York: New York University Press, 1970).

8. D. Right, *The American Indians of North Carolina* (Durham, NC: Duke University Press, 1947).

9. J. Mooney, *Myths of the Cherokees and Sacred Formulas of the Cherokees* (Nashville, TN: Charles Elder, 1972); J.P. Reid, *A Law of Blood* (New York: New York University Press, 1970).

10. L.A. French, *Psychocultural Change and the American Indian* (New York: Garland, 1987); L.A. French, *The Qualla Cherokee Surviving in Two Worlds* (Lewiston, NY: Edwin Mellen Press, 1999); and H. Kupferer, *The Principal People* (Washington, DC: Bureau of Ethnology Bulletin, 1966).

11. N. Browder, *The Cherokee Indians and Those Who Came After* (Hayesville, NC: Land of the Big Sky Press, 1974); and F. Gearing, *Priests and Warriors* (Masasha, WI: American Anthropological Association Press, 1962).

12. E. Stonequist, *The Marginal Man* (New York: Russell and Russell, 1937).

13. H. Malone, *Cherokees of the Old South* (Athens: University of Georgia Press, 1965); and R. Strickland, *Fire and the Spirit* (Norman: University of Oklahoma Press, 1975).

14. D. Bedford, *Tsali* (San Francisco, CA: Indian Historian Press, 1972); J. Brown. *Old Frontiers* (Kingsport, TN: Southern Publishers, 1978); G. Fleischmann, *The Cherokee Removal, 1838* (New York: Franklin Watts, 1971); W. Forrest, *Trail of Tears* (New York: Crown, 1956); J. Moone, *Myths of the Cherokees and Sacred Formulas of the Cherokees* (Nashville, TN: Charles Elder, 1972); and G.S. Woodward, *The Cherokee* (Norman: University of Oklahoma Press, 1963).

Chapter Four

(Note: Legal style is used by author Little Dog Reed for this chapter.)

1. The author uses the terms "American Indian," "Indian," "Native American," and "Native" interchangeably throughout this essay. None of these terms is correct. However, no matter which term is used, someone would be offended. These terms refer to the indigenous peoples of the continental United States, Hawaii, and Alaska.

2. Allison M. Dussias, "Ghost Dance and Holy Ghost: The Echoes of Nineteenth Century Christianization Policy in Twentieth Century Native American Free Exercise Cases," in 49 *Stanford Law Review* 773–852 (April 1997), at 775, quoting Frank Pommersheim, "Making All the Difference: Native American Testimony and the Black Hills (A Review Essay)," in 69 *North Dakota Law Review* 337 (19931), and Gloria Valencia–Weber, "American Indian Law and History: Instructional Mirrors," in 44 *Journal of Legal Education* 251 (1994). See also Mark A. Michaels, "Indigenous Ethics and Alien Laws: Native Traditions and the United States Legal System," in 66 *Fordham Law Review* 1565 (1998). Michaels observes that because Native Americans come from a "'plethora of cultural, religious, and linguistic traditions,'" it is "somewhat presumptuous to discuss these traditions in sweeping and general terms. . . . Nevertheless, all Indians in the Americas . . . share a historical experience that is fundamentally the same, and it is with that historical experience, above all else, that [lawyers representing American Indians] must contend." *Id.* at 1566.

3. See generally, Little Rock Reed, *The American Indian in the White Man's Prisons: A Story of Genocide* (Taos, NM: UnCompromising Books, 1993).

4. See *infra*, notes 51 and 61, and accompanying text.

5. M.J. Simpson, "Accommodating Indian Religions: Proposed 1993 Amendment to the American Indian Religious Freedom Act," in *Montana Law Review* 54 (1993), 19–55, at 21. See also, Mark A. Michaels, *supra* note 2. Michaels observes that "Native religious traditions generally stress responsibility for and accountability to one's community and one's elders and do not impose 'an external ethical system'; they emphasize ceremony rather than faith, the relatedness of all creation, and the sacredness of certain places." *Id.* at 1565. Michaels points out that the challenge for lawyers representing Native American religious claims " lies in maintaining this sense of accountability, relatedness and spiritual connection with the land while operating in a [judicial] system that is based on an antithetical world view." *Id.* at 1566.

6. In fact, from the beginning of the Union, the United States government employed Christian agents to carry out the task of converting Indians from their "heathenistic" and "pagan" ways to the "civilized" ways of Christianity. As early as 1776, Congress passed resolutions wherein Christian missions were established among the tribes and government-funded salaries were provided to the missionaries. See, e.g., R. Pierce Beaver, *Church, State and the American Indians: Two and a Half Centuries of Partnership in Missions Between Protestant Churches and Government* (1966).

7. The Rules for Indian Courts provided that first-time offenders could be punished for their participation in dances by the withholding of rations or by imprisonment. See Clyde Holler, *Black Elk's Religion: The Sun Dance and Lakota Catholicism* (1995), 120.

8. See, e.g., generally, the *1889 Annual Report of the Commissioner of Indian Affairs*.

9. Wovoka, Native prophet, quoted in James Mooney, *The Ghost-Dance Religion and the Sioux Outbreak of 1890*, Bison Book ed. (Lincoln: University of Nebraska Press, 1991), 764. Originally published in 1896.

10. *1882 Annual Report, Commissioner of Indian Affairs*, report of J.H. Fleming, Moquis Pueblo Agency. In his report, Fleming acknowledged that he had never personally witnessed any of the dances he referred to in the report.

11. See the *1883 Annual Report of the Secretary of Interior*, xi.

12. It is the custom of most tribes to have "giveaways," not unlike the giving of gifts at Christmas, as a part of their ceremonial life to show thanks for life and health. However, these giveaways were deemed by the government to interfere with the government's efforts to encourage a value system that included the accumulation of property, so the giveaways, too, were outlawed.

13. See the *1883 Annual Report of the Commissioner of Indian Affairs*, xiv–xv.

14. Peter Matthiessen, *In the Spirit of Crazy Horse* (New York: Viking, 1983). These religious activities were deemed to be "Indian offenses" punishable by the withholding of rations or imprisonment well into the twentieth century. See, e.g., *Secretary of Interior, Regulations of the Indian Office, effective April 1, 1904*, at 102–03. The ban on these dances was not lifted until 1934. See Walter Echo-Hawk, "Native American Religious Liberty: Five-Hundred Years after Columbus," *American Indian Culture and Research Journal*, 17 (1993): 33, 37.

15. Vine Deloria, Jr., *God Is Red* (New York: Dell, 1973).

16. Robert Burnette and John Koster, *On the Road to Wounded Knee* (New York: Bantam, 1974).

17. For example, the sun dancers did not make flesh offerings in the traditional way of the Lakota. In the Lakota way of understanding, everything in the universe already belongs to God, so if we are to give something in return for having our prayers answered, all that is truly ours to give is our flesh and our suffering.

18. Burnette and Koster, *supra* note 16.

19. Traditional hairstyles hold spiritual significance, and it is the belief of many tribal peoples that the hair should not be cut except when mourning the death of a loved one. There is a Lakota teaching that a long time ago, a man was walking in the woods, and he noticed that all the trees and plants had roots. This made him feel separated from his relatives, as he had no roots as they did. He cried in prayer, and at that time, the Creator grabbed a rainbow out of the sky and placed it on the man's head, whereupon it became long, dark beautiful hair. God then told him, "You now have your roots, for when you kneel down on your hands and knees as your four-legged relatives to enter the sweat lodge, your hair shall touch the earth, for it is your roots."

20. Steven Tullberg, Robert Coulter, and Curtis Burkey, for the Traditional Spiritual Leaders of the Hopi People. "Violations of the Human Rights of the Hopi People by the United States of America," in *Rethinking Indian Law* (New Haven, CT: Harvard University Press, 1982). Compiled and edited by the National Lawyers Guild Committee on Native American Struggles.

21. Kirk Kickingbird and Lynn Kickingbird. "A Short History of Indian Education, Part 2," *American Indian Journal*, September 1979, 17–21.

22. *Id.*

23. See *supra* note 20, at 161–68.

24. See, e.g., Estelle Fuchs and Robert Havighurst, *To Live on This Earth* (New York: Doubleday, 1972); Ann Beuf, *Red Children in White America* (Philadelphia: University of Pennsylvania Press, 1977); Sally McBeth, *Ethnic Identity and the Boarding School Experience of West-Central Oklahoma American Indians* (Lanham, MD: University Press of America, 1983); Burnette and Koster, *supra* note 16; Little Rock Reed, *supra* note 3.

25. Fuchs and Havighurst, *supra* note 24. See, e.g., Congress's "Regulations for Withholding

Rations for Non-Attendance at Schools," 27 *U.S. Statutes at Large*, 628, 635 (1983), 25 U.S.C. 283; and "Withholding Annuities from Osage Indians for Non-Attendance at Schools," 38 *U.S. Statutes at Large*, 96 (1913), 25 U.S.C. 285.

26. Quoted by Randolph Rice in "Native Americans and the Free Exercise Clause," *Hastings Law Journal* 28 (July 1977), 1509–1536.

27. Quoted from a pamphlet that was issued with the *1889 Annual Report of the Commissioner of Indian Affairs*. See Frederick Home, *A Final Promise: The Campaign to Assimilate the Indians, 1880–1920* (Lincoln: University of Nebraska Press, 1984).

28. Burnette and Koster, *supra* note 16.

29. Edgar Cahn, *Our Brother's Keeper: The Indian in White America* (Washington, DC: New Community Press, 1969).

30. Beuf, *supra* note 24. As Mark Michaels, *supra* note 2, points out, attempts to eradicate Native languages persisted as a matter of U.S. policy until the 1960s, and the policy was not formally abandoned until 1990, and federal grants for programs to preserve and to teach Native languages to Indian children only became available in 1992. *Id.* at 1571. Michaels explains the significance of this to Native religions: Because Native religions depend on the oral tradition for their transmission, the death of a language often means the death of a religion. Stories and ceremonies are at the core of most, if not all, Native religions, and these stories and ceremonies lose their context and meaning when translated. This connection between language and ceremony was made explicit in a communique written by the Traditional Circle of Indian Elders, a group that represents a number of different North American Nations: "[L]ong instruction and discipline are necessary before ceremonies and healing can be done. These procedures are always in the Native tongue; there are no exceptions." *Id.* at 1571.

31. *Id.*

32. McBeth, *supra* note 24.

33. William Coffer, *Sleeping Giants* (Lanham, MD: University Press of America, 1979).

34. Burnette and Koster, *supra* note 16.

35. *Id.*

36. *Id.* In 1969, Cahn, *supra* note 29, noted that at the Intermountain boarding school, "last Fall, a student thought to be drunk and unmanageable was carted off to jail, where he committed suicide by hanging himself with his sweater. The student was actually having convulsions and needed medical attention. . . . "

37. Cahn, *supra* note 29.

38. Burnette and Koster, *supra* note 16.

39. Cahn, *supra* note 29.

40. Dussias, *supra* note 2.

41. Dussias, *supra* note 2, points out that where Native American "free exercise rights conflict with property rights, courts resolve the conflict in favor of the property rights." *Id.* at 823. Dussias provides some shining examples, citing *Lyng v. Northwest Indian Cemetery Protective Association*, 485 U.S. 439 (1988) (in which the Supreme Court stated that whatever rights the Indians may have to exercise their religion at the sacred sites at issue, "those rights do not divest the Government of its right to use what is, after all, its land"); *Manybeads v. United States*, 730 F. Supp. 1515 (D. Ariz.1989) (in which the court followed the *Lyng* court in concluding that the plaintiff's rights "did not divest the government (or a property owner) of its right to use what is, after all, *its* land"); *Attakai v. United States,* 746 F. Supp. 13 95 (D. Ariz. 1990) (in which the court stated that "[t]he fact that a person's ability to practice their religion [sic] will be virtually destroyed by a governmental program

[that] does not allow them [sic] to impose a 'religious servitude' on the property of the government"); *Havasupai Tribe v. United States*, 752 F. Supp. 1471 (D.Ariz. 1990), *aff'd sub nom. Havasupai Tribe v. Robertson*, 943 F.2d 32 (9th Cir. 1991) (*per curiam*) (in which the court stated that whatever rights the Indians had, those rights did "not divest the government of its right to use what is, after all, its land"). A fundamental problem with most of these cases is that the government's property rights to the lands at issue are not conclusive, nor does any federal court's proclamation render it so. In fact, the only way any of the government's land claims in these cases can be sustained is by ignoring the well-documented history of how the sites at issue were attained by the government. These so-called "property rights" of the government exist only by consciously disregarding the treaties and well-established international legal doctrines which were violated in the process of acquiring the sites. See, e.g., generally, *Rethinking Indian Law*, *supra* note 20, which discusses the land title and history of many of these sites at issue.

42. Dussias, *supra* note 2, at 805–06. Dussias provides an excellent discussion of the difficulties prevalent in presenting Native American free exercise claims in the courts due to contrasts between Anglo and Native American views of religion and culture: "The First Amendment refers to the free exercise of religion, as if religion were wholly separable from other aspects of individuals' lives. Although this isolation of religion from other aspects of life may accurately reflect the Anglo-American perspective of the First Amendment's drafters, it is foreign to the Native American world view. While the Anglo-American world view tends to see law, religion, art, [politics,] and economics as separate aspects of society, the Native American world view tends to see them as interdependent parts of an organic, unified whole." *Id.* at 806.

43. Testimony before the United States Senate Committee on Indian Affairs, hearing held on the *American Indian Religious Freedom Act*, Los Angeles, CA, November 12, 1992.

44. *Sherbert v. Verner*, 374 U.S. 398 (1963).

45. *Wisconsin v. Yoder*, 406 U.S. 205, 215 (1972).

46. *Hobbie v. Unemployment Appeals Commission*, 480 U.S. 136, 141 (1987).

47. See, e.g., *Heffron v. International Society for Krishna Consciousness*, 452 U.S. 640, 654–56 (1981), and *Thomas v. Review Board of Indiana*, 450 U.S. 707, 718 (1981).

48. *Lyng*, *supra* note 41; and *Oregon v. Smith*, 494 U.S. 892 (1990).

49. 1n *Oregon v. Smith*, *supra* note 48, the Court wrote that "it may be fairly said that leaving accommodation [of religious practices] to the political process will place at a relative disadvantage those religious practices that are not widely engaged in; but that [is an] unavoidable consequence of democratic government." *Id.* at 890. This remark by the Court is ironically arrogant, in that most Native Americans do not consider themselves to be members of the "democracy" known as the United States, since federal citizenship was imposed upon them by Act of Congress in 1924 in which Natives played no role and in fact attempted to reject it. See, e.g., Mark Michaels, *supra* note 2, at 157–273. As Michaels observes, "[I]t seems likely that many of the [Indian Citizenship Act's] supporters voted out of a belief they were conferring a benefit on Native Americans; however, the legislation had the effect of forcing American Indians 'to live within a political/legal no man's land from which there seems to be no possibility of extrication.' To traditional [Native] people, the 'granting' of citizenship to Indians was but one act in a series of governmental efforts to strip Indian nations of their land and sovereignty by legal means." *Id.* at 1573, quoting Vine Deloria Jr., "The Application of the Constitution to American Indians," in *Exiled in the Land of the Free: Democracy, Indian Nations, and the U.S. Constitution*, ed. Oren Lyons and John Mohawk (Santa Fe, NM: ClearLight Publisher, 1992), 282. Native people continue to

struggle for the right to self-determination as distinct peoples with their own governments. An Act of Congress or a passing comment by the U.S. Supreme Court to the contrary does not alter that fact. See generally, *Rethinking Indian Law, supra* note 20; Vine Deloria Jr., *Behind the Trail of Broken Treaties* (New York: Dell, 1974).

50. 92 *U.S. Statutes at Large,* 470 (1978), 42 U.S.C. 1996.

51. See, e.g., *Fools Crow v. Gullet,* 541 F. Supp. 785, 793 (D. S.D. 1982)(the Act "does not create a cause of action in federal courts for violation of rights of religious freedom"), *aff'd,* 706 F.2d 856 (8th Cir. 1983), *cert. denied,* 464 U.S. 977 (1984); *Wilson v. Block,* 708 F.2d 735 (D.C. Cir.), *cert. denied,* 464 U.S. 956 (1983)(the Act merely requires that the government consult with Indians regarding the potential devastating effects its actions may have on Indian religious practices, but it does not require the opinions of the Indians to have any effect on the government practice); *Lockhart v. Kenops,* 927 F.2d 1028 (1991) (*The American Indian Religious Freedom Act* does not confer a cause of action for violation of Indian religious practices as it is merely a statement of federal policy), *cert. denied,* 112 S. Ct. 186, *rehearing denied,* 112 S.Ct. 670. See also, *Standing Deer v. Carlson,* 831 F.2d 1525 (1987); *Attakai v. United States,* 746 F. Supp. 1395 (1990)(*The American Indian Religious Freedom Act* did not create cause of action or judicially enforceable rights in favor of individual Indians).

52. United States Department of the Interior, Federal Agencies Task Force, *American Indian Religious Freedom Act Report* (August 1979), 1–8.

53. *Wilson v. Block, supra* note 51.

54. See *Wilson v. Block, supra* note 51; *Hopi Tribe v. Block,* 8 I.L.R. 3073 (D.D.C. June 1981), *aff'd,* No. 811912 (D.C. Cir. May 20, 1983).

55. See, e.g., *Badoni v. Higginson,* 455 F. Supp. 641 (D. Utah 1977), *aff'd,* 638 F.2d 172 (10th Cir. 1980), *cert. denied,* 452 U.S. 954 (1981); *Sequoya v. Tennessee Valley Authority,* 480 F. Supp. 608 (E.D. Tenn. 1979), *aff'd,* 620 F.2d 1159 (6th Cir.), *cert. denied,* 449 U.S. 953 (1980).

56. See, e.g., *Fools Crow v. Gullet, supra* note 41.

57. *Havasupai Tribe v. United States,* 752 F. Supp. 1471 (D. Ariz. 1990), *aff'd sub nom. Havasupai Tribe v. Robertson,* 943 F.2d 32 (9th Cir. 1991)(per curiam).

58. For example, in one case, *Badoni v. Higginson,* 455 F. Supp. 641 (D. Utah 1977), *aff'd,* 638 F.2d 172 (10th Cir. 1980), *cert. denied, Badoni v. Broadbent,* 452 U.S. 954 (1981), the court commented that the Rainbow Bridge National Monument, which lies within the Navajo Reservation, had "never actually been a part of the Navajo Reservation," *id.* at 644, and that "[a]ny aboriginal proprietary interest that the Navajos may have held in this land" was extinguished by "entry of the white man in earlier years." Based on this reasoning, the court agreed with the defendants' position that the Navajos' claim "did not come within a country mile of any cognizable legal theory upon which relief can be granted." *Id.* at 644. There are two fundamental errors in this position: first, the Rainbow Bridge National Monument was created by executive order without regard for the fact that it was within the boundaries of the Navajo Reservation, and second, it ignores the fact that aboriginal title, which is premised on a cognizable legal theory under international law, created a very clear "aboriginal proprietary interest" that the Navajos hold to these lands. See, e.g., *Rethinking Indian Law, supra* note 20.

59. *Lyng, supra* note 41.

60. *Id.* note 42.

61. Association on American Indian Affairs, "Supreme Court Rules That Sacred Areas on Federal Lands Have No Constitutional Protection," *Indian Affairs,* special Supplement: *Amer-*

ican Indian Religious Freedom, Summer 1988, vi.

62. *Supra* note 48.

63. *Id.* at 878–79.

64. In his dissent, Justice Blackmun noted that the plaintiffs' sacramental use of peyote appeared to be "closely analogous to the sacramental use of wine by the Roman Catholic Church," which the federal government exempted from its ban on possession and consumption of alcohol during the prohibition. *Id.* at 913, n. 6.

65. See, e.g., R.L. Bergman, "Navajo Peyote Use: Its Apparent Safety," *American Journal of Psychiatry,* 128 (6)(1971): 695–99; Pascarona, Futterman, and Halsweig, "Observations of Alcoholics in the Peyote Ritual: A Pilot Study," *Annals of the New York Academy of Sciences,* 273(1976): 518–24; Roy, Choudhuri, and Irvine, "The Prevalence of Mental Disorders among Saskatchewan Indians," *Journal of Cross-Cultural Psychology,* 1(1970): 383–92; Little Rock Reed, "Rehabilitation: Contrasting Cultural Perspectives and the Imposition of Church and State," *The American Indian in the White Man's Prisons: A Story of Genocide* (Taos, NM: UnCompromising Books, 1993); R.M. Underhill, "Religion among American Indians," *Annals of the American Academy of Political and Social Sciences,* 311(1951): 127–36; R.M. Wagner, "Some Pragmatic Aspects of Navajo Peyotism," *Plains Anthropologist,* 20(1975): 197-205; J. Weibel-Orlando, "Hooked on Healing: Anthropologists, Alcohol and Intervention," *Human Organization* 48(l) (1989); S.M. Stevens, "Alcohol and World View: A Study of Passamaquoddy Alcohol Use," *Cultural Factors in Alcohol Research and Treatment of Drinking Problems* (New Brunswick, NJ: Rutgers Center for Alcoholism, 1981).

66. 42 U.S.C. 2000bb *et seq.*

67. Citing *Sherbert, supra* note 44, and *Yoder, supra* note 45.

68. 42 U.S.C. 2000bb(b).

69. *Boerne v. Flores,* 117 S. Ct. 2157 (1997).

70. Public Law 103–344, *American Indian Religious Freedom Act Amendments of 1994* (October 6, 1994).

71. U.S. District Judge Karlton, in *Sample v. Borg, infra* note 99.

72. The survey is discussed in Reed, *The American Indian in the White Man's Prisons, supra* note 3, at 390–406.

73. The sweat lodge is the most commonly used religious facility/ceremony among the tribes of North America and is a central component of any adequate Native American religious program within the prison context. The sweat lodge is a dome-shaped structure made of willow branches and covered by tarps and blankets so that it is dark inside when the entrance is closed. The lodge itself represents the womb of Mother Earth and is used for purification ceremonies. It is an outdoor structure, which requires a fireplace (outside the lodge) in which to heat rocks, which are carried into the lodge to produce heat. When water is poured over the rocks, it produces steam, which the participants perceive as the breath of the Creator. The four sacred elements—fire, water, air and earth—are brought together in the ceremony for the purpose of purification and healing.

74. For an explanation of the spiritual significance of the wearing of long hair, refer to *supra* note 19.

75. There should be no dispute that these herbs and objects are held to be sacred within the Native American belief system. When necessary, questions regarding the spiritual significance of any item claimed by a Native American prisoner to hold religious significance should be directed to Native American spiritual leaders.

76. The items listed in the questionnaire included headbands, medicine bags, sage, cedar, sweet

grass, tobacco ties, drums, beading materials, gourd rattles, the sacred pipe and eagle feathers.

77. Little Rock Reed, *supra* note 3, at 394.

78. *Id.*

79. Those that responded were Alaska, Arizona, Arkansas, California, Colorado, Connecticut, Georgia, Illinois, Indiana, Kansas, Kentucky, Louisiana, Maine, Maryland, Massachusetts, Michigan, Minnesota, Mississippi, Nebraska, New Jersey, New Mexico, North Carolina, Pennsylvania, Rhode Island, South Carolina, South Dakota, Texas, Utah, Vermont, Virginia, Washington, and Wisconsin.

80. It is standard policy and practice throughout the federal and state prison systems to allow prisoners to remain at their job assignments and family visits during designated "count time" periods, which strongly suggests that it is unnecessary for officials to terminate Native religious ceremonies for count periods, so long as each prisoner is accounted for.

81. These isolated incidents are not evidence that sweat lodges are, per se, a threat to security or other penological objectives, any more so than similar incidents in prison Christian chapels are evidence that prison Christian chapels should be barred from the prisons. See, generally, Little Rock Reed, *supra* note 3. In October of 1992, when Reed appeared with Native American spiritual leaders for a meeting with the administrator of religious services for the Indiana Department of Corrections to discuss Native religious programming, the administrator defended the ban on sweat lodges by claiming that sweat lodges in other state prison systems were used for "dope parties." When asked to cite an example, the administrator replied that according to a newspaper article she read, this had happened in the Kansas Department of Corrections. However, the Kansas prison officials later verified that this simply was not true. *Id.* at 397.

82. One state that refused to allow Indian prisoners to wear long hair at the time of the survey, Pennsylvania, had previously allowed all prisoners to wear long hair, but adopted a short-hair rule just prior to the survey. According to correspondence to the NAPRRP from the Pennsylvania Commissioner of Corrections' office, no contraband had ever been found in a prisoner's hair, and there were no other instances in which the wearing of long hair had caused a breach of security. *Id.* at 397. It is worth noting that the instances in which contraband has been found in long hair suggest that standard prison searches are sufficient to meet the "compelling interest" of reducing contraband, which is the primary objective asserted by prison officials to justify cutting prisoners' hair in violation of First Amendment concerns. See, e.g., *Weaver v. Jago, infra.*

83. Arizona officials provided the following comment: "1992—Fort Grant—a minimum security institution—in attempting to examine a Native American inmate's medicine bag, an officer grabbed the bag from the inmate's possession and subsequently was attacked by the inmate for violating his religious possessions. (The outcome of this incident resulted in the rewriting of the procedures, an opportunity for the Warden to provide on-the-job training concerning proper methods of search in this area.)" *Id.* at 399.

84. *Id.* at 402–03. This information was based on the NAPRRP's and Reed's communications with Native American prisoners and prison officials at the time of the survey, as well as an examination of existing state policies and regulations at the time of the survey.

85. *Procunier v. Martinez*, 416 U.S. 396, 414 n. 2 (1974). See also, *Turner v. Safely*, 107 S. Ct. 2254 (1987); *O'Lone v. Shabazz*, 107 S. Ct. 2400 (1987).

86. The rehabilitation of prisoners is a "valid penological objective." See, e.g., *Pell v. Procunier*, 417 U.S. 817, 822–23 (1974), *Martinez, supra* note 84, at 412; and *O'Lone, supra* note 8.

87. D.E. Walker, "A Declaration Concerning the American Indian Sweat Bath and American

Indian Religion," prepared for the Native American Rights Fund, Boulder, CO.

88. *Id.*

89. Carol Sisco, "Indian Inmates Seek Right to Pursue Own Religions," *Salt Lake Tribune,* May 19, 1986. See also, Little Rock Reed, "The American Indian in the White Man's Prisons: A Story of Genocide," *Humanity and Society* 13(4): 403–20, and accompanying citations; Little Rock Reed, "Rehabilitation: Contrasting Cultural Perspectives and the Imposition of Church and State," *Journal of Prisoners on Prisons* 4 (2)(1993).

90. R. Seven, "Ritual of Rebirth: Sweat Lodge Reaffirms Indian Inmates' Heritage," *Seattle Times/Seattle Post Intelligencer,* January 24, 1988.

91. See the citations at *supra* note 84.

92. Case No. C87–0208 (U.S. Dist. Court, D. Utah, 1987).

93. *Id.,* unpublished decision of March 18, 1987.

94. Carol Sisco, "New Mexico Warden Says Prison Sweat Lodge No Problem: Utahns' Fear Conjuring Ghosts," *Salt Lake Tribune,* November 9, 1986.

95. *Supra* note 91.

96. *Turner v. Safely,* at 2261. Unfortunately for many Native American prisoners, the deference accorded prison officials has been nearly absolute, if not by the trial courts, then by the courts of appeal. For example, in *Brightly v. Wainwright,* 814 F.2d 612 (11th Cir. 1987), the Eleventh Circuit Court of Appeals consolidated the appeals of prison officials in numerous cases where the district courts ruled in favor of the prisoners on the hair length issue after careful analysis of the short-hair rules and the justifications asserted to justify them. In those cases, the prison officials argued, without elaboration, that the restriction on prisoners' free exercise rights by virtue of short-hair policies was a reasonable one designed to (1) aid in the recapture of prisoners following their escapes; (2) establish a uniform grooming policy; and (3) reduce the security risk inherent in maintaining prisons. These claims, which are nebulous at best, were entirely unsubstantiated by the prison officials except for their own self-serving "expert" opinions. Nevertheless, the *Brightly* court ruled that "the district court in each of the cases now before us erred in failing to accord appropriate deference to the judgment of prison officials." *Id.* at 613. See also, *Martinelli v. Dugger,* 817 F.2d 1499 (11th Cir. 1987)(reversed the lower court for failing to accord deference to prison officials); *Wilson v. Schillinger,* 761 F.2d 921 (3rd Cir. 1985) (reversed trial court, holding that prison officials need not present evidence beyond their "expert" opinions to substantiate their fears); *Reed v. Faulkner,* 842 F.2d 960 (7th Cir. 1988); *Pollock v. Marshall,* 845 F.2d 656 (6th Cir. 1988).

97. See, e.g., *Scott v. Mississippi Department of Corrections,* 961 F.2d 77 (5th Cir. 1992); *Martinelli v. Dugger, supra; Wilson v. Schillinger, supra; Reed v. Faulkner, supra; Pollock v. Marshall, supra.*

98. For example, the Ohio prison warden–defendant in *Pollock v. Marshall, supra,* Terry Morris, modeled his testimony, almost verbatim, on the testimony of Pennsylvania prison officials in *Wilson, supra,* but added one or two of his own fears. Since his testimony resulted in summary judgment against the prisoner, the Utah prison officials made sworn statements, modeled verbatim on the statement of Morris. See *Roybal v. DeLand, supra.* Likewise, other officials who have prevailed in this type of litigation have modeled their testimony, verbatim, on the testimony of Terry Morris, as if his statement was their own testimony. See, e.g., *Iron Eyes, infra; Powell, Scott, and Kemp, infra.* A serious error with these grants of summary judgment in favor of prison officials is that the prison officials' motions for summary judgment were supported only by the prison officials' affidavits containing unsubstantiated claims. The Rules of Civil Procedure require that such affidavits be

based on personal knowledge. None of these officials have ever allowed the wearing of long hair in their institutions, and therefore have no personal knowledge from which to draw their conclusions that the wearing of long hair will violate security objectives. And whenever the prisoners have raised an equal protection claim because female prisoners are allowed to wear long hair, the claims have been summarily rejected by the courts; yet the officials have never been required to explain why the hair on a male prisoners' head is perceived as more dangerous than the hair on a female prisoner's head. See *Little Rock Reed, supra.*

99. *Sample v. Borg,* 675 F. Supp. 574 (E.D. Cal. 1987).

100. *Id.* at 850–51, quoting *Turner v. Safely, supra* note 96. Emphasis added by Judge Karlton.

101. *Sample, supra* at 850–51.

102. *Turner v. Safely,* 107 S. Ct 2254 (1987).

103. 482 U.S. 78 (1987).

104. *Sample v. Borg,* 675 F. Supp 574 (E.D. Col. 1987).

105. *Roybal, supra.*

106. *Supra.*

107. The court's own note: "This court must observe that I can hardly believe that anyone would regard this as an untoward result: nevertheless, as noted [in *Turner*], in matters of security and burdens on resources, I am to defer to the judgment of prison authorities."

108. The court's own note: "In this trial, the defendants proved the remarkable ingenuity prisoners demonstrate in fabricating weapons out of anything they can lay their hands on. Indeed, it is difficult to fully credit this as a justification for the rule adopted by prison officials since it is they who have decided to doublecell inmates in [segregation]. . . ."

109. *O'Lone v. Shabazz,* 107 S. Ct. 2400 (1987).

110. It is not necessarily true that prisoners may engage in fasting without the state's permission, for as Reed has documented, one prisoner was placed in solitary confinement for 180 days and his security level was raised for five years solely and expressly as punishment for engaging in a fast. See *Reed, supra* note 3, at 251 n. 20.

111. The court's own note: "At the trial the court learned that the plaintiff's own cellmate is also a practitioner of Native American religion; thus fears concerning religious strife between cellmates also appears irrelevant to this case."

112. The court's own note: "If the answer to that question is 'yes, they can,' then the assertion that 'when a prison regulation or practice offends a fundamental constitutional guarantee, federal courts will discharge their duty to protect constitutional rights,' Turner, is a promise without substance."

113. *Sample v. Bora, supra.*

114. Tobacco ties consist of a pinch of tobacco placed inside a small square cloth and tied closed with a light string.

115. *Id.*

116. Interestingly, in further consideration of this requirement and the Turner factors, the court in *Sample v. Borg* observed: "In regard to the third factor, the courts are to defer to the informed judgment of prison officials . . . while the presence of the fourth factor is evidence that a regulation, rather than being reasonable, constitutes an 'exaggerated response' to prison concerns. . . . I pause here only long enough to note that such a formulation does not even allow the possibility of malevolence. I know of nothing in the history of prison administration in this country to provide such utter confidence. Moreover, this formulation does not recognize that extreme deprivations and perceived unfairness may themselves create profound security problems, as the histories of prison rebellions from Attica to the

recent incidents involving Haitian detainees clearly demonstrate. It may well be that considerations of this sort are initially for the responsible prison authorities, and that their determinations should be treated with deference. Nonetheless, as has been observed, deference to supposed expertise may be no more than a fiction."

117. *Id.* The court's own note: "Having made my determination under the applicable law, I will urge the prison administrators to further consider the question as to whether some rule regulating content or otherwise short of an absolute ban would not serve their security needs."

118. *Id.*

119. 946 F.2d 588 (8th Cir. 1991).

120. *Supra,* note at 588–89.

121. *Supra,* note at 814, emphasis added.

122. *Turner, supra.*

Chapter Five

1. F. Cohen, Section f: "Crimes in Indian Country by Non-Indian against Indian," Chapter 18: "Criminal Jurisdiction," *Handbook of Federal Indian Law* (Washington, DC: U.S. Government Printing Office, 1942), 364–65.

2. *Johnson v. McIntosh,* 21 U.S., (8 Wheat.) 534 (1823).

3. *Cherokee Nation v. Georgia,* 30 U.S. (5 Pet.) 1 (1831).

4. *Worcester v. Georgia,* 31 U.S. (6 Pet.) 515 (1832).

5. *Federal Enclaves Act,* 18 U.S.C.A., 1152 (1817).

6. *Assimilative Crimes Act,* 18 U.S.C.A., 13 (1825).

7. *Trade and Intercourse Act, U.S. Statutes at Large,* 4: 729–35 (June 30, 1834).

8. George Crooker's letter to President Abraham Lincoln concerning the Sioux outbreak, *The Minnesota Archaeologist,* 19 (1954): 3–17.

9. L.A. French; "Government Policy and Practices during the 'Indian War' Era," *The Winds of Injustice* (New York: Garland, 1994), 23–43; and R.W. Meyer, "Catastrophe," *History of the Santee Sioux: United States Indian Policy on Trial* (Lincoln: University of Nebraska Press, 1967), 109–32.

10. *Ex parte Crow Dog,* 109 U.S. Reports, 557, 571–72 (December 17, 1883).

11. S.L. Harring, *Crow Dog's Case* (New York: Cambridge University Press, 1994), 100–141.

12. *Major Crimes Act, U.S. Statutes at Large,* 23: 385 (March 3, 1885).

13. W.C. Canby, Jr., "Tribal Criminal Jurisdiction," *American Indian Law* (St. Paul, MN: West 1988), 133–42.

14. *U.S. v. Kagama,* 118 U.S. 375, 382–85 (May 10, 1886).

15. *Long Wolf v. Hitchcock,* 187 U.S. Reports, 553, 564–68 (January 5, 1903).

16. Courts of Indian Offenses, *Annual Report of the Secretary of the Interior,* Washington, DC, House Executive Document No. 1, 48th Congress, 1st Session, serial 2190, November 1, 1883, x-xiii.

17. *Rules for Indian Courts,* Washington, DC, House Executive Documents, No. 1, 52nd Congress, 2nd Session, serial 3088, August 27, 1892, 28–31.

18. Quote from the *Missouri Republican* (October 26, 1883) in G. Shirley, *Law West of Fort Smith: A History of Frontier Justice in Indian Territory, 1834–1896* (Lincoln: University of Nebraska Press, Bison Books, 1968), 145.

19. Shirley, *Law West of Fort Smith,* note 18.

Chapter Six

1. *Snyder Act of 1921,* 25 U.S.C. 13, 115, 42 *U.S. Statutes at Large,* 208 (November 2, 1921).
2. L. Meriam, et al., *The Problem of Indian Administration* (Baltimore, MD: Johns Hopkins University Press, 1928), 86–89.
3. *U.S. v. Sandoval* 231 U.S. 28 (1913), *rev'g* 198 Fed. 539 (D. N.M. 1912).
4. D. H. Getches, D.M. Rosenfelt, and C.F. Wilkinson, "Period of Indian Organization: 1928–1945," *Federal Indian Law: Cases and Materials* (St. Paul, MN: West, 1979), 79–86 (quote on 83).
5. F. Cohen, Section 9: "Tribal Powers in the Administration of Justice," *Handbook of Federal Indian Law* (Washington, DC: U.S. Government Printing Office, 1942), 145–49 (quote on 149).
6. W.C. Canby, Jr., Section D: "Present Criminal Jurisdiction," *American Indian Law* (St. Paul, MN: West, 1988), 119–42.
7. D.H. Getches, D.M. Rosenfelt, and C.F. Wilkinson, Section D: "'Public Law 280'—A Transfer of Jurisdiction in Some States," *Cases on Material on Federal Indian Law* (St. Paul, MN: West, 1979), 467–81 (quote on 468).
8. S.J. Brakel, "Trial Courts: History, Jurisdiction, and Current Status," *American Indian Tribal Courts: The Costs of Separate Justice* (Chicago: American Bar Foundation, 1978), 5–11.
9. *Williams v. Lee,* 358 U.S. 217, 79 S. Ct. 269, 3 L. Ed. 2d 251, 1959.
10. *United States v. Wheeler,* 435 U.S. 313 (1978).
11. *Oliphant v. Suquamish Indian Tribe,* 435 U.S. 191 (1978).
12. *Merrion v. Jicarilla Apache Tribe,* 455 U.S. 130, 144–45 (1982).
13. *Harding v. White Mountain Apache Tribe,* 779 F.2d 476, 478–79 (9th Cir., 1985).
14. *Duro v. Reina* (495 U.S. 696 (1990)).
15. Public Law 102–37, *Criminal Jurisdiction over Indians,* 105 *U.S. Statutes at Large* 646, 25 U.S.C. 1301 (4) 1991.
16. Chapter 38: "Indian Tribal Justice Support"; Subchapter 1: "Tribal Justice System," *United States Code—Title 25,* Sections 3611–3614.

Chapter Seven

1. N.J. NcCabe, Chief Justice of the Navajo Nation, *A Short Guide to the Courts of the Navajo Nation* (Window Rock, AZ: Judicial Branch of the Navajo Nation, n.d.), 1–2; emphasis added.
2. Title Seven, "Courts and Procedures"; Chapter 5, "Procedure (Tribal Code)", Sections 301 and 302; *Navajo Tribal Code* (Orford, NH: Equity Publishing Corporation, 1978), 145–46.
3. R. Yazzie, Chief Justice of the Navajo Court, *Judicial Branch of the Navajo Nation* (Window Rock, AZ: Judicial Branch of the Navajo Nation, n.d.), 5–7.
4. Title Seven, "Courts and Procedures"; Chapter 1, "Application of Code of Federal Regulations," Section 1: "Application and Purpose," *Navajo Tribal Code* (Orford, NH: Equity Publishing Corporation, 1978), 273.
5. Public Law 101–630; *Indian Child Protection and Family Violence Prevention Act, Title IV* (25 U.S.C. 3210, November 28, 1990).

6. Title Seventeen, "Law and Order," Chapter 5, "Procedures, Sections 1902 and 1904. "Grounds for Exclusion," *Navajo Tribal Code* (Orford, NH: Equity Publishing Corporation, 1978), 539–41.

7. Title Seventeen, "Law and Order"; Chapter 5, "Procedures," Section 1951, "Indians Committing Crime Outside Indian Country—Apprehension on Reservation," *Navajo Tribal Code* (Orford, NH: Equity Publishing Corporation, 1978), 543; and *United States Code Annotated,* Title 25, "Indians," Sections 441 to end, 2000 Supplementary Pamphlet covering years 1984 to 1999; 2000 General Index S to U; Section 1302, note 93 (St. Paul, MN: West, 2000), 289.

8. Title Nine, "Domestic Relations"; Chapter 11, "Juvenile Code," Sections 1001–1402, *Navajo Tribal Code* (Orford, NH: Equity Publishing Corporation, 1978), 352–83.

9. R. Yazzie, Chief Justice of the Navajo Nation, *The Navajo Peacemaker Court: Contrasts of Justice,* Public Document, Nov. 10 (Window Rock, AZ: Navajo Nation, 1992), 2–5.

10. J.W. Zion and N.J. McCabe, *Navajo Peacemaker Court Manual: A Guide to the Use of the Navajo Peacemaker Court for Judges, Community Leaders and Court Personnel* (Window Rock, AZ: Navajo Judicial Publication, 1982), 7–11, 100–109.

11. Judicial Branch of the Navajo Nation, *Fiscal Year 1999 Statistical Report: District Court Criminal and DWI Traffic Cases* (October 1, 1998 to September 30, 1999) (Window Rock, AZ: Navajo Nation, 2000).

12. Judicial Branch of the Navajo Nation, *Fiscal Year 1999 Statistical Report: District Court Civil and Civil Traffic Cases* (October 1, 1998 to September 30, 1999) (Window Rock, AZ: Navajo Nation, 2000).

13. Judicial Branch of the Navajo Nation, *Fiscal Year 1999 Statistical Report: Family Court Children's Cases* (October 1, 1998 to September 30, 1999) (Window Rock, AZ: Navajo Nation, 2000).

14. *Id.*

15. L.A. Greenfeld and S.K. Smith, "Highlights," *American Indians and Crime,* February, NCJ173386 (Washington, DC: U.S. Department of Justice, Bureau of Justice Statistics, 1999), v–viii.

Chapter Eight

1. L.A. French, "An Historical Analysis of Indian Justice," *Indians and Criminal Justice* (Totowa, NJ: Allanheld, Osmun, 1982), 1–17.

2. T. Horn, Chief of Scouts, *Life of Tom Horn: Government Scout and Interpreter* (Norman: University of Oklahoma Press, 1964), 138–39.

3. E.A. Hayt, *Annual Report of the Commissioner of Indian Affairs,* House Executive Document No. 1, 45th Congress, 2nd Session, Serial 1800, November 1, 1877, 398–99.

4. W.T. Hagan, *Indian Police and Judges* (New Haven, CT: Yale University Press, 1966), 101; and L.A. French, "The Apache," *Psychocultural Change and the American Indian: An Ethnohistorical Analysis* (New York: Garland, 1987), 69–91.

5. Curtis Act, *U.S. Statutes at Large,* 30: 497–98, 502, 504–5, June 28, 1898.

6. D.H. Getches, D.M. Rosenfelt, and C.F. Wilkinson, "Tribal Self-Government," Section C: "Tribal Courts," *Cases and Materials on Federal Indian Law* (St. Paul, MN: West, 1979), 315.

7. See L.A. French, "In the Spirit of Crazy Horse: Leonard Peltier and the AIM Uprising,"

and "Reservation Ills: Gambling, Mineral Exploitation, Toxic Dumps and Water Issues," *The Winds of Injustice* (New York: Garland, 1994), 77–112; 179–89.

8. See *Furman V. Georgia*, 408 U.S. 238, 345 (1972); and L.A. French and J. Hornbuckle, "Contemporary Social Issues: Do Cherokees Receive Death for Public Drunkenness?" *The Cherokee Perspective* (Boone, NC: Appalachian Consortium Press, 1981), 104–7.

9. Public Law 101–379, *Indian Law Enforcement Reform Act*, 25 USC Sections 2801–2809 (August 18, 1990).

10. Public Law 101–630, *Indian Child Protection and Family Violence Prevention Act, Title IV*, 25 U.S.C. 3210 (November 28, 1990)

11. *BIA Law Enforcement—Crime Statistics* <http://bialw.fedworld.gov/crimestats/95pt1.htm>.

12. Tony Hillerman, *Hunting Badger* (New York: HarperCollins, 2000)

13. W. Claiborne, "Violent Crime Grows on Indian Lands," *Washington Post*, October 11, 1998, 5A.

14. M. Kelley, Officer's Death Highlights Tribal Police Shortage," *Albuquerque Journal*, 119 (348) (December 14, 1999), C1.

15. M. Jorgensen and S. Wakeling, Policy Papers on "Fighting Crime in Indian Country," reprinted from *Indian Country Today* (March 30–April 6, 1998); and "The Cultural Renewal of Law Enforcement," reprinted from Indian Country Today (April 20–26, 1998). Both undated papers are distributed by the John F. Kennedy School of Government, Harvard University, Cambridge, MA.

16. See L.A. French, "Psychocultural Factors," *Addictions and Native Americans* (Westport, CT: Praeger, 2000), 35–43; and L.A. French, "Contemporary Indian Justice and Correctional Treatment," *Indians and Criminal Justice* (Totowa, NJ: Allanheld, Osmun, 1982), 179–86.

Epilogue

1. M. Kelley, "State Party Wants Governments Ousted," *Albuquerque Journal*, 12 (201) (July 19, 2000), A7.

2. R. Weller, "Site of Sand Creek 1864 Indian Massacre Remains Unmarked," *Albuquerque Journal*, 120 (219) (August 6, 2000), B6.

3. Nelson A. Miles to George W. Baird, November 20, 1891, Baird Collection, WA-S901, M596, *Western Americana Collection*, The Beinecke Rare Book and Manuscript Library, Yale University, New Haven, CT.

4. R. Costo and J. Henry, "The Council of State Governments Resolution on the American Indian Policy Review Commission," *Indian Treaties: Two Centuries of Dishonor* (San Francisco, CA: Indian Historian Press, 1977), 235–37.

5. See M. Weber, *The Protestant Ethic and the Spirit of Capitalism*, T. Parsons, trans. (New York: Charles Scribner's Sons, 1930); L.A. French, "Reservation Ills: Gambling, Mineral Exploitation, Toxic Dumps, and Water Issues," *The Winds of Injustice: American Indians and the U.S. Government* (New York: Garland, 1994), 179–205; and *Navajo Timeline: Self-Determination (1970 to Present)* <http://www.lapahie.com/Timeline_USA_1970_Present.html>, December 26, 2000.

6. S. Ross, "Clinton Seeks Racial Healing," *Albuquerque Journal*, 120 (70), A6.

7. J. Reno, *Department of Justice Policy on Indian Sovereignty and Government-to-Government Relations with Indian Tribes* (Washington, DC: Office of the Attorney General, 1995), 1–6.

8. "300,000 Indians Sue Federal Government for Mismanaging Their Money," *NARF Legal Review*, 21 (2) (Summer/Fall 1996), 1.

9. *Elouise Pepion Cobell, et al., v. Bruce Babbitt, Secretary of the Interior, Lawrence Summers, Secretary of the Treasury, and Kevin Gover, Assistant Secretary of the Interior* (U.S. District Court, DC, Civil No. 96-1286 (RCL), December, 1999) (*Cobell v. Babbitt*), 30 F. Supp. 2d 24 (Nov. 5, 1988).

10. M. Kelley, "It's a Matter of Trust," *Albuquerque Journal*, 120 (337) (December 2, 2000), E1.

INDEX